VOLUME EDITORS

JESSE R. STEINBERG is an assistant professor of philosophy and the director of the Environmental Studies Program at the University of Pittsburgh at Bradford. He has been a visiting professor at Victoria University in New Zealand, at the University of California at Riverside, and at the University of Illinois Urbana-Champaign. He has published a number of articles on topics including philosophy of mind, metaphysics, philosophy of religion, and ethics.

ABROL FAIRWEATHER is an instructor at San Francisco State University and the University of San Fransisco. He has published in the area of virtue epistemology and sustains interests in philosophy of mind, metaphysics, and philosophy of language. He has contributed to popular culture volumes on Facebook and Dexter. The guitar, vocals, and lyrics of Lightnin' Hopkins and Mississippi John Hurt are major influences.

SERIES EDITOR

FRITZ ALLHOFF is an associate professor in the philosophy department at Western Michigan University, as well as a senior research fellow at the Australian National University's Centre for Applied Philosophy and Public Ethics. In addition to editing the *Philosophy for Everyone* series, he is also the volume editor or co-editor for several titles, including *Wine & Philosophy* (Wiley-Blackwell, 2007), *Whiskey & Philosophy* (with Marcus P. Adams, Wiley, 2009), and *Food & Philosophy* (with Dave Monroe, Wiley-Blackwell, 2007). His academic research interests engage various facets of applied ethics, ethical theory, and the history and philosophy of science.

PHILOSOPHY FOR EVERYONE

Series editor: Fritz Allhoff

Not so much a subject matter, philosophy is a way of thinking. Thinking not just about the Big Questions, but about little ones too. This series invites everyone to ponder things they care about, big or small, significant, serious… or just curious.

Edited by Jesse R. Steinberg and
Abrol Fairweather

BLUES
PHILOSOPHY FOR EVERYONE
Thinking Deep About Feeling Low

A John Wiley & Sons, Ltd., Publication

This edition first published 2012
© 2012 John Wiley & Sons, Inc.

Wiley-Blackwell is an imprint of John Wiley & Sons, formed by the merger of Wiley's global
Scientific, Technical and Medical business with Blackwell Publishing.

Registered Office
John Wiley & Sons, Ltd., The Atrium, Southern Gate, Chichester, West Sussex, PO19 8SQ, UK

Editorial Offices
350 Main Street, Malden, MA 02148-5020, USA
9600 Garsington Road, Oxford, OX4 2DQ, UK
The Atrium, Southern Gate, Chichester, West Sussex, PO19 8SQ, UK

For details of our global editorial offices, for customer services, and for information about how
to apply for permission to reuse the copyright material in this book please see our website at
www.wiley.com/wiley-blackwell.

The right of Jesse R. Steinberg and Abrol Fairweather to be identified as the authors of the editorial
material in this work has been asserted in accordance with the UK Copyright, Designs and Patents
Act 1988.

Library of Congress Cataloging-in-Publication Data

Blues – philosophy for everyone : thinking deep about feeling low / edited by
Jesse R. Steinberg and Abrol Fairweather.
    p.   cm. – (Philosophy for everyone)
  ISBN 978-0-470-65680-8 (pbk. : alk. paper)
1. Blues (Music)–Social aspects.   2. Music and philosophy.   I. Steinberg, Jesse R.
II. Fairweather, Abrol.
  ML3521.B64 2012
  781.64301–dc23

                                                    2011026137

A catalogue record for this book is available from the British Library.

This book is published in the following electronic formats: ePDFs 9781118153253;
Wiley Online Library 9781118153284; ePub 9781118153260; Mobi 9781118153277

Set in 10/12.5pt Plantin by SPi Publisher Services, Pondicherry, India
Printed in Malaysia by Ho Printing (M) Sdn Bhd

1   2012

This book is dedicated to the folks that have produced the greatest music on Earth. Thank you!

CONTENTS

FOREWORD

The blues is an art of ambiguity, an assertion of the irrepressibly human over all circumstances, whether created by others, or by one's own human failing.
(Ralph Ellison)[1]

The blues is a form of magic. Yes, magic, not just music. It is incredibly simple, usually involving somewhere between one and five chords; usually in 4/4 time; with verses rarely more than sixteen bars long; and often with only two lines of words, often one repeated, in a verse. Yet the blues is infused with a subtlety and power of emotion that transcend even the listener's ability to understand the meaning of the words. The passion, the humor, the sorrow, the joy all seem to communicate on a subliminal, non-intellectual level that defies explanation.

Amazingly, the blues, a music that has won a worldwide audience, was created by an incredibly isolated group of people, an almost-invisible and often despised minority population with little interaction with the white majority in their unchosen home country. They were dragged in chains from their homes in Africa and deposited in a strange land under the control of owners who often literally worked them to death, enforced illiteracy, divided their families and original tribes, and often even banned them from owning musical instruments. Even after the legal end of slavery, the sharecropping system made it virtually impossible for African-Americans to emerge from dire poverty, to own land, or to create a future for their children. In their own country, they were (and still often are) the ultimate 'other.' All this in the 'land of the free.'

How did these isolated, oppressed, often illiterate people manage to create a music that has reached beyond their own culture to find an audience among not only the white majority in the United States but also among people around the world? What is it about this music that can inspire fans and musicians in Argentina, China, India, Russia, and Singapore to adopt the blues as their favorite music? What is it about the blues that has fueled mainstream rock and pop music? And what is the 'inside' of the blues, the part that audiences have such a hard time understanding, even when they can identify and enjoy the structures and sounds of the 'outside' of blues?

For almost 300 years, African-Americans' choices for brief relief from endless work and poverty were found either on Saturday night or Sunday morning. If they chose the church (the religion of their captors, which they transformed into something very much their own), then the ultimate brighter future was found after death, in the arms of Jesus, as so often expressed in song. If they chose Saturday night in the country juke joint or city blues bar, then the songs were secular and spoke, as does all blues, in literal terms about everyday life. Often these songs were of the disappointments of living, especially the failure of love to survive, either because of the cruelty of the beloved or the foibles of the singer, and, by extension, the members of his or her audience: 'It's my own fault, babe, treat me the way you want to do' (from 'It's My Own Fault' by John Lee Hooker). Sometimes they were about the positive attributes of the singer and again, by extension, the members of his or her audience. These were the attributes to which poor people could relate – primarily that of being a good lover, which could be suggested by the blues artist's singing and playing ability, or the audience members' dancing ability. And sometimes the songs were nothing but a release, a rhythmic excuse to party, to forget the hopelessness of daily life and just whoop and holler and try as hard as possible to attract a sexual/romantic partner. But, under any circumstances, the songs and the spirit of the songs were about reality, not the glories of the life in heaven to come. No wonder the preachers declared that the blues was 'the devil's music.' Not only did the blues imply that the here and now were more important than the afterlife, but also those who spent their meager income on Saturday night had nothing for the collection plate on Sunday morning!

The continuing power of the blues is rooted in how strongly the music and the creators of the music (by which I mean not only the blues musicians but also the culture that created and nurtured them) had to fight for an iota of joy and a sense of community in the face of overwhelming odds – to be someone and not 'the other.' Even now, when the conditions that created the blues, at least those specific to the rural South, have almost disappeared, the power of the music that those conditions engendered lives on. Imagine a prize fighter who has built himself up to a level of incredible strength for the fight of his life. Even if the fight happened years before, the power of those muscles is still there. Thus, the power of the blues lives on.

Explaining the emotional, spiritual effect of the blues is almost impossible. Even defining the blues is a challenge. But here's what we can perhaps agree on: The blues is a folk music form that was created primarily by African-Americans, probably evolving out of unaccompanied work songs. It generally involves both singing and playing instruments. It often has twelve bars and three chords arranged in a I-IV-I-V-VI-I structure. It usually contains flatted thirds and sevenths, the so-called 'blue notes.' Its lyrics speak of secular rather than religious or spiritual matters, though it shares many structures and vocal techniques with gospel music. Most blues has a strong, danceable rhythmic pulse. (Note that the inclusion of the long, flashy guitar solo is something that mostly happened after white fans adopted the blues. For black people, the blues was always first about words and groove.)

Okay, so we now have a vague but functional historical and musical definition. But then there's that other quality, the emotional/psychological one that's generally called 'tension and release.' How does that work, the part that 'hurts so good'? Some psychologists say that the chord movement from V to I is somehow soothing to people on an elemental level. But there is that same chord movement in plenty of other types of music that don't create the tension and release of the blues.

Often tension is created in the blues by things happening late: The voice will start a verse a beat after the instruments begin it. If there is drummer, he or she will generally be playing the snare drum on the second and fourth beats of a 4/4 measure, but will create tension by not playing squarely on the beat but intentionally a nanosecond behind. Singers and instrumentalists will intentionally hit a note that is below the 'correct' pitch (if you were writing out the parts on sheet music) and bend their note or voice up to the correct pitch, creating tension by entering 'wrong' and release by finally being 'right.' The longer it takes to get to the 'right' pitch, the more the tension and the greater the release. Listen to Albert King's guitar or Muddy Waters' slide to hear this technique done to perfection. These techniques are almost unknown in European classical music. They are all about Africa, where moving

BRUCE IGLAUER

pitches are considered very much 'correct.' All these things speak to how the blues creates musical tension and release. But still, this doesn't speak to how the blues works on *us* – that 'healing feeling.' That's the eternal, wonderful magic of this music.

The blues certainly wasn't created as a self-conscious 'art form' and most blues musicians, past and present, would describe themselves as entertainers, not 'artists.' The blues existed for decades as folk music, passed from person to person, before it was first recorded in 1921. But, in the country juke joints of Mississippi or the South and West Side black clubs of Chicago where I first got my blues education, the idea of discussing, dissecting, and analyzing the blues would have been laughed at. It was party and dance music, music for people who had literally picked cotton until their hands were raw or chopped animal carcasses in a slaughterhouse or cleaned houses (as Koko Taylor told me, 'I spent many hours on my knees, and I wasn't praying ... I was scrubbing rich folks' floors' – from the blues standard 'Five Long Years,' originally cut and recorded by Eddie Boyd) or worked in a mill, 'trucking steel like a slave.' It was music to celebrate their mutual roots, to hear someone else singing the story of their lives, their loves, and their losses, so they didn't feel so alone in their struggles. These people had almost everything in common. When I spent a Sunday afternoon at Florence's Lounge on Chicago's South Side, listening to Hound Dog Taylor, I was one of the few people in the bar who hadn't been born in the South, who hadn't labored in the blazing sun, who hadn't come north with a few dollars in a pocket or purse, no education, and the hopes of finding a labor job and having a better life.

There's a joke that says 'all blues starts "woke up this morning."' Yes, that's a cliché of the blues. But for the people at Florence's this meant more than 'I opened my eyes in bed as the sun came up.' It meant that they were bonded by the mutual experience of 'I woke up this morning knowing that in half an hour I'll be pushing a massive plow behind a farting mule or bending over to hoe weeds, and I'll be doing that until it's too dark to see. And tomorrow and the next day and the next day, I'll do it again, until, most likely, I work until I die, broke, just like my parents and grandparents.' That was the shared subtext, the other information hiding in those simple lyrics.

As one essay in this book points out, the blues is no longer a popular music for most African-Americans. Even when I came to Chicago in 1970, when there were forty or fifty clubs in the black ghetto that regularly presented blues bands, younger blacks dismissed the blues as old-time,

Southern music, and often used dismissive descriptions such as 'Uncle Tom music' or 'slavery time music.' Older blacks with roots in the South were often blues fans, but, even during the commercial heyday of the blues, from the 1920s through the early 1960s, many blacks preferred other forms of music, from jazz to gospel to vocal groups and even to white pop and country music. The blues was (and is) seen in the black community as blue collar music, music for the uneducated, the hard-drinking, the occasionally violent patrons of lower-class bars. The white parallel would be hillbilly music, the poor, moonshine-drinking, toothless, embarrassing cousin of commercial country music. Even though black people have defined the blues much more broadly than whites, and have included artists such as Dinah Washington, Louis Jordan, Sam Cooke, Johnnie Taylor, Otis Redding, and other black pop and soul singers under the mantle of the blues, blues was never the only popular music in the black community, and it has been decades since it was among the most popular. Meanwhile, audiences that know little of the culture that generated the blues have adopted and adapted the blues, morphing it into British blues and hard arena rock, and even injecting the structures of blues into punk rock.

Since the blues emerged from the Southern juke joints and Northern bars into the mainstream of American and world music, it has become more of a form of entertainment and less of a shared community folk music. When I sit in white blues clubs and primarily white festival audiences, rarely do I see fans stand up and holler, or wave their arms over their heads when the lyrics hit that familiar spot, the way the fans showed their appreciation in the black clubs. They may love the music but will generally wait until the end of the song to applaud or whistle their approval. The bluesmen and blueswomen present the music to the audience and the audience receives their presentation – the sharing of mutual experience isn't there, even though the audience can still feel the tension and release. Does the blues work the same way on an audience of middle- and upper-class 'blues cruisers' as it did on an audience of black Southern sharecroppers or urban factory laborers? Of course not. But does that make its emotional impact less legitimate, or just different? Can audiences around the world, audiences that didn't grow up in the blues culture, still feel the primal blues urge to survive the pain of real life by sharing it, and to glory in the joy of simply being alive, as the creators of the blues intended? I believe so.

With this book, we have a series of reflections, ruminations, and dissections of the blues as both a form of music and as a cultural force.

BRUCE IGLAUER

Certainly these can give us some insight into the blues. But for a truer insight than any of these authors, myself included, can give, I urge you to dive into the very, very deep and endlessly invigorating well of blues music itself. Buy some blues recordings (I could suggest a good label if I weren't so modest). Attend some live performances by blues artists, white or black, who have some sense of the tradition. Immerse yourself in this wonderful, invigorating, life-affirming music. It won't hurt... or, if it does, it will be the kind of hurt that 'hurts so good.'

NOTE

1 Ralph Ellison, 'Remembering Jimmy,' *Saturday Review* XLI (July 12, 1950), p. 37.

JESSE R. STEINBERG
AND ABROL FAIRWEATHER

IT GOES A LITTLE SOMETHING LIKE THIS...

An Introduction to *Blues – Philosophy for Everyone*

The blues is deep. Philosophy is deep. Combined, they are doubly deep. However, you may be wondering whether these seemingly different enterprises really have any strong connection to one another. Is philosophy bluesy? Is the blues philosophical? A glance at the dominant figures in the history of each clearly reveals strikingly different colors – black and white, respectively. Moreover, blues and philosophy seem to focus on very different topics. Blues lyrics talk about women, whiskey, suffering, death, and the devil. The feel of the music is loose, gritty, raunchy, and rolling. Philosophy lacks a musical tone or tempo and avoids all mention of sex, drugs, and rock 'n' roll unless absolutely necessary. The feel of philosophy is tight, logical, and prim and proper. So the connection between blues and philosophy is not as apparent as that between Muddy Waters and McKinley Morganfield, or, as an example that philosophers are fond of, between Clark Kent and Superman. Blues and philosophy are definitely not one and the same. Yet the essays in this book make the case that there is a lot of connective tissue. These connections have to do with a shared approach and response to the many profound and enduring questions of human nature, knowledge, and existence.

Let's start our exploration of the relationship between the blues and philosophy by examining the blues. Blues songs typically have a strong back-beat and a characteristic pulsating rhythm. The blues typically involves a three-line AAB verse form. It often has characteristic 'blue notes,' which are slight drops of pitch on the third, seventh, and sometimes the fifth tone of the relevant scale. But this barely begins to plumb the depths of the blues. The people and their lives tell us more.

It's hard to pin down our favorite list of blues legends. We love Sam Lightnin' Hopkins, Bessie Smith, Mississippi John Hurt, Son House, Howlin' Wolf, B. B. King, Albert King, Muddy Waters, Little Walter, Buddy Guy, Junior Wells, and both artists that went by the name Sonny Boy Williamson. Not only did these figures produce fantastic music, but their lives are fascinating and provide a lens into what the blues is really all about.

If you like guitar, you definitely love Lightnin' Hopkins. In addition to being one the most gifted musicians and performers, he recorded albums in seven decades (from the twenties to the eighties); spent time on a work camp for an unknown crime; wrote an amazing number of songs about whiskey and women; and has been cited as the key inspiration and idol of Eric Clapton, Jimmie Page, and Keith Richards. And in all of his music there is a wicked wink and a knowing smile underneath.

Son House was the classic fallen preacher of the blues and one of the founders of the Delta blues. In the words of Michael Bloomfield, 'Son House *is* the blues.' Son House gave up preaching for the blues and led a life of binge drinking that included fifteen years of hard labor for taking another man's life, supposedly in self-defense. Son House is not considered a great guitarist, but his voice and the content of his lyrics are powerful and intensely fierce. Religion is a common theme in his music, giving us the great contradiction of the whiskey-filled hard life of a blues preacher.

Howlin' Wolf is the great figure of the Chicago blues. He was a big, big man. It was said that the way he got the crowd worked up and his raw power on stage scared away all the white record company execs that had been interested in signing him and his band. At the same time, he was a savvy and caring business manager who paid his band when they were not gigging.

B. B. King is probably the hardest-working blues artist of all time. He has famously gigged for hundreds of days each year, well into his golden years. B. B. still plays far more shows than many younger musicians and does it all with the same twinkle in his eye, bravado, and mellow voice, along with the ever-present piercing wails emanating from his guitar, Lucille. Borrowing from greats such as T-Bone Walker, he introduced an amazing style of guitar solo based on string bending and heart-wrenching vibrato that has influenced virtually every modern electric blues guitarist.

Let's now see how *philosophical* the blues is by looking at some ideas found in some of the legends of philosophy such as Plato and Descartes. Imagine a suffering, worried soul in difficult circumstances internally and externally striving to understand itself and find a better way. The blues and philosophy both have a lot to say about this soul, and thus a lot to say to each other. Blues souls and souls studied by philosophy come together in many ways. Lightnin' Hopkins thoroughly embodies this image. You can feel the forlorn, suffering vibe in the slow, wandering riffs of 'Down Baby,' and the lyrics of 'Gin Bottle Blues' and 'Thinkin' and Worryin'' beautifully express the spiritual turmoil caused by excesses of booze and women, respectively. But, in his famous 'Mojo Hand,' Lightnin' is clearly on top of this trouble. It's that mojo hand that you gotta find when you got the blues. Lightnin' went to Louisiana to get his. And you just might find an expression of yours in his music.

Think about Plato. In Book IX of his masterpiece *The Republic*, written over 2300 years ago, Plato presents the striking image of the human soul composed of three elements engaged in a primordial, distinctively human struggle within itself – man's inner struggle. According to Plato, the biggest part of the soul is a many-headed beast: appetite, urge, and craving. It is the impulsive, desiring part of the self that occupies this bottom part of one's soul. The smallest part the soul is a man on the very top: the rational element (*nous* in Greek). This part is the executive, decision-making part of the self. In the middle is spirit (*thumos* in Greek). This is the part that involves feeling and emotion. Things get interesting when Plato says that reason and desire both aspire to control and take over the middle part. Our emotions will either be in service to our passions or to our reason. Thus is born a fundamental tension that lies at the heart of being human. Inside all of us there is this battle. We usually just call it 'living.' Lightnin's great electric piece 'Lonesome Dog' is all about the dog in his back yard that howls every time his baby is gone. We don't think that dog has four legs. Rather, the 'dog' is that bottom part of the soul Plato is talking about. The blues soul has an essential tension within. It's that bent note inside of us.

This tension also gives rise in philosophy to accounts of *how best to live* given the inner struggle among the elements that make us up. This has to do with human flourishing and how one can be fully happy. Plato goes on to say that the well-ordered soul, the virtuous and happy soul, is the harmony that results when reason is large and in charge, controlling and directing the other parts of the self. For Plato, reason creates harmony in the soul and in society. But this is clearly not a blues harmony. Something has gone wrong in the blues. Things are not as they should be – not what a rational mind would propose. It might seem like a blues soul would be disordered one in Plato's sense. Lightnin's dog is getting fed. Conditions on the outside are far from fair. But there's something beautiful in a way not fully described by the rational point of view here. This beauty is expressed by, and even understood through, the music. It's not a Platonic harmony, it's a blues harmony. It achieves a different sort of resonance between the parts of the soul, and there is something deep to the way the blues does this.

But this difference between Plato's philosophical harmony and a blues harmony may not be huge. First, Plato knew that most people do not perfectly achieve or even approximate this ideally harmonious soul. Plato's teacher, Socrates, went around urging an increasingly decadent Athenian society to examine themselves and their beliefs. He encouraged them to care about the condition of their soul more than about wealth and power. He was killed for this, a point we will return to. There were plenty of differently ordered souls in ancient Athens – and there are still plenty around today. That's why they needed philosophy – and that's why we still need it today.

Where we get more disagreement between blues and philosophy is in the therapy, or the solution, to the suffering of conflicted souls. As noted, Plato puts reason large and in charge. The blues, on the other hand, makes suffering *into* music. It looks it straight in the eye, makes it artistic and beautiful, and transcends it in the process. Though in different ways, philosophy and the blues provide us with a perspective from which to understand the struggling soul and the wisdom to become more. That's a deep connection.

A second connection can be found in the work of moral philosophers such as Jeremy Bentham, who famously thought that what matters morally about any being is whether it can suffer. Blues offers musical and lyrical insight into suffering and misfortune. The music itself is a way of knowing that part of the world. If you could see suffering and worrying from the inside, it would sound like Lightnin's classic, 'Last Night.' It's a slow, dusty suffering. That song is authentically and deeply dark. Although the medium is different and gives us a unique way of knowing it, the blues is very much about what moral philosophy is about – suffering. So the blues wrestles with the same sort of deep issues plaguing humanity and human nature as philosophy.

Despite this general connection with suffering, we have to appreciate the very specific nature of blues suffering. It's not just any troubled mind that has the blues. It's 300 years of slavery, Jim Crow, segregation, sharecropping, oppression, poverty, prison camps, and worry. It's acoustic in the Mississippi Delta and Texas in the early twentieth century. And it's electric in Chicago, Detroit, and St. Louis just a few decades later. It's black. The blues is very specific suffering. This raises the interesting question of whether blues experience can be authentically had or understood only by people that have a share of this very specific history. Can the general principles of philosophy really penetrate this unique, particular experience? Is the wisdom contained in the blues available to us all? This is one of the great questions raised when thinking about the blues, and it is a question many of our essays address.

One thing is for sure: the blues has been one of the most significant forces in popular culture in the United States, and, in great measure, the world. Whether or not we can all participate in this authentically (you'll have to read the essays to determine that!), we are all touched by it. It is in us and the way we experience the world. Blues is thus a form of self-understanding for large swaths of humanity. It's how we got here and the sorts of beings that we are. Blues, like philosophy, is a source of knowledge about very important aspects of human existence.

So far, we have considered what is philosophical about the blues. Let's finish by considering what is bluesy about philosophy. Does the philosopher have a bluesy sensibility? Existentialists such as Kierkegaard and Camus worry about the absurdity of the human condition, grappling with despair and forlornness as the undercurrent of human experience. Descartes, and every philosopher since he wrote his *Meditations On First Philosophy*, has a worried mind because a certain evil demon might be out there trying to make him wrong in everything he believes, making the very project of philosophizing futile. The philosopher pursuing knowledge has to make his peace with this devil and realize that the world is not entirely hospitable. Despite the best efforts we can make to be fully rational, there is always failure lurking, and it's not even our fault.

Socrates might have a bluesy sensibility. As mentioned, he was killed by his fellow Athenians for trying to get them to improve their disordered souls – such a fine aim with such an unjust and unfitting end. We might expect that in his last known conversation, as presented in Plato's *Phaedo*, Socrates would have had the blues. But the friends that gathered around him on his last day were amazed to find him in such good spirits, right before his execution. In fine form, Socrates dispelled the commonly held view that there is any reason to fear death. In Socrates' world, much has gone wrong; it looks like a world full of the blues. But Socrates rises above fear and worry through philosophizing. Lightnin' doesn't use *modus ponens* or *modus tollens* like philosophers are apt to do, but his music raises him above what is wrong in himself and the world. That's why he has that smile! Our point is that philosophers like Socrates have a lot more in common with blues artists like Lightnin' – and *vice versa* – than you might think.

At bottom the blues is positive, very positive. Not in the way that Disneyland is positive, but more like the way Nietzsche is positive. Despite the dark themes and hard experiences, the blues is empowering and smoothly triumphant. This is a subtle and very important feature of the music and it explains part of its enduring impact. It's not just about overcoming, it *is* overcoming. It's what makes the hard, disordered experience of the world understandable and bearable. But it doesn't do it by denying that the world is that way. Rather it acknowledges and, in a sense, embraces such hardships. Something has gone wrong, and it's beautiful and inspiring. The blues creates meaning for real, disharmonious lives in a world gone wrong in all kinds of ways. The universal appeal and cultural impact of the blues shows that it does this particularly well. Since philosophers worry about such issues and wrestle with these features of human existence, the blues and philosophy are, perhaps surprisingly, close kin.

***

In this part of the introduction we give a brief tour of what will unfold in this volume. In doing so, we will sketch some of the main issues and themes that will be addressed. There are four main parts, with a number of fascinating essays in each.

Part I – How Blue is Blue? The Metaphysics of the Blues

The essays in this first section examine the basic question of what the blues really is. To say that the question is basic is by no means to imply that the answer is simple or easy. A number of possible characterizations of the blues have been put forward – that a description of the musical form typically found in most blues music is easy enough to produce; that the blues occupies a nicely defined place in history, preceded by black minstrel music and leading to jazz; that you just know the blues when you hear it, or when you feel it in the music – but none of these easy solutions work.

Bob Dylan famously said that 'the times they are a-changing.' In 'Talkin' To Myself Again,' Joel Rudinow shows us that the blues continue to change, which shows that the historical definition will not work; the blues is not just a blip in history. We also see how the great evolution of the blues will challenge our ability to pin down any complete set of features that defines the blues. This leads us to see the blues as a continuing process in the world. Rudinow is part of this process, as he has been a blues musician for years.

You might have heard of 'throat singing.' That's what Ken Ueno does, in addition to being a professor in the Music Department at the University of California, Berkeley. In 'Reclaiming the Aura,' Ueno introduces the idea of the 'aura' of a piece of music, which goes beyond and may be only loosely connected to the notes. Every piece of music likely has both, and we see classical music as defined by the score – a more tangible, consistent basis via which different orchestras can determining how the same piece of music should be played. However, this is not how it works in the blues. In order to play the same blues song as someone else, you don't have to be playing the same set of notes. You have to capture the aural aspect of the song. Ueno brings out this distinction with a great example from B. B. King.

In 'Twelve-Bar Zombies,' Wade Fox and Richard Greene provide examples of music that is undoubtedly blues but also clearly does not fit the canonical musical form we call the blues. In fact, they argue that there is no set of conditions that all and only blues satisfies. But to say that the blues cannot be defined in the exact way philosophers often aim to define concepts such as 'truth,' 'goodness,' and 'beauty' is not to say that it cannot be understood. Fox and Greene propose that all things that count as blues will bear some 'family resemblance' to other things that count as blues. Some set of overlapping features will be shared between them. This way of capturing both what is similar and what is different across the broad range of blues music is a very nice application of the philosophy of Ludwig Wittgenstein.

Jenkins shows a different kind of difficulty in defining the blues in 'The Blues as Cultural Expression,' when he introduces the distinction between musical form and cultural expression. Jenkins says that authentic blues is a form of cultural expression. Unlike musical form, cultural

  JESSE R. STEINBERG AND ABROL FAIRWEATHER

expression cannot be achieved by anyone with sufficient training and talent. You have to have the right kind of experience to produce that distinct cultural expression that is the blues. So-called 'cultural outsiders' cannot do it. One interesting implication, it would appear, is that white people cannot play the blues, at least not blues-as-cultural-form.

Part 2 – The Sky is Crying: Emotion, Upheaval, and the Blues

The blues is a way of feeling, a way of feeling life, the world, and yourself. As such, it reaches into some of the deepest and most important aspects of human existence. The blues isn't a happy, shiny feeling. It's clearly on the darker side of the color spectrum as far as feelings go. This raises the question of why we would want to listen to the blues and why it's been so popular and influential. If it not only is about feeling low but also brings out those feelings in us when we listen to it, why would we want to play and listen to it? This is complicated. Maybe feeling bad in this sense isn't all that bad after all. Maybe we all really want and even relish feeling blue in that sense. Conversely, we might think that no one wants such feelings. It might not seem that anyone would *want* to feel blue. Regardless of the side of this debate on which you stand, such feelings are obviously inevitable. The down feeling in the blues is thus about that down part of life that we cannot avoid. We might not want it, but, given that it's here, we want to understand it and how to deal with it. How exactly does blues put us in touch with these down feelings and that down part of life?

In 'The Artistic Transformation of Trauma, Loss, and Adversity in the Blues,' Alan M. Steinberg, Robert S. Pynoos, and Robert Abramovitz propose the fascinating hypothesis that the structure and function of the blues mirrors the structure and function of psychotherapy. Specifically, they examine therapeutic forms of coping with trauma, loss, and adversity, and find analogous themes in the lyrics, notes, rhythm, and tonality of the blues. They argue that this aspect of the blues constitutes a major reason for its popularity and endurance. Given the inevitability of low-down feelings, the blues represents a universal therapeutic and artistic way of communicating and addressing those feelings. The blues is then a forum and setting for coming to terms with these aspects of harsh emotional life.

The down feelings of the blues might turn out to be a pleasurable experience of a sort – pleasurable in the sense that experiencing beauty is pleasurable. David C. Drake argues for the beauty of the blues in 'Sadness as Beauty,' saying that not just the musical talent exhibited but also the sadness itself is beautiful. Looking at theories of aesthetic beauty philosophers have developed, it turns out that the down feelings of the blues are beautiful. Not just any and all sadness is beautiful; it is the way blues does sadness that makes it beautiful. The unique achievement of the blues is making sadness beautiful.

In 'Anguished Art,' Ben and Owen Flanagan bring out other ways in which the down feelings are the upside of the blues through the concept of anguish. Tragedy, operatic disaster, and sad poetry are pleasing precisely because of the anguish they produce in us. These are expressions of an essential tension in humanity. To feel anguish is to be authentically human. To deny that feeling is less than authentic, and the pleasantness that might come from denial is temporary and shallow at best. The blues is part of this tradition, in a particularly modern way. It has always been important for human beings to feel negative emotions, and the blues carries on this timeless tradition.

In 'Blues and Catharsis,' Roopen Majithia shows us how the experience we have in the blues performs an important cleansing of the modern, urban soul. Life builds up pent-up feelings in us and these need release – only to build up and require release again. This is a healthy process of coping with the inevitable residue of human existence. Aristotle and the Greeks were aware of this. The process Aristotle calls 'catharsis' explains why the Ancient Greeks held yearly festivals in which they would watch gruesome and horrible tragedies (think of Oedipus). The value of experiencing these gruesome portrayals is the release of feelings – the art form becomes a catalyst for purgation and cleansing. Now, we might not get the same release from a Greek tragedy as its original audience did, and they might not obtain the same release from listening to a blues show as we do, but the art forms perform similar functions: cleaning house.

Part 3 – If it Weren't for Bad Luck, I Wouldn't Have No Luck at All: Blues and the Human Condition

The cause may not be 'original sin,' but human life inevitably brings with it disappointment, suffering, and betrayal. We wouldn't consider a being that never felt these emotions *one of us*. These feelings are some of the basic principles of our frame, experienced in different ways by different people at different times. There are surely some upsides to the human condition, and the blues looks at some of these aspects too. But the blues is primarily focused on the darker parts of the human condition. It does the dirty work.

Disappointment, suffering, and betrayal are all part of the human condition. Some philosophers have argued that the way out of this predicament is to stoically control your emotions. In 'Why Can't We Be Satisfied?' Brian Domino argues that the blues offers us a defiant response to Western philosophy's characteristic stoicism.

In 'Doubt and the Human Condition,' Jesse R. Steinberg argues that a pervasive part of the human condition and a major theme in blues music is *doubt*. Descartes and other philosophers have provided arguments for a view called skepticism – the view that we don't know very much at all about the world around us – that relies on this unfortunate part of the human condition. Steinberg argues that blues music surprisingly provides support for skepticism.

In 'Blues and Emotional Trauma,' Robert D. and Benjamin A. Stolorow find deep parallels between psychologically coping with trauma and connecting with blues music. Blues provides a therapeutic, visceral-linguistic conversation in which universally traumatizing aspects of human existence can be communally held and lived through.

When it comes to religion and the blues, one name reigns supreme – Son House. If you haven't listened, the time is now. The music is powerful, very powerful. House is often considered the least musically talented of the great early bluesman but perhaps the purest, deepest, and definitely the most deeply connected to religion. Though he was a preacher, he was a fallen preacher. In 'Suffering, Spirituality, and Sensuality,' Joseph J. Lynch chronicles this fallen preacher's relationship with the blues and religion to find an essential commonality between the two in the alleviation of sin, suffering, and oppression, despite the seeming contradiction between House's piety and hard bluesman life. Lynch finds a similar Son House-like bluesmanship in Marx, the Buddha, and Kierkegaard.

In 'Worrying the Line,' Kimberly R. Connor explains how blues lament is imbued with religious elements and how much of the deep power of the blues comes from the divine power invoked. This divine power comes amidst some less-than-divine, imperfect, impure aspects of human existence. But this is precisely the root of the power. We are not gods or angels; we are mere mortals. But we also have the power of the divine, which is much more powerful when we mere mortals experience it.

The blues as Connor describes it is essentially a vehicle of transcendence, and it is this transcendence that we are reacting to when we hear the blues.

Part 4 – The Blue Light was my Baby and the Red Light was my Mind: Race and Gender in the Blues

You can't talk about the blues without talking about being black and about men and women. The original blues musicians were almost all black. Gender becomes relevant because of the amazing number of blues songs written and performed by men about women, and the trouble thereby caused. But there have been and are very significant female figures in the blues, even right at the beginning, and the social history of women may make them equally suited to singing the blues.

When considering women and the blues, the many, many blues songs written about women by men may initially spring to ming. Women are the second person in the blues. In 'Lady Sings the Blues,' Winsby argues that women have a more central place as the subject – the first person, not the second person – of the blues. She makes the case that a certain (partially non-black) population has the right kind of cultural experience and history to play the blues authentically, namely women. Women have a history and experience of social frustration, subjugation, and silencing that brings with it the emotional center of the blues aesthetic. The female voice is very much the voice of the blues, even though most of what you hear sounds like a male voice.

Regarding the color of the blues, Douglas and Nathaniel Langston, in 'Even White Folks Get the Blues,' contend that many a great bluesman has conceived of the blues in a way that leaves it open for non-black musicians to be authentic blues musicians. Whatever differences can be claimed between the world views of black sharecroppers and their descendants and people of white Northern European descent, they are not inseparable. The blues is, then, not the province of the cultural experience of African-Americans. In an important sense, blues is colorblind.

In 'Distributive History,' Neumann challenges the very idea that blues is 'black music,' and thus the oft-cited claim that rock and roll ripped off the blues. Rock and roll did indeed borrow much from contemporary black music, but it did so by tapping into what had long ago become virtually a shared heritage. If one listens to Clapton, Keith Richards, and

Jimmie Page and then goes back and listens to bluesmen such as Lightnin'
Hopkins and Muddy Waters, one gets an 'aha!' feeling. These white rock
legends, seemingly pioneers, were just modifying the blues. They made a
lot more money, and this might lead to the idea that rock and roll ripped
off the blues, which sounds like yet another injustice on top of the injustices that prompted the blues in the first place. But Neumann debunks
this 'rock ripped off the blues' account.

In 'Whose Blues?' Ron Bombardi offers a philosophical portrait of
blues music as a social narrative – a story of American life with familiar
episodes of bondage, liberation, and denial and restitution. He argues
that the story of blues music is beset by bad habits of thinking about differences between people – habits that stem from a mistaken confidence
in the notion that a people's music will tell the tale of their shared identity. Not only does this confidence ignore importantly stubborn facts
about the makers of blues music, but it also conspires to perpetuate
exactly the sort of material and emotional oppression from which blues
songs have always sought deliverance.

We invite you to engage your mind and your soul as you read the
philosophical investigations into the blues collected here. You can
approach these essays musically, culturally, historically, racially, emotionally, or religiously. Along the way, you may develop your own philosophy
of the blues, or perhaps a *bluesy philosophy*!

ACKNOWLEDGMENTS

Jesse R. Steinberg

I think my first concert was the Long Beach Blues Festival in southern California. I must have been only one year old, but it turned out to be the beginning of a love affair. I've been hooked ever since! My parents are deserving of thanks for more than I can express, but one thing that I'll be eternally grateful for is the fact that they introduced me to the blues and exposed me to such great music over the years. Some of my fondest memories are of getting to see the likes of Albert King, B. B. King, John Lee Hooker, Etta James, Buddy Guy, and Junior Wells. What a lucky kid I was. And I even have fond memories of doing chores – such as scrubbing the kitchen walls and spending hours painting my house – thanks to the blues music I was listening to at the time. So, Alan and Bernice, thanks so much for giving me something that I'll savor for the rest of my life.

I should thank my friend, Fritz Allhoff, the editor of the *Philosophy for Everyone* series. He encouraged me to apply my love of the blues to my love of philosophy. Others at Wiley-Blackwell are deserving of thanks too. I especially want to acknowledge Jeff Dean and Tiffany Mok for all their help. I'd also like to thank the contributors to this volume. You've each been a pleasure to work with and have produced some fascinating essays.

I've been fortunate to have some great friends who love the blues just as much as me and with whom I've had penetrating conversations about music (and with whom I've seen some great shows). I'm lucky to know Louie Gallian, Anand Vaidya, and Tony Brueckner. I've learned quite a bit about the blues from other musicians too. I'd like to thank my old band mates from college and graduate school, and, more recently, Josh Spence and the Sugar Prophets for all the many hours of fun playing in Illinois. I miss all of you.

I'd like to also thank my wife, Erica. Her patience, support, and encouragement are boundless. She's the sweetest little angel there ever was.

Finally, with as much gratitude as I can muster, thank you to all the blues musicians that have worked so hard, and who have overcome so many obstacles, to create the music that we love so much.

Abrol Fairweather

I would like to thank the music most of all. Next to becoming a parent, nothing has affected me so deeply. Rock with a little blues thrown in was, as for many of us, an essential element for me in growing up – Zeppelin, Hendrix, the Rolling Stones, The Who, Clapton. Pretty standard. I knew there were lingering deep blues influences in the music I grew up on, but it was only a decade after I moved out on my own, went to college, and started studying philosophy that I really met the blues. It was a passing comment made by my friend Willow that she doesn't even remember making – 'you should check out Mississippi John Hurt.' And so I did, and that was it. For years I just drank in his sweet soul, heavenly voice, and unbelievable pickin', and the lyrics, the stories, the images, the experiences, and the emotions – all of it, all the way, all the time. I felt as though I truly, truly loved him, and constantly thanked him out loud. What a beautiful man. Another passing comment by Robert Conrad – 'if you like John Hurt, you'll like Lightin' Hopkins' – led to years of complete immersion in his spontaneous, dusty, whiskey-bottle blues. I came to truly love Lightnin', but it's a little different from how it is with Hurt. I thought this palpable difference in how I related to Hurt and Hopkins was really interesting, and it got me thinking about how it is that I can feel so intimately moved and connected to music made by people that I would be hard pressed to find anything in common with in my actual life. That, in turn, got me thinking about the blues in all kinds of ways. I started exploring more and different blues, and in time came to see that the blues has all kinds of philosophy going on. This deeply formative fifteen-year period culminated in the present collection.

I have listened to and learned many other blues, but I always go back to Mississippi John Hurt and Lightnin' Hopkins. Thanks guys!

I also want to thank the great team at Wiley-Blackwell: Fritz Alhoff, Jeff Dean, and Tiffany Mok. You were great to work with, and I am a better editor for the experience. I love my daughter Barbara and fiancé Michelle, and to Michelle I owe great thanks for her support and patience.

PART I

HOW BLUE IS BLUE?
THE METAPHYSICS OF THE BLUES

CHAPTER I

TALKIN' TO MYSELF AGAIN

A Dialogue on the Evolution of the Blues

It is unlikely that [the blues] will survive through the imitations of the young white college copyists, the 'urban blues singers' whose relation to the blues is that of the 'Trad' jazz band to the music of New Orleans: sterile and derivative. The bleak prospect is that the blues probably has no real future; that folk music that it is, it served its purpose and flourished whilst it had meaning in the Negro community. At the end of the century it may well be seen as an important cultural phenomenon – and someone will commence a systematic study of it, too late.

(Paul Oliver)[1]

Me: Remember when blues historians were all worried about the blues surviving the rock era?

Myself: Absolutely. Paul Oliver actually said he didn't think that the blues would survive through the 1960s. The way he saw it, the blues was essentially rooted in time and place – a variety of folk music indigenous to the post-reconstruction American South. In that unique context the music served an essential social function within its community of origin. Removed from that cultural context the blues is severed from its essence, resulting in music that is at best merely 'sterile and derivative.'

Blues – Philosophy for Everyone: Thinking Deep About Feeling Low, First Edition.
Edited by Jesse R. Steinberg and Abrol Fairweather.
© 2012 John Wiley & Sons, Inc. Published 2012 by John Wiley & Sons, Inc.

Me: Shows how much they knew! Check it out – we're now ten years into the twenty-first century and it's quite apparent that the blues has survived, thrived, and arrived. And I mean *ARRIVED*!

Myself: Wait a minute. Just *what* do you mean, 'arrived'?

Me: Well, just look around. Blues is big global biz – maybe not *quite* as big as hip-hop, or the NBA, but no less global, and pretty damn big. The blues is everywhere now! The blues has its own 'Oscars,' or 'Grammys.' The Blues Foundation, like the Academy of Motion Picture Arts and Sciences and the National Academy of Recording Arts and Sciences in Hollywood, hosts an annual Blues Music Awards ceremony and banquet (formerly the W. C. Handy Awards) drawing thousands of visitors from all over the world to Memphis, Tennessee. And they sponsor an annual international talent search, attracting entrants from far and wide: Australia, Canada, Croatia, France, Israel, Italy, Norway, Poland, and all fifty US states. Blues tourism is now a growth industry in the Mississippi Delta and beyond. Nowadays you can go on a Caribbean Blues Cruise – a floating week-long round-the-clock blues festival aboard an eleven-deck five-star cruise-ship – stopping in Aruba, Curacao, St. Barts, and other exotic vacation destinations. And look here! There is even now a recognized academic specialty in blues scholarship. By the time you get a book of philosophical essays published about the blues, under the Wiley-Blackwell imprint, no less, the blues has, like I said, *ARRIVED*!

Myself: Well, if that's what you mean by 'arrived,' what do mean by 'thrived' and 'survived'?

Me: Well, isn't the blues 'thriving' as commerce?

Myself: Depends on who you ask. I know a lot of players can't get a gig and others can't keep a band together because of blues clubs and festivals closing down all over the place or changing their format to something more 'contemporary.' Did you know that the San Francisco Blues Festival, the longest running blues festival anywhere, shut down two years ago for economic reasons? And lots of smaller regional festivals have had to do the same, and in this economy…

I: Look, in the twenty-first century the whole music industry is in deep turmoil. At this point, none of the old business models seem viable even short-term. So what's the point of debating the commercial viability of one particular genre of music?

Myself: Okay. Let's skip the economics. But the still deeper question, about 'survival,' remains whether commercially successful 'blues' is really blues. Go ahead and assume that the blues *has* been successfully commercialized. How does it survive that transformation *as blues*? Isn't successfully commercialized blues essentially 'dead on arrival?'

Me: I hope you're not assuming some sort of radical incompatibility between the blues and show business success. Surely you're not going to discredit B. B. King because he made it from the chitlin' circuit to the world stage and his own chain of nightclubs!

Myself: Don't trivialize the point. B. B.'s career speaks for itself. I'd say the same for Buddy Guy – these are two good (indeed *exceptional*) examples of bluesmen surviving and thriving. But that's the point. These are the *exceptions* that prove the rule. There's a huge difference between B. B. King's Beale Street Blues Club in Memphis or Buddy Guy's Legends in Chicago and, for example, the national corporate chain known as the House of Blues.

Me: Specifically?

Myself: Well, for starters, look at the locations. It makes sense for Buddy Guy to have his own club in Chicago, and for B. B. King to erect a shrine to the blues on Beale Street in Memphis. But what's up with the House of Blues on Disneyland Avenue in Anaheim (smells like a theme park to me) and the Boardwalk in Atlantic City (smells even worse: like a casino)? Then look at the ownership structure, if you want to get more deeply into it. The House of Blues chain is part of Live Nation, arguably now the world's largest global entertainment conglomerate, controlling events, concert tours, festivals, and the largest venues in major markets all over the world (and now ticket distribution, including scalping – what a racket!). Music, monster trucks, golf – they don't care. They promote anything! If you can draw a crowd, they'll promote it. And now that they own the House of Blues, do you really think it's a chain of blues clubs anymore, *if* it ever was? Just check out the music lineup. Maybe it includes *some* blues, but damn few and far between! The concert listings are dominated by Live Nation touring acts, just as you'd expect: Anvil, Nickelback, Killswitch Engage, Timbaland. C'mon! No disrespect to Anvil or anybody, but it ain't the blues or even close! House of *Blues*?! They've got their 'blues' logo plastered all over their useless schwag – it's got nothing whatsoever to do with the blues. It's nothing but a corporate entertainment franchise operation sloppily copping a 'blues-theme,' very much in the mold of the Hard Rock Café (which makes *some* sense, by the way – the same entrepreneur, one Isaac Tigrett, started both). That's commercialization for you: completely devoid of soul.

Me: Slow down, man! You're getting carried away. Whatever Live Nation may be doing with it now, that's not how the House of Blues started out, and Live Nation would never have been interested in acquiring the House of Blues if the latter hadn't demonstrated that there's a viable commercial market for the blues.

Myself: I'm not so sure. Live Nation seems bent on global domination and ready to gobble up whatever they can use and whatever stands in their way, regardless. But let's talk about the origins of the House of Blues. The first House of Blues opened in Harvard Square (!) in 1992. Tigrett's original partner in the venture was Canadian comedian Dan Aykroyd, of *Saturday Night Live* fame. Aykroyd and his *Saturday Night Live* co-star John Belushi had developed two characters: the Blues Brothers – two white guys fronting a blues band. Belushi, as 'Jolliett Jake' Blues, was the singer (imagine Belushi's samurai warrior character dressed like a Chicago hit man in shades with a microphone). Aykroyd, in matching outfit, as Elwood Blues, played harmonica. What began as a comedy sketch and then developed into a running gag was so successful (popular) that within a couple of years Belushi and Aykroyd had rounded up a backup band of A-list Memphis session musicians, had recorded and released a full-length album (*Briefcase Full of Blues*), and had a script for a Hollywood feature-length comedy in production (*The Blues Brothers*, 1980). They even opened a bar in Chicago called *The Blues Brothers Bar*. The bar didn't have an actual liquor license so it got shut down pretty quickly, but there's your prototype. And there you have it: the original House of Blues – a spin-off of a successful comedy act about a couple of white guys fronting a blues band.

Me: Now look who's trivializing. The impulses behind the original House of Blues were complex, not simply comedic. And it's worth noting that the comedic impulses animating the Blues Brothers as comic personae have more than a little complexity and depth as well. Aykroyd was a committed blues fan from his high school and college days in Ottawa, where he got to hear all the great touring bluesmen of the 1950s and early 1960s: Muddy Waters, Howlin' Wolf, James Cotton, Junior Wells, Buddy Guy. He even jammed with Muddy Waters. Aykroyd turned Belushi on to the blues, and Belushi grew to be a committed blues fan himself, his interest growing deeper through his encounters with Curtis Salgado and Robert Cray during the production of *National Lampoon's Animal House* in the late 1970s in Eugene, Oregon (Cray wound up appearing as the bass player in the band that performs as 'Otis Day and the Knights' in the roadhouse and frat-house party scenes). So both Aykroyd and Belushi got some serious schooling in the blues from some

JOEL RUDINOW

pretty unimpeachable sources. And, if you look closely you begin to see that what the Blues Brothers were *really* making fun of was *themselves* as white guys getting into the blues.

Myself: I love it when people make my point for me. See, we're back to Paul Oliver's bleak assessment of the future of the blues. Aykroyd and Belushi are just part of a cultural process in which the blues is simultaneously appropriated, exploited, and left behind. I suppose it's nice, even somewhat 'redeeming,' that these guys were able to make fun of themselves and of their own role in that process.

Me: But you're now talking as though the blues can be neatly separated and distinguished from what you call the 'process' of commercial appropriation and exploitation. Don't forget: all the great blues singers took part in that process. In the 1930s weren't they expanding their audiences through recordings and radio performances? In the 1960s weren't they playing college towns and folk festivals, reaching new generations of fans? Then didn't they go to the West Coast and play the Fillmore, and open for the Stones in Europe, expanding their audiences even further? You can see these same processes at work all the way back to 1903 with W. C. Handy, who transcribed the blues for sale as sheet music. So what exactly is it about these processes that you see as being especially in need of 'redemption'? Is it the commerce, or the roles and racial identities of those involved in it?

Myself: Both! The black bluesmen and women that performed on the radio, made recordings, and went out on tours were generally being exploited commercially by businesses controlled mostly by white people.

I: I thought we were going to skip the economics, but apparently not. Do you sense the discussion expanding to greater and greater levels of complexity? We're now confronting not only the economics and business ethics of the entertainment industry and the arts but also the complexities of American history and race in the even larger context of the Heraclitean flux of culture formation, and…

Me and Myself [in shocked unison]: What the… ?!

I: … how can we even *begin* to comprehend the massive network of dynamic forces (economic, social, political, and more) constantly shaping culture at any moment in time and place? Don't you wonder where to find *any* reliable standard for predicting and assessing the trajectory of a culture and its contents? Who was it that said, when asked for an opinion about the future of jazz, 'If I knew where jazz was going, I'd be there already'?

Myself: Trumpeter Humphrey Lyttelton said that.

Me: But what was that hurricane cluster flap, or whatever that was you said? What *are* you talking about?

I: Heraclitus: the Greek philosopher who held that everything is always changing (in flux). He's the source of that famous saying that you can't step twice into the same river. So, isn't culture a lot like a river – always flowing and changing, affecting and affected by everything with which it comes in contact?

Me: Okay. So we get the metaphor.

Myself: But where are you headed with it?

I: Well, suppose we consider the blues as a cultural phenomenon, something that arises as part of what we call culture. As such the blues is 'alive,' constantly changing and developing – that is, of course, until it 'dies.' Now, how do you tell whether the blues is living or dying? How *do* you determine which changes and developments constitute continuations or extensions of the blues as a living tradition and which ones constitute departures from or betrayals of that tradition? And doesn't it get more complicated and difficult with each new generation of change and development?

Me: How about an example?

I: Okay. Here's one. When Muddy Waters moved from Mississippi to Chicago, it wasn't long before he was playing amplified electric guitar and surrounded by a full band. That was a change, a development. And he was playing to audiences of factory workers in an urban nightclub, instead of sharecroppers in a Delta juke joint. That's a change, more development. Does anyone wonder whether the blues is surviving through *these* changes?

Me: Not me.

I: Now take the example a step further. By 1969 Muddy was playing in larger and more opulent venues spread out across the United States and overseas. He was playing to larger and younger crowds, including more and more white people. And he made an album for Chess Records entitled *Fathers and Sons*, now surrounded by a full band including three white guys: Paul Butterfield, Michael Bloomfield, and Donald 'Duck' Dunn (who also played bass behind the Blues Brothers). These are the guys Paul Oliver is talking about as having a 'sterile and derivative' relationship to the blues. More change, more development; but now doubts are being raised about whether the blues will survive.

Myself: Well, the obvious difference is the growing presence of white people in the picture – a difference that *makes* a difference to how the music is made, presented, received, and understood, and, of course, to how it is treated commercially.

Me: How long are we going to stay bogged down in this tired old debate over white people and blues 'authenticity'? That's so twentieth century![2]

Myself: The debate may be 'old' and 'tired' but it's far from settled. And if you only look you'll see this very same debate raging right in the middle of the twenty-first-century hip-hop wars.[3]

Me: If you ask me, the fact that this tired old debate is now raging around hip-hop shows that the music is evolving but not the debate.

I: Then you're not studying the debate closely enough. The debate over the authenticity issue has indeed continued to evolve – mostly in the direction of greater complexity, just like the issues (of race and racism) that continue to animate it.[4]

Myself: I don't see what's so 'complex.' Look, you can go to any city (or area of suburban sprawl) in America right now and find the local 'blues society,' which will almost inevitably be a sort of amateur musicians' 'bowling league' populated by aging white people who sell insurance for a living and have a 'band room' in their garage where they think up formulaic band names like 'Hardhat Harry the Home-Wreckers' and play endless lame versions of 'Sweet Home Chicago' and (gag) 'Mustang Sally.' What a caricature!

Me: What you just said is a caricature. You should remember who you're talking to! And choose your words carefully. You're talking about *me*, you know!

I: Can we clear the air in here? It's getting a little funky. You know, usually there's *some* truth in caricature – also oversimplification and selective exaggeration. Now, would you like to know what I mean by 'complexity?'

Me: Suits me.

Myself: Speak for yourself.

I: Alright, first tell me what we're talking about.

Me: The evolution of the blues?

Myself: More like the 'evolution' of the 'blues' (choosing my words carefully).

I: Oh, goody! A subtle distinction! Now, scare quotes or not, in order to understand what it is we're talking about, do we or don't we need a definition of 'the blues?'

Me: Question: We're talking about the music (not the feeling), right?

I: As you wish.

Myself: Question: Supposing that we're talking about the music, are we talking about it in the sense that musicians use the term, or the sense used in the marketing end of the music industry (because they're not the same)?

I: Again, as you wish.

Myself: Well, this is already kind of confusing, because a musician might say something like 'Okay, let's play a medium blues shuffle in 'A' with a quick four starting from the five,' and what they would mean by 'blues' is a song structure based on a twelve-bar chord progression in one of several standard variations. But, if you go on iTunes, 'blues' turns up as a genre category second from the top (right between 'alternative' and 'children's music'). And if you browse around in this category you're going to find a whole lot of music that doesn't fit that structure or *any* of its standard or even non-standard variations.

Me: That's because the iTunes category is organized on the basis of the blues canon, and the reason that musicians use the more restrictive meaning is for convenience. It's a kind of shorthand for one of the central conventional song forms in the canon.

I: So, it seems that what we've been arguing about is how to specify the blues canon, and how the blues canon may or may not evolve?

Me and Myself [in surprised unison]: Exactly!

[three-beat pause]

Myself: Having positioned myself as a 'conservative' in defense of the blues canon, I must confess now that it seems a little odd to be speaking of a 'blues canon,' and even to utter the words. I mean, suddenly I'm struck by the paradox of being invested in the 'canonical' status of 'old school' blues.

Me: Can you explain that? I'm not so sure I follow you.

Myself: Well, 'canon' comes from medieval Catholic scholasticism, and...

Me: Right! Talk about 'old school'!

Myself: ... and originally it meant a kind of ecclesiastical rule or law based on the officially authorized holy texts – the texts that the priesthood had 'authenticated' as coming from God. Then that concept got imported into more modern secular disciplines of scholarship. But it still carries most of that weighty freight of official authority. So, for example in the study of English literature you get the distinction between the 'canonical' works of Shakespeare, meaning the texts that the expert literary scholars have decided were actually written by him and are thus 'authentic,' and the 'apocryphal works,' meaning the 'inauthentic' or 'spurious' imitations. And furthermore you get the notion of an English literary canon, meaning the Great Books list of literary works that, again, the expert scholars have decided are the 'best' or the 'most important' or the 'most worthy of serious study,' and are thus understood to definitively establish abiding standards of literary value and taste. You know, the stuff in the *Norton Anthology of English Literature*. And this makes me cringe a bit.

Me: I still don't get it, especially coming from you. I mean, look, your guy Paul Oliver is one of the editors of *The New Blackwell Guide to Recorded Blues*, isn't he?[5] What *is* that if not analogous to the *Norton Anthology of English Literature*? Don't you orient yourself to the blues canon by reference to it?

Myself: Indeed. But what's now making me cringe is how alien all of this 'canonization' business is to 'old school' blues (and even mid- to late-twentieth-century blues-rock) and the cultures that produced them.

Me: Maybe you'd feel more comfortable if you adopted a more flexible and ecumenical attitude toward the evolving blues canon. Take Robert Johnson's 'Cross Road Blues' as an example. Surely this has to count as a canonical blues tune! Have you heard John Mayer's slick new version?[6] As polished and contemporary as it sounds, you can trace a direct line from there straight back through Eric Clapton's classic long jam versions with Cream to the original 1936 recording.

Myself: Sorry, but it's not a very convincing example. The *tune* may belong to the blues canon (still assuming that it makes sense to speak of such a thing), but Mayer's new version of it is quite another matter. The link to Clapton is obvious. But Clapton's version(s) belong to the blues-rock guitar canon, not really to the blues canon as such.

Me: But why do you insist on dividing 'old school' blues from blues-rock?

Myself: Because they're different. I rather suspect that Clapton himself would make the same distinction. When he plays the blues canon, which he does from time to time, as for example on *Me and Mr. Johnson*, Clapton is very 'old school' in his approach. He's paying open and faithful homage to the original compositions and recordings.[7] But with Cream, although he was using blues materials (most famously Robert Johnson's 'Crossroads'), Clapton was moving in a whole new musical direction: the guitar-centric rock power trio. The same goes for Jimi Hendrix. Of course, this music could hardly have been conceived without the blues as a foundation, but it is quite distinct from the blues in so many ways, beginning obviously with the shift of focus from the singer and the lyric to the instrument and its virtuosic manipulation!

Me: Canons to the left of me, canons to the right. And only moments ago one canon was making you cringe.

Myself: It still does seem odd to me to be talking about a blues canon. But given that we are, I still see a clear break between the blues and the psychedelic blues-rock of the 1960s.

I: Do you really mean a 'clear break'? Or is the relationship more of a 'branching off'?

Myself: Well, I suppose it's more of a 'branching off' sort of relationship, in that there's continuity going from psychedelic blues-rock back to the blues roots, but why do you ask?

I: Well, suppose we focus more closely at the 'crotch' where the branch is most integrally connected to its root source and is just beginning to develop in its own separate direction. So, for example, how would you want to characterize Clapton's 1966 version of 'Crossroads'? I'm referring to the one he recorded for Elektra Records in a one-off band with Steve Winwood called 'Eric Clapton and the Powerhouse'?[8] On this recording the ensemble is not a 'power trio,' but is structured and behaves rather in the mold of a 'Chicago blues band.' Clapton doesn't even play the solo. The instrumental break is taken by Paul Jones on harmonica. Now, how is this related to the blues canon? Is it blues or is it blues-rock? Is the blues canon evolving or dividing? And, if we are divided over *this* question, are we divided over an 'aesthetic' question ('a matter of taste')? Or are we divided over a political and moral question (a matter of conscience)? Or both?

Myself: I'm not sure *how* to answer these questions – at least not all of them at once. But suppose we begin by noting something important about the *nature* of a canon: even if canons *do* evolve, this can only be at a slow and stately pace. Otherwise they cease to serve their essential canonical functions.

I: And these are… ?

Myself: Well, it would appear that, if we *are* to have any kind of serious conversation about the blues as an art form, it will inevitably be by reference to a canon. So, I guess a canon is either a pre-condition or an inevitable by-product of the kind of discourse we're engaging in here and now.

I: That's an interesting observation, though not entirely decisive, and it leaves the question of essential functions unanswered. Let's go slowly now. The observation seems to be that the emergence of a canon is a symptom of the phenomenon of academic scholarship. When a *scholarly*

community assembles around a given art form, talk of the canon and the canonical arises. One wonders whether the emergence of a canon is a by-product of the of the advancing evolution of the art form, a symptom of the art form having achieved a level of depth and maturity worthy of serious scholarly attention.

Me: What I'm sayin'!! But don't overlook the possibility that the blues had enough depth and maturity to merit serious attention before the academic scholars started coming around.

Myself: Wait a minute. Didn't academic scholars start coming around about a hundred years ago? Both John and Alan Lomax were academic scholars, and, even before them, there was Howard Odum, who thought of his research as social science. They were all pioneers in the application of emerging audio recording technology to the process of documenting the blues. So, scholarly interest in the blues as an art form is clearly as old as recorded blues.

I: So, is talk of the canon and the canonical with reference to the blues as old as scholarly interest in the blues as an art form or not?

Myself: I'm going to say not, because the first generation of academic scholars to take an interest in the blues as an art form thought of themselves as folklorists, or cultural anthropologists, and thought of the blues in terms remote from those reserved for the discussion of 'literature.' And only in later generations of scholarship – the blues 'revivals' of the 1960s and 1980s – did the blues begin to be assimilated to literature. Then we began to really obsess over the blues canon.

I: So, you're now saying that the emergence of a canon is a symptom of the art form having achieved academic recognition for levels of depth and maturity worthy of serious scholarly attention *as literature*? But now one begins to wonder whether the emergence of a canon is symptomatic of a peculiar need that scholarly communities and their members have for 'foundations' upon which to rest their conflicting claims and assessments of 'literary value'?

Myself: That's *my* worry.

Me: Now *I'm* going to say 'wait a minute.' I think you *can* trace talk of the blues canon (in effect, if not in so many words) all the way back to the first generation of blues scholarship. Or maybe we should say the first and second generation. I'm thinking of the rift that developed between John and Alan Lomax toward the end of the former's life over what properly constitutes folklore. John was apparently quite dismayed when his son Alan undertook to survey the commercially recorded blues that black people were collecting and listening to in the Delta in the 1940s. He thought what you were supposed to do as a folklorist was to go out and find the 'pure' pre-industrial rural music at the source and then record it in the raw for the archives. *And* John was equally dismayed at how his greatest discovery, Huddie 'Leadbelly' Ledbetter, was changed and 'corrupted' by exposure to white urban audiences. Leadbelly was apparently getting too heavily invested into 'showmanship' for the elder Lomax's taste.[9]

I: So, do you now see what I mean by 'complexity'?

Me: I think I'm *beginning* to.

Myself: At least in the sense that I'm somewhat confused about where we are in the discussion.

I: Well, that's not too bad. At least it's honest. So, what do we think about this year's new crop of blues albums? I'm thinking in particular of one of the most surprising, Cyndi Lauper's *Memphis Blues*.[10]

Myself: Well, I think it's doubtful that it will be nominated for a Blues Music Award.

Me: I agree, but what does that indicate about the Blues Music Awards and the Blues Foundation – institutions that some would argue are too heavily invested in the past to recognize (or even allow) the evolution of the blues as a living art-form? You can hear the critics sharpening their knives, writing Cyndi Lauper off as just another shape-shifting publicity-seeking pop icon, trying to compete with Madonna and Lady Gaga by projecting a blues diva avatar, and so on, before they even listen to the record.

Myself: And what does all of this indicate about the future of the blues, the question Paul Oliver raised back in the 1960s?

I: Hard to say (in advance). Even the past keeps looking different with each passing season.[11] A lot depends on what we bring to the music. I really like how Mike Mattison – the vocalist in Derek Trucks' band (a band that is really stretching and extending the blues, and, despite winning the contemporary blues Grammy, is yet to be recognized by the Blues Music Awards) – put it when he said on behalf of the band, 'The now-popular conception of blues is that it's niche music, old people's music. But like any Southern band worth its salt, the Derek Trucks Band knows that the blues are the fount of American music itself – and that's how we treat it.'[12]

NOTES

1 Paul Oliver, 'The future of the blues: Looking back at looking forward,' in *Blues Off The Record: Thirty Years of Blues Commentary* (Tunbridge Wells, UK: Baton Press, 1984), pp. 285–289.

2   Cf. Amiri Baraka (LeRoi Jones), *Blues People* (New York: William Morrow, 1954); Ralph J. Gleason, 'Can the white man sing the blues?' *Jazz and Pop* (August 1968), p. 28. My critique of these arguments was published as 'Race, ethnicity, expressive authenticity: Can white people play the blues?' *The Journal of Aesthetics and Art Criticism*, 52 (1994), pp. 127–137. See also the exchange in Paul C. Taylor, 'So black and blue: Response to Rudinow' and Joel Rudinow, 'Reply to Taylor' *The Journal of Aesthetics and Art Criticism*, 53 (1995): pp. 313–317. For an update on my position, see Joel Rudinow, *Soul Music: The Spiritual Roots of Pop from Plato to Motown* (Ann Arbor, MI: University of Michigan Press, 2010), Chapter 6.

3   Cf. Michael Eric Dyson, *Know What I Mean? Reflections on Hip-Hop* (New York: Basic Civitas Books, 2007).

4   Complementing a growing literature in what is known as 'race formation theory,' an emerging field of 'whiteness studies' is now gaining respectful attention. See, for example, Crispin Sartwell, *Act Like You Know: African-American Autobiography and White Identity* (Chicago, IL: University of Chicago Press, 1998); Rich Benjamin, *Searching for Whitopia* (New York: Hyperion, 2009); and Nell Irvin Painter, *The History of White People* (New York: Norton, 2010). For a review of the latter two titles, see Kelefa Sanneh, 'Beyond the pale: Is white the new black?' *The New Yorker* (April 12, 2010), pp. 69–74.

5   John Cowley and Paul Oliver (Eds.), *The New Blackwell Guide to Recorded Blues* (Cambridge, MA: Blackwell, 1996).

6   John Mayer, *Battle Studies* (Columbia Records, 2009); see also Cream, *Wheels of Fire, Disc 2: Live at the Fillmore* (Polydor, 1968).

7   Eric Clapton, *Me and Mr. Johnson* (Reprise, 2004); see also *Sessions for Robert J* (Reprise, 2004).

8   Eric Clapton and the Powerhouse, 'Crossroads,' *What's Shakin'* (Elektra Records, 1966).

9   See Marybeth Hamilton, *In Search of the Blues: Black Voices, White Visions* (London: Jonathan Cape, 2007), pp. 114–124.

10 Cyndi Lauper, *Memphis Blues* (Mercer Street Records, 2010), with guest performances by B. B. King, Jonny Lang, Charlie Musselwhite, Ann Peebles, and Allen Toussaint. Lauper dedicated the album to Ma Rainey, channeling Tracy Nelson.

11 See Elijah Wald, *How the Beatles Destroyed Rock 'n' Roll* (New York: Oxford University Press, 2009), pp. 8–9.

12 The Derek Trucks Band, *Roadsongs* (SONY Masterworks, 2010).

CHAPTER 2

RECLAIMING THE AURA

B. B. King in the Age of Mechanical Reproduction

*That which withers in the age of mechanical repro-
duction is the aura of the work of art.*

(Walter Benjamin)[1]

Years ago, when I was a graduate student in music
composition at Harvard, I heard B. B. King present a lecture. It was the most amazing lecture on
music I had ever experienced – experienced, rather
than heard, because what he demonstrated about
sounds forced me to question my values about listening, and helped me form new paradigms about
how to hear. As a contemporary composer being educated in the Western
classical tradition, a B. B. King lecture was not really part-and-parcel of
my doctoral curriculum. To be sure, composers such as Ravel and
Gershwin were influenced by the popular music of their time. Moreover,
composers today find themselves delineated into countless hyphenated
niches – avant-garde, neo-classical, post-modern. In the university system, though, composition students generally analyze more Beethoven
than blues. An education in music composition, in the strictly classical
sense, equips the student with the tools of the Western canon, and generally emphasizes an understanding of where one's budding voice fits in

Blues – Philosophy for Everyone: Thinking Deep About Feeling Low, First Edition.
Edited by Jesse R. Steinberg and Abrol Fairweather.
© 2012 John Wiley & Sons, Inc. Published 2012 by John Wiley & Sons, Inc.

the scheme of things, and the historical responsibility of writing music after the eras of your Mozarts and Prokofievs. Yet, for all the compositional theory and score analysis, all the performances given and attended, there was something missing that seeing B. B. King illuminated for me. His lecture revealed an aspect of music that I had heretofore never recognized, for all my classical training.

It was a snowy evening in Cambridge, Massachusetts in December, the last week before winter break. Arriving a little late, I was surprised (but enthralled) to find the hall totally packed. Of course, the hall should be packed for B. B. King, but I remember my expectations being colored by Harvard's reputation as an ivory tower, where you might expect the separation of high art (such as opera and symphonic music) and pop music to be guarded. The band played for a full ten minutes while we waited for B. B. to come onstage, heightening our anticipation of B. B.'s appearance. When he did finally walk into the hall, he immediately received a standing ovation – the first musician I had ever witnessed receiving that honor. He went over to his guitar and sat down. The band stopped to let him talk, and, with that characteristic equator of a smile – one that seems to embrace the circumference of life's wisdom – he delivered to us some important lessons on musical authenticity. 'I go around the country,' he began, 'and many guitar players want to play for me. So, I listen. One thing I don't understand is, why they want to sound like A or B. I tell them, if I wanted A or B, I can *get* A or B!'

Having grown up emulating Jimi Hendrix (one of the few As that B. B. can't get), I – like anyone who has ever been inspired by someone else – identified with that ambition to sound like one's hero. If King had contented himself with only imitating his mentor, T-Bone Walker, is reputation likely never would have extended beyond the borders of his Mississippi home. As he had decades earlier, B. B. was inspiring us to go find our own voice.

Midway into his presentation, B. B. asked members of his band to play solos. Some of the band members were young hot shots with lots of technical proficiency, able to solo with exotic, modern scales and play extremely fast. 'You see?' he said, 'I like having young people in my band, because I learn things from them.' B. B.'s own style, he frequently reminded the audience, is not about flash and technical prowess. 'But you know,' he continued, fingering the neck of his 'Lucille,' 'there is no beating experience.' Compared to the young guns, B. B. played slower, with fewer notes. He languished in the space around the notes. The soulfulness of his soloing handily beat the younger guys' dexterous virtuosity.

The evening's highlight came when B. B. demonstrated how he improvises. First, having his band vamp on a twelve-bar blues (a standard harmonic pattern for the blues – more on this later), B. B. showed he could play the 'right' notes and proceeded to solo for twelve bars. The notes he played were restricted to the appropriate scale and harmonies of the twelve-bar progression in which the band was vamping – everything was in the right key, nothing out of place, very straightforward. It sounded pretty cool – relaxed but still creative. Then he said, 'I can play the same notes, but I can turn it *on*!' Wow! It was like someone had hit the flood lights. What followed was some of the most amazing live guitar I have ever heard. The notes came alive! B. B. miraculously transformed into the B. B. of legend.

It is hard to explain exactly how B. B. 'turned it on.' The notes he was playing were more or less the same as before, except now they had personality, bending over and under the 'right' notes of the scale. The rhythms were sharper, too, picked with an energy B. B.'s first solo had lacked. There were subtle technical differences, certainly – more creative use of space, sharper attacks, sexier slides – but the underlying motivation was a change in the man himself: B. B. was expressing something, telling us a story. His heart was in it.

Amazingly, everyone watching felt the same shift in expression, and we all knew the temperature change was collectively felt. It was almost like in the first solo B. B. had been merely reciting text whereas in the second he was preaching a sermon. The experience of this phenomenon challenged and seemed to contradict how I was being trained as a classical musician – how do you transcribe someone's personality?

One of the things you are taught in classical training is to analyze the works of the masters by looking at their scores. We look at how individuals such as Beethoven and Brahms created intricate musical structures by splicing, elongating, and inverting themes – using the same notes in different permutations. A venerable respect for the written score is developed through this kind of analysis, and we begin to think that the answer to all the genius and magic of the masters' music is in the score. B. B. King's demonstration taught me that the key to tracing his genius was beyond the scope of thinking about music in this kind of textual way. B. B.'s expression defied representation in a written score. Instead, we felt his genius by tracing his aura, his very personality.

In his influential essay, 'The work of art in the age of mechanical reproduction,' the German-Jewish philosopher, Walter Benjamin (1892–1940), theorized that the feeling of the presence of a work of art – its uniqueness, which he termed *aura* – would be diminished through mechanical reproduction (in the case of music, this translates to audio recordings), but that new modes of perception would be made possible. My feeling, however, is that recordings can help prepare us to identify the aura of our favorite artist, and that this is especially important in our contemporary engagement with the blues.

As influential as Benjamin was in delineating how attitudes toward art changed in the Industrial Age, he was not as specifically revelatory in the potential of mechanical reproduction to revolutionize *listening*. To be fair, 'The work of art in the age of mechanical reproduction' mainly investigated the impact of photography and film on contemporary society. The history of recording technology has helped to create a new paradigm of listening to music, one that gives voice to artists working outside the domain of Western art traditions such as the blues. Furthermore, with the advent of recordings, the source of the identity (aura) of a piece of music shifts from the composer to the performer. An example of this in my own listening is how the song 'Wild Thing' is much more associated with Jimi Hendrix's performance at the 1967 Monterey Pop Festival than with the Troggs' hit record or Chip Taylor as the composer.

In classical music, however, the written score is paramount. One could even go so far to say the score transmits the will of the composer. Moreover, the culture of performance practice surrounding classical music exists to preserve the intentionality of the composer, by being faithful to the score. The following statement by Gunther Schuller, a Pulitzer-prize-winning elder statesman of American classical music, exemplifies the privileged place the written score has in classical music. When he was first starting out as a conductor, Schuller developed a tremendous respect for the written score, and understandably so, since much of the music he was conducting was contemporary and no recordings existed at the time. Schuller writes:

> I was learning to respect rigorously the content of the score – by whomever – and the score became a kind of sacred document to me. In all the intervening years I have seen no reason to change my views on this matter, whether in standard or contemporary repertory.[2]

By extension, this means that a work of classical music is transportable, that many people can perform the work, that the identity of the work outlives (or survives) any one interpretation or performer. This is the special means by which the aura of classical composers has been transmitted through the ages – through a physical reproduction, from generation to generation. A player performing a work today invokes the legacy of a work. The performer is often expected to channel the composer's original intentions, or the intentions we ascribe to the composer via historical research.

The written classical score also results in the privileging of certain aspects of sound in music, because it is limited in the amount of information it can convey. Only those frequencies that are playable on the piano are generally considered usable as material in classical music. These pitches (frequencies that have letter names such as 'do,' 're,' 'mi') are also the notes that can be notated in the system of Western music notation. The notated relationships between these notes in a work of music, expressed in a score, emanate its identity. This is Schuller's sacred text. Sounds that do not express these frequencies with names are expunged from the system and are often not considered music. When a sound is too dense for a pitch to be clear, it is considered noise. If a frequency lies between the notes playable on a piano, it is considered to be out of tune, though the music of many non-Western cultures (e.g., Indian *raga* or the *maqam* of the Middle East) has different tuning standards.

The radical twentieth-century American composer John Cage said that 'if a sound is unfortunate enough to not have a letter or if it seems to be too complex, it is tossed out of the system on the grounds: it's a noise or unmusical.'[3] So which sounds exactly are 'unmusical'? What about bent notes on a guitar, which are common in the blues? Or the slippery sounds of a slide guitar? What about the transcendent presence that B. B. King demonstrated in his lecture? These are sounds that do not have names, and, therefore, would be 'tossed out of the system,' as Cage says. The blues also often features noise elements in timbre (the color of the sound) that distort the clarity of pitches: the vocalist's rasp and the distortion of the guitar sound. Furthermore, the blues, in contrast to classical music, is an aural, unwritten tradition. Since there is no score, one cannot depend upon faithfulness to a score to judge accuracy of intent, or locate its identity.

The basic structure of the blues is an AAB lyrical form, sometimes called bar form. (A bar of music is, in the usual case of the blues, a grouping of four pulses, or beats.) In AAB form, the first line is stated over four bars (A) and repeated over the next four bars (A), then a concluding line is stated over the final four bars (B). This call-and-response cycle of an AAB stanza adds up to twelve bars of music, thus giving the name to the most common form of the blues. The 'Star-Spangled

Banner' is one of the most famous examples of AAB form. Another example is in 'How Blue Can You Get?' (1963), one of B. B. King's signature songs, composed by Leonard Feather:

> (A)
> I've been down hearted, baby
> Ever since the day we met
>
> (A)
> I've been down hearted, baby
> Ever since the day we met
>
> (B)
> Our love is nothing but the blues
> Baby, how blue can you get?

The harmonic progression that accompanies AAB twelve-bar blues form comprises only three basic chords. All songs that follow the twelve-bar blues form share the same harmonic progression. From the perspective of classical music, this is problematic in tracing a song's unique identity. Since the chord changes are the same from standard to standard, in order to distinguish songs you have to track the lyrics or melody rather than the harmonic progression.

Let's put it another way. Whereas in classical music one has to listen to the content of the words that are spoken to trace the identity of the speaker, in the blues, one traces the identity of the speaker by identifying the sound of the voice. If a blues singer picks up a phone and says 'hello,' we cannot tell who is speaking based on *what* is expressed, but by *how* it is expressed. By tracing the sound of the voice, we can trace the identity of the speaker. In the same way that we might tell the mood of a loved one from a single 'hello,' we can feel the emotive power of the blues from a similar sense of unique, performative presence.

Identity in the blues is expressed by the aura of the individual artist. In this way, the listening paradigm is expressly opposite to that of classical music: the text, the song as material, is not as important as how the song is being sung by that particular performer. When B. B. King sings 'How Blue Can You Get?' I am not tracking how faithful he is being to songwriter Leonard Feather's intentions; I am listening for how the song is a vehicle for B. B.'s aura.

Benjamin thought that the aura of an original work of art would be diminished through mechanical reproduction. Ironically, however, for an aural tradition, like the blues, mechanical means of reproducing sounds (i.e., recordings) have helped not only to preserve the legacies of performances but also to shape the listening values of contemporary culture. Audio recordings preserve and transmit bent notes on a guitar, B. B. King's voice, the tone of his guitar, and all the special sounds that classical notation fails to transmit. In effect, audio recordings are a superior mode of notation because they are more democratic than written scores. Furthermore, recordings aid in our emotional investment in the aura of our favorite artists. For example, I had seen countless cover bands perform my favorite Rolling Stones songs, but when I saw the Rolling Stones themselves play live I felt that I was in the presence of the authentic, the true aura of the Rolling Stones, even though I had only previously heard them through recordings. Listening to Rolling Stones albums prepared me for the live experience. It is true that aficionados of classical music have their favorite recordings, and they too can revel in the aura of their favorite performers; but the traditional hierarchy privileging the intentionality of the composer still holds true. Symphonic recordings, for example, are still catalogued by composer. Ergo, the larger revolution is the effect technology has had on non-notated music.

Recordings not only prepare us to receive the unique voice of a specific performer but can also help to teach us to appreciate the nuance of a specific performance. This is especially important for the blues, as it is a form expressed through improvisation. In comparing different performances by our favorite artist we can develop sensitivities to their improvisatory styles and their characteristic quirks as well as realizing that some performances capture something more special than others. This kind of familiarity with the history of differences in performances further distances us from the classical notion of fixity. An ideal classical performance is a clean rendering of the score, whereas we expect each blues performance to be somewhat different.

While I am thinking about the impact recordings have had on listening, I want to point out an additional, important effect they have on listeners to pop music. I am thinking of the numerous times my non-musician friends have related to me how much they enjoyed a concert of their favorite pop stars by saying 'It was great! I sounded just like the CD!' This statement fascinates me. It reveals further developments in the psychology of listening in the post-Benjamin era. In these cases, when a listener is assessing a live performance and comparing its quality with a CD, they are comparing what used to be the authentic (the live) to what used to be a reproduction of the authentic (the recording) and reversing the aspect of authenticity, in that the recording trumps the live and becomes the new standard of authenticity. The live experience is still, of course, the original, and a recording is still, in actuality, a document – a reproduction of the original – but, effectively, the roles of the two in terms of authenticity have been reversed. The recording still serves, as in the blues, to help the listener develop a relationship with the voice of an artist – helping them to recognize the voice – but the piece of music or song becomes fixed in identity, like a classical music score, to the point that the listener quantifies his or her enjoyment of the live experience by tracking how faithfully it compares to (replicates) the recording. Several factors play into creating this reversal of authenticity. First, it is increasingly common to be introduced to an artist's music through recordings before experiencing a live performance. Second, and perhaps more powerfully, recordings allow and in fact invite repeated listenings. Through repeated listenings we begin to memorize the many details of a performance of a particular song. Along the way, strong emotional attachments are developed to the song and the artist, and that recording becomes fixed as the true identity of a song. What is therefore different now, as opposed to periods before the invention of recordings, is that often attending the live experience is a way to confirm and amplify the emotions we have developed listening to recordings of our favorite songs and artists. By saying all this, though, I must admit that it is increasingly harder to define exactly what pop music is. And there must always be allowance retained for differences in individual listening, no matter the genre. With these caveats stated, for me, when I listen to the blues, no matter how familiar I am with a particular recording, I still feel that a recording somehow reminds me that the authentic is retained by the live person, that somehow I am missing something by not experiencing the live performance, and that there are limitations to human experience that are mediated through technology. The blues still evades fixity.

In writing this essay, my intention is not to elevate the merits of one genre over another. As a classical composer, I am deeply indebted to the legacy of classical music, and the paradigms of listening that it proposes have shaped me tremendously. I am also a lover of all kinds of rock and pop music. My main aim here has to do with the imperious nature of the paradigms of classical music in academia. In many spheres in American academia, classical music holds a privileged place in terms of pedagogy and prestige, to the extent that non-classical cultures of music are evaluated through the lens of classical music. An example of this hierarchy is the still-prevalent practice of transcribing non-classical, and even non-Western, music using classical notation. This has the effect of quantizing[4] frequencies and rhythms into values Cage called 'the privileged tones,' in order to make scholarship of those other musics more conveniently palpable to Western academics. A further consequence is that classical notation might then filter out the special microtonal (frequencies between the notes of the piano), timbral, or rhythmic features of a musical culture that is non-classical. The effort to capture an aural tradition in this way runs the risk of misrepresenting it completely. The biggest crime is that classical notation does not take performance practice considerations into account: it disregards how these other people are thinking about performing their music. My hope in calling attention to what is special about listening to the blues is that we might begin to make a space to honor differences in paradigms of listening, rather than trying to force all listenings to be subsets of one dominant paradigm. Listening is too diverse and beautiful for it not to be more democratic in this day and age.

The aura of a great blues artist transcends the cultural jadedness we have accumulated over a history of art reproduced through mechanical means. The B. B. Kings of the world reconnect us to a soulfulness that is necessarily transmitted through live performance. The uniqueness of a blues performance in time and place also courageously says to us that life is ephemeral and beautiful because it is ever changing, and that we must embrace the now, rather than fetishizing fixity and promoting a fear of death. The blues is authentic and not transportable. Through this we are reminded how an individual life – and, by extension, how all of our individual lives – can be so meaningful.

NOTES

1 Walter Benjamin, 'The work of art in the age of mechanical reproduction,' in *Illuminations* (New York: Schocken Books, 1968), p. 221.
2 Gunther Schuller, *The Compleat Conductor* (New York: Oxford University Press, 1997), p. vii.
3 John Cage, 'Julliard lecture,' in *A Year from Monday* (Hanover, NH: Wesleyan University Press, 1963), pp. 96–97.
4 Quantizing is the process of calibrating and adjusting a frequency to the nearest equal tempered pitch, or the nearest metric beat in rhythm.

KEN UENO

CHAPTER 3

TWELVE-BAR ZOMBIES

Wittgensteinian Reflections on the Blues

We (your faithful authors) have long been huge fans of various forms and iterations of the blues, but have both tended to strongly dislike more recent forms, even when the blues is played as a sort of homage to earlier forms. Oddly, neither of us have had this reaction to other contemporary homages, for example when film makers pay homage to earlier genres. In this essay we would like to begin by briefly looking at what makes something the blues. We will then argue that a standard conceptual analysis in terms of necessary and sufficient conditions is doomed to fail, but that a Wittgenstein 'family resemblance' approach will do the trick. We will end by applying this Wittgenstein analysis to paradigmatic cases of 'good' recent blues (e.g., Robert Cray, Stevie Ray Vaughn) in the hope of explaining just why we find ourselves less than enthusiastic about where the genre has gone (and is headed!). Specifically, we will address the question 'what is it about contemporary blues that is lacking, given that many of the elements that people typically associate with the blues are present?'

Blues – Philosophy for Everyone: Thinking Deep About Feeling Low, First Edition.
Edited by Jesse R. Steinberg and Abrol Fairweather.
© 2012 John Wiley & Sons, Inc. Published 2012 by John Wiley & Sons, Inc.

Playing the Blues

When we were in college we played in a pop music combo. Both of us were guitarists. Occasionally we would cover blues songs. Though neither of us had any formal training on the guitar, it was pretty easy to play the blues. In fact, we sort of just 'knew' how to do it. The chord progressions seemed obvious to us. We just needed to agree on a key, follow the singer to determine the number of measures that were going to be played, and listen to the drummer for the tempo. In fact, we usually didn't even discuss the key we were going to play in – unless someone said otherwise, the song was played in A (it's a guitarist thing). Using a 'do-re-me' scale, we'd strum the chord that corresponds to 'do' for four bars, then 'fa' for two bars, 'do' for another two bars, 'so' for a bar, 'fa' for a bar, and finally 'do' for two bars. Once this pattern had been repeated a handful of times, the song was over. That's how we played a twelve-bar blues song. We played eight-bar and sixteen-bar blues songs as well, which were slight variations on the basic twelve-bar theme. Of course the singer would sing something that was depressing and repetitive (more on this later) and the rhythm section (bass and drums) would round things out with a walk, a shuffle, or a boogie-woogie (or some such), but the essence of the blues number was found in the chord progression described above.

We were living in the San Francisco Bay Area at the time, where there is no shortage of places to hear the blues. Sometimes we would go to Eli's Mile High Club in Oakland (which sadly closed recently, a few years after the murder of founder Eli Thornton at the hands of a jealous mistress) or to any number of the many blues clubs situated in San Francisco's North Beach region. Our experiences in these venues, along with hearing blues covers by contemporary pop, punk, and alternative artists, only served to reinforce our conception of what the blues is. Even though there is much a band can do with the basic blues riff (e.g., adding horns, extra percussion, keyboards, or melody instruments), at root the blues is an eight-, twelve-, or sixteen-bar chord progression. Given this, providing a philosophical account of just what constitutes a blues song is likely to be pretty easy. So it seems, anyway.

Defining the Blues

So just what is it that makes a blues song a blues song? Here we want to give a philosophical definition of the blues. A philosophical definition

WADE FOX AND RICHARD GREENE

differs from other definitions in that other types of definition just serve to pick out or identify the referent or, perhaps, referents of a term, whereas a philosophical definition goes further than this. In addition to picking out the referent(s) of a term, it serves to explicate what makes something the kind of thing that it is; that is, it identifies the essential or defining characteristics of a thing. One could give an ostensive definition of the blues by pointing (literally or figuratively) to a paradigmatic instance or two of the blues. For example, one might give an ostensive definition by instructing someone to listen to Blind Lemon Jefferson's 'Rising High Water Blues' or to Muddy Waters' 'You Can't Lose What You Ain't Never Had.' Ostensive definitions, while useful in a number of instances (usually when one already has a certain concept), don't tell exactly what we want to know in this case: what is it that makes a blues song a blues song. Dictionary-type definitions typically define things in terms of synonyms, which might help one understand what a particular word means but doesn't provide any sort of conceptual analysis of that word. Dictionary definitions of the blues don't even go that far (as there are no actual synonyms for blues songs). They typically provide a little information about the origins of the blues and then mention something that characterizes many blues songs, such as being melancholy, having a twelve-bar structure, and so on. Such definitions do not, however, get at the heart of the matter.

Our interest, of course, is in determining just what constitutes a blues song – identifying the essential characteristics of a blues number, or explicating what features blues numbers have that distinguish them from other songs. This is what a successful philosophical definition will accomplish.

Over the centuries philosophers have gone about giving philosophical definitions in a variety of ways. The Greeks primarily gave philosophical definitions in terms of genus and species, the idea being (broadly) that the blues would be placed in a certain category, such as folk music or popular music (this identifies the genus), and then distinguished from other things that fall into that same category (this identifies the species). In modern times philosophers are more apt to provide definitions by making reference to necessary and sufficient conditions. As these activities amount to roughly the same thing – highlighting or identifying an essential feature of something – and the modern way of doing things is somewhat less rigid in its implementation, we'll go with the modern approach.

Necessary conditions are conditions that must be met in order for something to be a thing of a particular kind. For example, a necessary condition for someone to be a certified public accountant (CPA) in the United States is for them to have passed Section I of the CPA exam. Having done so does not make them a CPA, however, because they also need to have passed the other sections and to have had so many hours of on-the-job training, and so on. Sufficient conditions are conditions that, once they are met, serve to make something a thing of a particular kind. For example, a sufficient condition for traveling at a speed greater than one hundred miles per hour is driving a properly functioning Indy race car at or near top speed. This is sufficient because it will do the trick, but one needn't drive an Indy race car in order to go over one hundred miles per hour; one can ride in an airplane, on a high speed train, and so on. Each of these is a sufficient condition for traveling at a speed greater than one hundred miles per hour.

One way to give a philosophical definition of something is to explicate all the necessary conditions for that thing. The set of individually necessary conditions, if all goes according to plan, will then constitute a jointly sufficient condition for the thing being defined. For example, the following are thought to be necessary conditions for something being a triangle: (1) it must have three sides, (2) it must be a single plane, (3) it must be a closed figure, (4) each of its sides must be straight lines, and (5) its interior angles must add up to 180 degrees. Anything that satisfies each of these five conditions will be a triangle, so this set of individually necessary conditions constitutes a jointly sufficient condition.

So what are the individually necessary conditions and jointly sufficient conditions for something being a blues song? Let's begin by removing from consideration some of the clear nonstarters. Certain wines, for example, are defined by the region in which they are produced. The thing that makes a Bordeaux a Bordeaux is that it is produced from grapes grown in the Bordeaux region of France. The blues, of course, doesn't derive from a single region. The blues is perhaps most closely identified with the Mississippi Delta region, but there are equally distinctive styles of blues associated with Chicago, New Orleans, St. Louis, and many other parts of the United States. Another nonstarter is instrumentation. If one had only heard certain Mississippi Delta blues artists, one might be tempted to think of the blues as an acoustic-guitar-based art form, as it frequently is. However, big bands, jazz bands, rock and roll bands, orchestras, pianists, mandolin players, saxophone players, and zither players have all performed and recorded blues numbers. Thus, the temptation to define the blues in terms of either its geographic origins or the instruments most frequently used to play it should be resisted.

A natural candidate for a necessary condition is the twelve-bar chord progression (and its eight- and sixteen-bar variants) detailed above. Recall that, for us, playing the blues was a matter of adhering to this format; it's what we took ourselves to be doing when we played a blues number. There is no shortage of blues songs that follow these progressions. Son House's 'Preachin' the Blues,' Frank Stoke's 'Downtown Blues,' and Leadbelly's 'Leaving Blues,' for example, all make use of standard blues chord progressions, as do thousands of other blues songs. Right off, however, it should be clear that having one of these progressions, while possibly constituting a necessary condition for a song being a blues song, won't provide both a necessary and a sufficient condition, as lots of non-blues songs also make use of these progressions. Chuck Berry's 'Johnny B. Goode' and Elvis Costello's 'Mystery Dance,' to name a couple, each use a standard blues progression but are pretty clearly not blues songs. (Actually, this is true of almost all Chuck Berry songs.) So, having a blues chord progression is not enough by itself to make a song a blues song.

Perhaps whether a song is a blues song is a matter of its having a blues chord progression in combination with some other essential feature. In other words, the existence of non-blues songs utilizing blues chord progressions does not rule out the possibility that having a certain chord progression is a necessary condition for a song to be a blues song; rather, we've just ruled out that it is the *only* necessary condition. (If it were the only necessary condition, then it would also be a sufficient condition, which we've already seen by way of counterexample is not the case.) The problem, however, with defining the blues in terms of any particular set of narrowly defined chord progressions is that a large number of paradigmatic blues songs don't, in fact, follow these progressions, even though they are what folks most often have in mind when they think of the blues. Consider, for example, Blind Blake's 'He's in the Jailhouse Now,' Barbeque Bob's 'Goin' Up the Country,' and Mississippi John Hurt's 'Spike Driver Blues,' none of which are confined to the three chords (i.e., do, fa, and so) found in most blues riffs, or Charley Patton's 'Mississippi Bo Weavil Blues,' which only has one chord (do) in the entire song; or Bill Broonzy's 'Terrible Operation Blues' and Blind Willie McTell's 'Ticket Agent Blues,' each of which makes use of the standard blues chords but in an inverted sequence. In fact, a number of blues songs don't even closely resemble eight-, twelve-, and sixteen-bar blues songs. Many musicians, such as Blind Blake, played ragtime tunes such as 'Diddie Wah Diddie' and 'Come on Boys Let's Do That Mess Around.'

And many bluesmen included folk and popular tunes in their repertoires. Robert Johnson was known to sing 'My Blue Heaven' and 'Yes Sir, That's My Baby.' Leadbelly included folk tunes such as 'The Grey Goose' on his recordings. Each of these would constitute a counterexample to any definition of the blues that had the standard blues chord progressions as a necessary condition.

Since the ubiquitous eight-, twelve-, and sixteen-bar chord progressions come up short as essential or defining characteristics of the blues, let's turn to lyrical content as a possible source of necessary conditions. Here there are a couple of things we can focus on: structure and topic. As was mentioned above, many blues songs have a certain repetitive structure: each verse consists of a line repeated twice followed by a second line. Examples of this can be found in Blind Joe Reynolds' 'Outside Woman Blues' (1967):

> When you lose your money, great god, don't lose your mind
> When you lose your money, great god, don't lose your mind
> And when you lose your woman, please don't fool with mine

and in Robert Johnson's 'Cross Road Blues' (1937):

> I went to the crossroad, fell down to my knees
> I went to the crossroad, fell down to my knees
> Asked the Lord above 'Have mercy, now save poor Bob, if you please'

While this pattern is common to a great number of blues songs, it is certainly not a feature of *most*, and, consequently, cannot be a necessary condition of blues songs. (Furthermore, as was the case with chord progression, many non-blues songs also have this structure.)

It may be that the best candidate for a necessary condition is lyrical content. Perhaps the thing that makes a blues song a blues song is the fact that, when one sings one, one is literally expressing that one has the blues. Blues songs are melancholy or mournful. They are about pain, strife, suffering, difficulty, being generally doomed, and so forth.

Again, we see the same types of worries arise. Plenty of non-blues songs will also have these lyrical elements. We see this in virtually all genres: opera, pop, jazz, country, folk, rock and roll, rap, hip-hop, punk, and so on – perhaps most notably in the torch song genre, which, like the blues, is dominated almost completely by melancholy and mournful lyrics. Moreover, a great number of blues songs, such as Jelly Roll Morton's

'Original Jelly Roll Blues,' have no lyrics; they are instrumentals. There are also a number of blues songs, such as Joe 'King' Oliver's 'West End Blues,' that were written and originally performed as instrumentals but had lyrics added later. (If you've not heard Louis Armstrong and his Hot Five's recording of 'West End Blues,' stop what you are doing immediately and proceed to the nearest music store.). Also, many blues songs, such as jug band blues, are quite cheerful. So it would appear that blues lyrics do not fare any better as a candidate necessary condition.

So where does this leave us? It would appear that the blues as a genre resists philosophical definition in terms of necessary and sufficient conditions (and, by extension, in terms of species/genus), as there is no single defining characteristic that is found in all blues songs or even in all paradigmatic blues songs. So we can't define the blues in terms of either musical features or lyrical features, or some combination of the two.

It is always open to one to offer a stipulative definition in terms of necessary and sufficient conditions. For example, one could just dig one's heels in and maintain that any song that (1) does not have the aforementioned eight-, twelve-, or sixteen-bar structure, (2) does not have the aforementioned repetitive line structure, and (3) is not sufficiently mournful is just not a blues song. This is what purists tend to do. The problem with this is that it fails to be descriptive in the appropriate way. This definition would not adequately describe what the blues is, nor would it capture what blues musicians often took themselves to be doing when they wrote, sang, and played the blues. Such a definition would be normative, in a pretty false way (analogous to stipulating that only activities that utilize balls and pucks are really sports). So, at this point we are left without a philosophical definition of the blues.

Wittgenstein to the Rescue

Socrates famously (or perhaps infamously) acted on the assumption that, if one could not provide an airtight and counterexample-proof philosophical definition of a term, one did not know what that term meant. Counterexamples to this assumption abound in the philosophical literature. Philosophers working in the theory of knowledge, ironically, have not been able to define the word 'know' in a fashion that resists counterexamples, yet even very young children know what the word 'know' means. This error in reasoning is now known as the 'Socratic fallacy.' An inability to philosophically define a term or concept does not, contrary to the admonitions of Socrates, indicate a failure to grasp or understand that concept. So, our inability to explicate the individually necessary and jointly sufficient conditions for a song being a blues song does not indicate that there is not an actual category to which the blues and only the blues belongs, nor does it indicate that persons incapable of defining the blues fail to know what the blues is. Perhaps the right thing to say (roughly following Supreme Court Justice Potter Stewart) is that we can't define the blues but we know what it is when we hear it. This conclusion, however, seems too hasty. There is one treatment of the blues that we've yet to consider: Wittgensteinian family resemblance.

In the early twentieth century, philosophers of language and linguists were concerned with (among other things) providing an account of how language functions. More specifically, they were concerned with addressing the question of how expressions and sentences manage to be meaningful. Wittgenstein, for example, in his *Tractatus Logico-Philosophicus*,[1] argued that sentences are meaningful in virtue of the fact that they constitute pictures of reality. This view came to be known as the 'picture theory of meaning.' Eventually Wittgenstein came to reject this view. According to a popular story, the veracity of which we cannot vouch for, a colleague of Wittgenstein with whom Wittgenstein had an acrimonious relationship on one occasion made an obscene gesture toward Wittgenstein (something akin to 'flipping the bird'). It occurred to Wittgenstein that this gesture had linguistic meaning, yet was not accounted for by the picture theory of meaning. Rather than replace the picture theory of meaning with some similar theory that attempted to capture in a single thought how language manages to be meaningful, Wittgenstein rejected conceptual analysis altogether.

The picture theory of meaning was replaced by the notion of family resemblance. In his *Philosophical Investigations*,[2] Wittgenstein argued that language functions in a variety of ways that, while similar to one another, are not reducible to a single function; rather, they are 'a complicated network of similarities, overlapping and criss-crossing.' He provided an analogy between the uses of words and families. Members of a particular family might all resemble one another even though there is no particular characteristic common to all members of that family. So, for example, most of the members might have similar noses, but not everyone has a similar nose, and most of the members might have similar eyes, but not everyone has similar eyes, and so forth. Thus, it may be the case that each

WADE FOX AND RICHARD GREENE

member of the family has much in common with each other member, even though there is no single trait or characteristic common to all. Wittgenstein held that the same was true of the ways in which language functions. Moreover, on Wittgenstein's view, we recognize these similarities, just as we recognize that family members look alike, without actually running down the list of traits at a conscious level – we just recognize the resemblance.

Wittgenstein's notion of family resemblance can be employed in capturing what it is that makes the blues the blues. We saw that none of the candidates for necessary conditions of the blues were acceptable as necessary conditions, because each was subject to counterexamples – there were instances of the blues that failed to have those features. While this is a problem for conceptual analysis in terms of necessary and sufficient conditions, it is not a problem for conceptual analysis in terms of family resemblance, because there is no expectation that any particular blues song will have any of the particular features that are ubiquitous in blues songs. So, for example, a failure to have the eight-, twelve-, or sixteen-bar chord progression does not exclude a song from the category of blues songs, provided that the song has a number of the other elements commonly found in blues songs, such as mournful lyrics that repeat in certain patterns; an actual expression of feeling blue; a certain kind of melody; a certain kind of piano, banjo, or guitar fill; and so on. So the best way to understand the blues is in terms of a set of features, some number of which must be present in the song. The exact number required, of course, is dependent on which features are present; sometimes having a couple of the major features is sufficient.

Good Blues, Bad Blues, Walking Dead Blues

The idea of family resemblance makes it easier to define the blues because it does not require an exact definition. Many songs and styles that might not be included in the genre if we were to take a purist's approach to can now be included in the category of blues. Family resemblance, however, creates another problem with definition. We broaden what can be considered blues, but at a certain point we must reach a hazy middle ground in which a song appears to be a blues but is missing some essential element that makes it a good blues. In this way, much contemporary blues is reminiscent of a zombie, an animated corpse of the blues.

A zombie looks like a living person. It moves, acts, and reacts, but slowly, with a clumsy gait. It has a limited range of expression. Some essential characteristic of humanity is missing; it has lost its soul. In a similar fashion, contemporary blues has certain attributes in common with older blues, just as the zombie of a family member may look like your family member. Contemporary blues may use a twelve-bar blues pattern. It may include themes that are common to blues. The singer's vocal patterns may suggest blues. All these characteristics may create a family resemblance to the blues of the early blues generations, but all these signifiers are empty, creating a living shell of the dead blues.

Although contemporary blues frequently duplicates the tropes of blues, just as a zombie lacks a certain spark of authentic humanity, the form often lacks the authenticity of the earlier generations of blues players. Musicians today are performing the roles of bluesmen – wearing the right clothes, singing the right lyrics, performing the correct riffs – but they are incapable of authentically being bluesmen. Now, authenticity is not necessary to all forms of music. Rock music seems to thrive on created personae, and authenticity may not be important to all blues, but inauthenticity can make a good blues unbelievable. And believability and authenticity have always been important in the emotional impact of blues. The blues came out of a certain social and cultural scene, from the African-American culture of the American South. Although blues was widely distributed across regions, most of the blues musicians, even in different regions and at different times, came out of that culture. Even early greats of the electric Chicago blues, such as Muddy Waters, began as acoustic musicians in the Mississippi Delta. That culture and time, with its racism, poverty, inequality, and injustice, created a need for the blues, and from this came the music's style and much of its subject matter. Many of the earlier generations of the blues had spent time in prison, worked at farming, and lived actual lives of hardship and wandering. Leadbelly, the son of a sharecropper, was actually first recorded in prison. Bukka White, whose early recording career was a victim of the great depression, was rediscovered at Mississippi's infamous Parchman Farm, the prison farm that was temporary home to some of Mississippi's greatest bluesmen, including Son House. When Skip James sings 'Hard Time Killin' Floor Blues,' he suggests a deep experience of pain. These were men who experienced hardship and poverty.

The songs of blues musicians well into the sixties came out of an experience that contemporary blues musicians cannot experience. Musicians who are not from that period and place may sing blues, but they lose an important characteristic of good blues. As an extreme example, the teenage white blues prodigies that began appearing in the nineties, such as Kenny Wayne Shepherd and Jonny Lang, seem to have little credibility as singers of the blues, although they are both exceptional musicians. When Jonny Lang sings 'Wander this World,' a listener is likely to wonder how much of the world Lang has actually seen. Critics of his early albums marveled at Lang's maturity and technical ability, but their surprise suggests a disconnection between message and messenger. As a seventeen-year-old white boy from Fargo, North Dakota, Lang could play the licks, but his music and lyrics did not and could not come out of lived experience. Even older contemporary blues musicians, such as Robert Cray or Keb' Mo', come across as performers only. Robert Cray, from Tacoma, Washington, began his musical career playing rock before he became interested in blues. Keb' Mo', one of the few recent blues musicians influenced by acoustic Delta blues, was born Kevin Moore in Los Angeles. His early musical career included a stint as a steel drummer in a calypso band and a job as a staff writer for A&M Records. These musicians may sing about mournful experiences or hard times, but they are unlikely to have actually experienced the hard times they sing about or to genuinely have come out of the culture of the blues. When Keb' Mo' wears an outfit reminiscent of a Delta bluesman, he does not become a bluesman. He is performing the role of a bluesman, as he played the role of Robert Johnson in the documentary *Can't You Hear the Wind Howl* and in Martin Scorsese's series on the blues.

Another issue is the limited range of most contemporary blues. Like the reanimated dead, contemporary blues lacks the ability to grow and change of a living form. Older blues was a vital and lively popular form of music, like rap today, and it borrowed from many sources – country, jazz, folk ballads, gospel and religious music, and even advertising jingles such as the Nugrape Twins' 'I've Got an Ice Cold Nugrape.' Now, blues has become a traditional form, and, because it is a traditional form, it has become limited by the expectations of those that respect the tradition. Tradition requires that a performer must play blues that sounds like blues, which means it must follow strict rules – clichés of what a blues song means. The purists hold blues to a conditional definition. It must follow specific riffs and certain topics, and, without them, a blues would not be considered a blues. A contemporary blues musician could not play like Mississippi John Hurt today, with his sweet voice and cheerful fingerpicking, and be accepted as a blues musician. Furthermore, electric blues has solidified the structure so that most blues we hear today, if played within the blues tradition, is derived from a very small part of that tradition. Much of blues in the early days was acoustic and played on a variety of instruments – Yank Rachell played mandolin with Sleepy John Estes; the Mississippi Sheiks, one of the most popular blues acts of the thirties, were a fiddle and guitar duo; Reverend Gary Davis frequently played banjo (and, in fact, the banjo was probably the instrument on which much blues was played prior to the twentieth century); Skip James played both piano and guitar; and the earliest recorded blues women, for example Bessie Smith, were accompanied by pianos and a variety of wind instruments, such as trumpets, trombones, and saxophones. Even guitar players had more instrumental variety. Big Joe Williams played a homemade nine-string guitar. Leadbelly played a twelve-string, and Papa Charlie Jackson, one of the first blues musicians to be recorded, played a guitar with a resonator like a banjo. Most blues today is played on electric guitar only. And it tends to ignore the diversity of the tradition. Almost all electric blues is borrowed from Chicago blues, so the Piedmont blues, Delta blues, ragtime, jug band, Texas blues, and the many other forms are ignored. We are left with the shambling corpse of the blues, incapable of the immense variety of expression of earlier forms, beyond a few simple grunts and groans.

Finally, it is questionable whether much of contemporary blues can still be called blues. It still bears a family resemblance to blues (as do jazz, rhythm and blues, soul, rock, and nearly every popular form of American music), but it is more the resemblance of a distant relation or bastard child. Much that is called blues now bears a stronger relation to other genres. For example, Stevie Ray Vaughan – who was an outstanding guitarist – played music that often had the structure and subject matter of a blues, but his music was more closely related to rock. As he said himself, his leads were heavily influenced by Jimi Hendrix:

> I actually learned to play from Jimi's records. I remember getting my little stereo – an Airline with the cardboard satellite speakers – and I would mike that up with a Shure PA that I had in my bedroom. For some of my first gigs, I'd rent four separate reverbs, and I'd have all this set up in my room. Of course, the parents were at work. I would go in there and floorboard it, dress up as cool as I could, and try to learn his stuff.[3]

There is no doubt that Jimi Hendrix was influenced by the blues and played in blues structures, but he is the quintessential rock guitarist. And the image of young Stevie Ray playing along to his hero is one any suburban rock fan can identify with. Vaughan also borrowed heavily from Chuck Berry (like nearly every other rock guitarist). His 'Love Struck Baby,' from the album *Texas Flood*, is rhythmically very similar to 'Johnny B. Goode,' and its leads are clearly derived from Chuck Berry's classic rock 'n' roll sound. Vaughan was hardly unique in his strong allegiance to forms other than the blues. This was common to many members of his generation. Robert Cray, another blues crossover success, borrows from soul for his singing style and owes his light, lyrical sound to pop-style production that belies the stories he tells. We are left, with much of contemporary blues, with a confusion of styles related to blues with the blues.

Thus we are left without the vitality, variety, and experience of authentic blues. Often, instead, we are left with something that is blues in appearance only. The style and signifiers of blues allow musicians to pass off music that is only distantly related to blues as blues. This confusion of styles can sometimes lead to unspeakable horrors. In the most extreme case, in the late seventies, John Belushi and Dan Aykroyd donned black shades and fedoras and performed as the Blues Brothers, playing songs such as Sam and Dave's 'Soul Man,' music that was actually from the Stax/Volt Records-style rhythm and blues and soul (and playing with members of the Stax/Volt house band). The success of their act may have led to a resurgence of interest in the blues and to the success of performers such as Cray and Vaughan in the eighties, but it also further removed contemporary blues from its true tradition, leaving us with the corpse of the blues, shuffling into the future to a walking bass line, blues in name only.

NOTES

1 Ludwig Wittgenstein, *Tractatus Logico-Philosophicus*, trans. C. K. Ogden (London: Routledge & Kegan Paul, 1922).
2 Ludwig Wittgenstein, *Philosophical Investigations*, G. E. M. Anscombe and R. Rhees (Ed.), trans. G. E. M. Anscombe (Oxford, UK: Blackwell, 1953). See especially remark 66.
3 From an interview in *Guitar Player* (May 1989).

CHAPTER 4

THE BLUES AS CULTURAL EXPRESSION

In a filmed 1966 performance of his song 'How Many More Years,' Chester Arthur Barnett, a.k.a. Howlin' Wolf, introduced the tune as follows:

A lot of people's wonderin' 'what is the blues?' I hear a lot of people sayin' 'the blues – the blues.' But I'm gonna tell ya what the blues is. When you ain't got no money, you got the blues. When you ain't got no money to pay yo house rent, ya still got the blues. A lot of peoples holler about 'I don't like no blues.' But when you ain't got no money, and can't pay yo house rent, and can't buy you no food, you damn sure got the blues […] cause you're thinkin' evil […] Anytime you thinkin' evil, you thinkin' about the blues.[1]

Does one really have to be thinking bad thoughts, 'evil' thoughts, to play the blues?

Think of a recording artist whose persona one would not easily associate with 'thinkin' evil'. For instance, imagine Barry Manilow playing guitar (or, more realistically, piano) in a tiny, dingy blues club, belting out Son House's 'Death Letter Blues'. Is that image clear in your mind? No? If not, it could be because it's difficult to think of Barry Manilow as someone whose hard

Blues – Philosophy for Everyone: Thinking Deep About Feeling Low, First Edition.
Edited by Jesse R. Steinberg and Abrol Fairweather.
© 2012 John Wiley & Sons, Inc. Published 2012 by John Wiley & Sons, Inc.

life has resulted in an evil-thinking attitude. Perhaps we can think of him as being annoyed or even mad that his limo hasn't arrived on time or his concert tux wasn't starched properly. But Barnett's 'thinkin' evil' – an extreme attitude toward the world and one's own position in it – is a kind of thinking one may be unable to *even conceptually* attribute to Barry Manilow.

Could Barry Manilow, or for that matter any other white musician – for example Eric Clapton, Lou Ann Barton, Stevie Ray Vaughn, or Leon Russell – truly play the blues? Some writers interested in this issue emphatically say yes, and others just as emphatically say no. In fact, in recent years, a debate has surfaced over whether non-African-American musicians can play the blues authentically. Everyone agrees that the blues is a musical art form that arose out of the African-American experience of slavery and its appalling aftermath. But some argue that the blues is strictly a musical style that anyone can play, regardless of their cultural background, while others argue that only people with a certain cultural heritage can authentically play the blues. Why the disagreement? In this essay, I argue that blues musical formalists have underappreciated the role that a particular kind of experience plays in performing the blues authentically, a kind of experience that only a member of African-American culture can have. This essay is divided into three parts. First, I will make a distinction between two categories of blues: the blues as musical form and the blues as cultural expression. Second, I propose a theory of cultural expression that I hope clarifies what blues expressivists have been saying. Third, I will argue that what lies behind objections to expressivism is a too-loose definition of culture, one that does not take into account certain aspects of African-American cultural experience important to delivering an authentic blues performance.[2]

Two Categories of the Blues

In *Blues People*, Amiri Baraka argues vehemently that white people cannot play the blues because they have not had the right cultural experiences to draw upon. Baraka writes,

> The idea of a white blues singer seems an even more violent contradiction of terms than the idea of a middle-class blues singer. The [experiential] materials of blues were not available to the white American, even though some strange circumstance might prompt him to look for them. It was as if these materials were secret and obscure, and blues a kind of ethno-historic rite as basic as blood.[3]

A little later in the book, he says that 'the white musician understood the blues first as music, but seldom *as an attitude*, since the attitude, or world-view, the white musician was responsible to was necessarily quite a different one.'[4] Elsewhere, jazz music critic Ralph Gleason makes the stronger claim that 'the blues is black man's music, and whites diminish it at best or steal it at worst. In any case they have no moral right to use it.'[5] What appears to motivate these strong views is what I will call 'the blues as cultural expression,' which attracts strong adherents who urge that blues is the collective possession of African-Americans alone. In this view, Manilow cannot play the blues authentically because he has not had the experiences necessary for having *the right attitude*.

In contrast, in a 1994 article for *The Journal of Aesthetics and Art Criticism*, Joel Rudinow argues against the idea that the blues can be authentically played only by African-Americans by criticizing what he calls 'the experiential access argument.' This argument 'says in effect that one cannot understand the blues or authentically express oneself in the blues unless one knows what it is like to live as a black person in America, and one cannot know this without being one.'[6] According to Rudinow, the experiential access argument maintains that, because of the deep, hidden nature of the unique experience, cultural outsiders will inevitably give a shallow and superficial musical interpretation of it. Such an argument, says Rudinow, is dubious. Most contemporary African-Americans have only a remote experience of slavery or sharecropping in the Mississippi Delta, and thus can have no more access to these unique experiences than outsiders.

In a 2008 book entitled *Cultural Appropriation and the Arts*, James O. Young proposes several arguments against the view that a cultural outsider cannot produce aesthetically valuable works in the style of another culture. Young, in response to the claim that a white person cannot play the blues, says that the blues can be learned by virtually anyone. He writes, 'Being able to work in a given style is like learning a language and there is no reason why outsiders cannot learn this language every bit as well as insiders.'[7] Rudinow and Young therefore seem to hold the view that the blues is not something that can only be authentically played by a particular group (i.e., by 'cultural insiders') but rather is first and foremost a musical form that anyone, in principle, can play (i.e., even 'cultural outsiders'). This view I call 'the blues as musical form' because it maintains that the blues is really nothing more than sound patterns or forms that require only the ability to manipulate the instruments (including the voice) in the right way by playing the right chords,

PHILIP JENKINS

singing the right melodies, reconstructing the right rhythms, and so on. Notice that the right musical form can be performed merely by imitating the structure of the work, regardless of the attitude, or personal history, of the performer.[8]

One reason that there is so much disagreement is that there is no easy definition of the blues. Looking for answers, I naturally consulted Answers.com, where the following definition appears:

> The blues: A style of music that evolved from southern African-American secular songs and is usually distinguished by a strong 4/4 rhythm, flatted thirds and sevenths, a 12-bar structure, and lyrics in a three-line stanza in which the second line repeats the first.[9]

Interestingly, this definition contains key assumptions from both sides of the debate: the blues as an evolved cultural style, and the blues as a formal musical sound structure. So, unfortunately, a dictionary definition is not going to decide things for us. What we need is a clearer definition of cultural expression that can make sense of what people are talking about when they claim it is necessary to be a cultural insider in order to authentically perform music developed by cultural insiders.

When Baraka and others talk about the blues as the communication of a particular cultural experience, what do they have in mind? Could Barry Manilow sing the blues as authentically as Muddy Waters? What is it about the blues that makes 'the right attitude' important, and where does this attitude come from?

What is Cultural Expression?

One of the unspoken principles of doing philosophy (well, okay, sometimes it is spoken, like now) is that before we go very far in a conceptual inquiry we first need to put the terms of disagreement before us and become clear on their meaning. In light of this, let's try to understand what 'cultural expression' might mean, especially as it relates to music. For Rudinow and Young, the term doesn't seem to have much meaning beyond perhaps the following formalist definition:

> Cultural expression in music is the act of anyone performing in a given musical form.

The problem with this way of putting it is that it makes Baraka's point seem silly, and a characterization of an opponent's view that makes it look implausible on its face (*prima facie* is the Latin form preferred by philosophers) is regarded as uncharitable, and violates a second principle of philosophy: always provide the most charitable version of your opponent's argument. In light of this, let's see if we can strengthen the meaning of the phrase in a way that takes Baraka's statements into account:

> Cultural expression in music is the expression of feelings through a musical form, where those feelings are only available to one who has had experiences in virtue of being a member of the social group responsible for creating that musical form.

This sounds like a description that Baraka might agree with, but of course, Rudinow and Young would not. Which description is the more plausible one?

The difference between these two characterizations is that the first would allow performers to 'act' according to the style of the music while the second would only allow 'expression.' An example of 'acting' would be my telling you that it is raining when I have no acquaintance with current weather conditions. So an 'actor' is someone who is concerned first and foremost with appearances. An example of 'expressing,' on the other hand, would be my telling you it is raining when I have just been outside and have experienced the rain first hand. So 'expressing' implies that what I am communicating is in fact true, in 'reality.' Thus, the 'acting' and 'expressing' dichotomy mirrors the famous 'appearance' and 'reality' distinction philosophers love to talk about. The main problem with 'appearance' and 'reality' is that one often can't tell the difference between them.

In this way, the blues formalists are content with music that appears to be expressing something experienced by cultural insiders, and so it makes sense that cultural outsiders can do it, in many cases as well as insiders can. The blues expressivists, conversely, will not be satisfied with the *appearance* of cultural expression but rather only with the *reality* of blues expression. In other words, expressivists are purists: only music that expresses the cultural experience of being black in America will count as real. How can such experiences be expressed? This is a difficult problem, perhaps even more difficult than the previous one. Nevertheless, for good or ill, I have a theory.

Many of my acts take a form that is characteristically mine. The way I walk across a room, hold my pen when I write, talk about my past, greet people on the street, strum a guitar – these are all behavioral performances with a certain style, a certain way of doing those acts. It follows too that my style of doing things will be manifest in the tools that I use: my handwriting, my word phrasing, my playing of a musical instrument – all will carry my particular manner of carrying out those activities. The behaviors are patterned, and so will carry my mark, so to speak, in those patterns. Furthermore, with experience, some people may even become good 'critics' of the products of my actions, simply by making certain inferences from those products to me. My point is that my unique take on the world is expressed by the way I do things, and the way I make things. Where does this 'unique take,' this attitude, come from?

My attitudes about the world had to have come from somewhere. It seems to me that there are three clear sources: (1) my innate temperament, (2) personal experiences, and (3) the attitudes of the people who belong to the social groups I most identify with. Now, the third of these is only available to me through the expressions of those group members. I can only know of their attitudes from how they express them. And, as it seems plausible that these attitudes are communicated to me from the time I am very young, they would have to be conveyed to me in simple ways, which I would tend to imitate. In addition, socially communicated expressive attitudes, as much as or more than the other two, tend to pervade my outlook on the world in a way that makes them invisible to me. Plausibly, my temperament and personal experiences will often be noticeably different from those of my group co-members. But social group attitudes, manifested in the way 'we' in our group express ourselves, will tend to be more uniform, unquestioned, taken for granted, and therefore opaque to my notice.

Now here's the leap in my theory. These imitated expressions will tend to foster the internalizing of those very attitudes that my fellow group members have. Another way to put this might be to say that the 'expressive resources' possessed by any one individual are shaped through systematic interactions with one's cultural group co-members. For instance, one's characteristic expressions of joy, sorrow, hope, and anger are learned by modeling the behaviors of one's parents, family, and other social group members.[10] Thus, the set of expressions one learns in this way comes from the set of expressions shared by the social group. Following Sue Campbell, I will call these collective expressions that one takes on one's 'expressive options.'[11] The only problem with this term is that it makes it appear that one has a choice in choosing which expressions to take on from one's group, and I don't think there is much choice. However, the phrase does bring out the idea that any social group will contain minimal variation of expressive behavioral patterns. For instance, women's attitudes toward oppressive situations with which they are faced may be shaped by angry outbursts, emotional breakdowns, stoic refusal to submit, denial of the circumstances, or rational explanatory strategies, though which option is chosen will have much to do with other factors, such as temperament and social location. Still, it should be remembered that the options are relatively limited. Attitudes of group members will tend to fall into characteristic patterns.

This is one interpretation of cultural expression I propose that helps us to understand what writers such as Amiri Baraka might mean when they claim that the blues cannot be played by a non-black person. A non-black person cannot communicate the kinds of attitudes that the blues was developed to express, and so the performance of the blues by a cultural outsider will tend to be aesthetically poorer. The blues was shaped by the cultural expressions of many generations of African-Americans, so much so that performances of the music today by non-black musicians will tend to be inauthentic. Of course, two things are also true: (1) some African-Americans *may not* have learned the culturally expressive options that the blues was made to express and 2) some non-black musicians *will* be able to learn the style and feel of the music in such a way as to 'fool' even a cultural insider into thinking the white musician is playing authentic blues.[12] In fact, these two outcomes are compatible with, and more easily explained by, the model I have proposed. Cultural insiders will tend to be the ones most apt to authentically play the blues, and cultural outsiders those most inapt to authentically play the blues.

So, that is my theory. Certainly anyone can play a blues-derived style, and play it very well, but Barry Manilow can't play the blues authentically because he doesn't have the right experience. In the next section I address what I think is the main problem with the formalist definition of cultural expression.

A Too-Loose Definition of Culture

Most formalist objections to the idea that cultural outsiders can't play authentic blues derive their plausibility from a too-loose definition of culture. The tendency of such definitions is to identify culture with external traits, such as language, religious practices, customs, and laws,

  PHILIP JENKINS

though some internal traits are sometimes included, for instance beliefs and knowledge.[13] One formalist, James O. Young, says he is 'not too fussy' about how we divide up cultures, and goes on to argue that nothing is lost aesthetically when a type of artwork that began in one culture is taken up by cultural outsiders. This approach may be adequate when trying to define cultures in general, but it seems relevant to a treatment of authenticity that some cultures are more experientially cohesive than others. The experiences of members of 'the drug culture' or 'the alternative music culture' are bound together by many shared experiences to be sure, but membership is quite voluntary compared to other groups. One enters the drug culture by taking drugs, associating with group members, and adopting some characteristic modes of dress and slang. Similarly, one need only listen to a certain kind of music, associate with other group members, attend live performances of alternative bands, and, again, learn some jargon to be a member of the alternative music culture.

Imagine too that one were to maintain that white males belong to a culture. Is white male culture as cohesive as African-American or Hispanic culture? Arguably, one of the defining features of being a member of black, Hispanic, or Jewish culture involves having been discriminated against by non-members because of negative stereotypes, or having knowledge that one's ancestors were ruthlessly oppressed. Memberships in drug, alternative music, and white male 'culture' (if one chooses to define the term loosely enough) primarily come about through a set of voluntary preferences, while memberships in African-American, Hispanic, or Jewish culture come about through involuntary systematic oppression.

Let me hasten to add that I am not claiming that one from outside the culture could not *understand* this oppression, at least in one sense. To be sure, if one is very empathic, imaginative, and sensitive, and perhaps in close relationship to one or more people who have gone through some of the experiences characteristic of African-American culture, one could conceivably understand black oppression in such a way as to allow one to bring to mind the experiential feelings in music that might capture the experience in ways that even group members would be unable. Group members might even find that those musical works represent their experiences better than those of cultural insiders. But, even though other people may be able to explain my experiences in ways I am unable to, because of their perspective, because of their training in techniques of explanation, and so on, no one will have the embodied physical knowledge about me that I have. Because, no matter how much extrinsic talent someone else brings to the representation of my life, I will always have something more, something inaccessible to them: my lived experience.

But perhaps the point isn't that one must belong to a group in order to produce authentic music from that culture. Why not allow that, if one can fool cultural insiders, one has produced authentic music? Young writes, 'Cultural outsiders can fool cultural insiders. Stevie Ray Vaughn, John Hammond, Marcia Ball, Johnny Winter, and others, have won blues awards and some blues players have said they have "got it" just as much as any insider.'[14] To be sure, these musicians are some of the best non-African-Americans to play the musical form of the blues. But if fooling people were sufficient justification for someone from one group to be considered a member of another group, then any man who could dress as a woman who fooled another woman would have to be considered a woman himself! The obvious response to this counterexample is that what people see when they look at Dustin Hoffman in *Tootsie* is not the determining factor in being a woman. That is, one may have to 'look closer' to find the man in the woman's clothing, but it is just silly to maintain that the defining feature is not there. (I leave it to the reader to figure out how one might go about finding out that a man dressed as a woman is man.) Similarly, the defining feature of the blues must be sought by 'looking more closely' at the music. For the blues, just as in the case of *Tootsie*, the defining feature is not immediately apparent. The example is meant to illustrate the point that authentic blues includes features not always discernable even to a cultural insider.

Conclusion

My aim in this essay has been to make explicit the distinction that I find implicit in these debates about the blues, and that I fear gets lost in the arguments of both parties: the distinction between the blues as *form* and the blues as *expression*. I have given an account of the two sides of the debate between blues formalists and blues expressivists, and argued that the expressivist position has not been adequately expounded. In making this case, I have offered the outlines of an explanation of cultural expression to help explain why certain styles of music will tend to be best performed by members of the cultural group in which that music originated. In addition, I have identified where I think the difficulties have arisen, namely in a too-loose definition of culture. However, what has been said should not be construed as a claim about the morality of cultural appropriation or racialist interpretations of artistic performance. I am not maintaining that only African-Americans should be allowed to perform the blues. The point is only that blues authenticity depends upon group membership. While cultural outsiders can sing the blues, it should be understood that what is being sung in these cases is a variant of a cultural expression derived from a very different kind of experience. If the ideas presented here are for the most part sound, then the culturally expressive nature of music may not be as mysterious or as simplistic as was once thought.

NOTES

1 Don McGlynn (Dir.), *The Howlin' Wolf Story* (Los Angeles, CA: Arista, 2003). The clip is also available as 'Howlin' Wolf – How Many More Years' (http://www.youtube.com/watch?v=4Ou-6A3MKowz).

2 By 'authentic' I mean 'authoritative,' 'original,' and 'pure.' Think of how a Civil War re-enactment that stays close to the facts of the way it 'really was' could be called 'authentic.'

3 Amiri Baraka, *Blues People: Negro Music in White America* (New York: Harper Perennial, 1999), p. 148.

4 Baraka, *Blues People*, p. 148 (emphasis mine).

5 Ralph J. Gleason, 'Can the white man sing the blues?' *Jazz and Pop* (1968), pp. 28–29.

6 Joel Rudinow, 'Race, ethnicity, expressive authenticity: Can white people sing the blues?' *The Journal of Aesthetics and Art Criticism* 52 (1994), p. 132.

7 James O. Young, *Cultural Appropriation and the Arts* (New York: Blackwell, 2008), p. 41.

8 It may be thought that 'style' is a perfectly good word for what I am driving at here, but 'style' has connotations that sometimes result in ambiguities in the distinctions I want to make. If 'style' were to be equated with 'form,' then I would have no problem with using the word.

9 'Blues' (n.d., http://www.answers.com/topic/blues).

10 For the universality of facial expressions see Charles Darwin, *The Expression of Emotion in Man and Animals* (New York: Oxford University Press, 2002 [1872]) and Paul Ekman, 'Afterword: Universality of emotional expression? A personal history of the dispute' in the same volume. For an alternative view, see James A. Russell, 'Reading emotions from and into faces: Resurrecting a dimensional-contextual perspective.' In James A. Russell and José Miguel Fernández-Dols (Eds.), *The Psychology of Facial Expressions* (Cambridge, UK: Cambridge University Press, 1997), pp. 295–320.

11 I have appropriated the terms 'expressive resources' and 'expressive options' from Sue Campbell, *Interpreting the Personal: Expression and the Formation of Feelings* (New York: Cornell University Press, 1997).
12 This point addresses Young's argument about a cultural insider who misidentified the cultural origins of performances by a cultural outsider. See Young, *Cultural Appropriation and the Arts*, pp. 38–39.
13 Young, *Cultural Appropriation and the Arts*, pp. 9–17.
14 Young, *Cultural Appropriation and the Arts*, p. 39.

PART 2

THE SKY IS CRYING: EMOTION, UPHEAVAL, AND THE BLUES

ALAN M. STEINBERG, ROBERT S. PYNOOS,
AND ROBERT ABRAMOVITZ

CHAPTER 5

THE ARTISTIC TRANSFORMATION OF TRAUMA, LOSS, AND ADVERSITY IN THE BLUES

People keep asking me where the blues started and all I can say is that when I was a boy we always was singing in the fields. Not real singing, you know, just hollerin', but we made up our songs about things that was happening to us at the time, and I think that's where the blues started.

(Son House)[1]

The blues was the facts of life, a heritage of the black people, a thousand generations of poverty and starvation.

(Willie Dixon)[2]

For blues lovers, blues music is among the most evocative music in the world. From its early beginnings until today, at its best it is raw in lyrics, sound, and style, gushing with many of the most profound emotions in the human repertoire. The sound of a bent, sustained, and vibrating note on an electric guitar can literally take your breath away; the anticipation of an expected chord change can seem like an anxious eternity; the wailing cry of a harmonica can tear at your heartstrings; the relentless

Blues – Philosophy for Everyone: Thinking Deep About Feeling Low, First Edition.
Edited by Jesse R. Steinberg and Abrol Fairweather.
© 2012 John Wiley & Sons, Inc. Published 2012 by John Wiley & Sons, Inc.

deep pulsating rhythm of a bass guitar and bass drum can progressively deepen and escalate emotions; and the raspy growl and moan of the blues singer can evoke sustained, yet unalleviated, empathic distress. In concert with the music, blues lyrics deal with many of the most basic human experiences and emotions, and in particular, for a significant portion of the genre, those experiences most difficult to endure, including violent, terrifying circumstances, intolerable and hopeless predicaments, and irreversible losses and separations. These are some of the keys that make the blues what it is.

Trauma, loss, and extreme adversity have been ubiquitous throughout human history. The literary and visual arts provide a great many impressive artistic expressions attesting to the devastating impact of catastrophic experiences on individuals and communities, along with the powerful human reactions and responses to those experiences. A good deal has been written about these expressions of the tribulations inherent in the human condition. This essay provides a welcome opportunity to delve into some of the special techniques that blues writers and performers have used to express and struggle with devastating experiences to make some kind of meaning out of them; in other words, to artistically, creatively, and aesthetically express, define, preserve, transform, and ultimately transcend them.

Artistic expression and transformation not only involve the communication of dreadful circumstances and situations along with attendant suffering, helplessness, melancholy, disillusionment, and alienation. They also often involve themes of triumph over tragedy and adversity. This essay will describe a variety of selected themes regarding trauma, loss, and adversity as these have been artistically and creatively expressed and transformed in the medium of the blues. It will describe how these themes are illustrative of aspects of our current scientific understanding of all-too-human traumatic and loss experiences, including post-trauma reactions (such as post-traumatic stress disorder), separation anxiety and distress, difficulties in forming and maintaining close interpersonal relationships, depression, and grief, and ways that human beings try to cope with the experience, its impact, and how they tolerate and manage associated reactions. Those familiar with the blues will readily recognize the transformation of trauma through the use of disguised references and humor. The lyrics of the blues often represents the expression of trauma, loss, and adversity as thoughts of revenge, and failed preventive or protective action. By relating these negative or danger-oriented expectations regarding the self, others, the world, and the future – summed up in the lyric 'if it wasn't for bad luck, I'd have no luck at all' – trauma and

ALAN M. STEINBERG, ROBERT S. PYNOOS, AND ROBERT ABRAMOVITZ

loss are transformed. The passionate intensity of blues lyrics also conveys trauma's disruptive impact on the ability to regulate strong emotions, such as rage, shame, guilt, and fear. The multitude of songs about jealousy, rejection, and revenge reflect trauma's severely detrimental impact on maintaining enduring and satisfying intimate relationships. The overarching sense of alienation associated with trauma and its consequences has been poignantly expressed by Leroy Carr in 'Blue Night Blues' with the hauntingly disturbing lyric:

> I just feel dissatisfied baby,
> Now sometimes I don't know what to do.
> I just feel dissatisfied baby,
> Sometimes I don't know what to do.
> Have you ever had that same feeling, babe
> To come over you?

We will conclude this essay by taking the opportunity to briefly comment on the use of blues lyrics, combined with chord progressions and delayed notes, as another potent technique of artistic expression and transformation.

The Roots of the Blues in Trauma, Loss, and Adversity

Blues music throughout its history has been strongly influenced by the centuries of catastrophe experienced by African-Americans. Its roots, extending back to the late nineteenth century in the Mississippi Delta cotton fields and gin houses, include spirituals, work songs, and field hollers. As has been well documented, Delta blues originated on share-cropping plantations such as the Docherty at the end of the nineteenth century after reconstruction failed to deliver on social equality and the promise of increased political participation and economic advancement. The music captures the massive scale of exposure to painful trauma, loss, and adversity associated with enduring the humiliation and brutality of slavery and its transition to sharecropping. This painful legacy was intimately intertwined with societal racism, either sanctioned by Jim Crow laws or instigated through lynchings and beatings. Unrelenting extreme poverty and harsh lives on the streets, and frequent arrest, incarceration, and the experience of prison road gangs, compounded by devastating and uprooting natural disasters (including droughts, floods, and hurricanes) perpetuated the pain. Its musical expression followed the massive displacement of large populations from the plantations of the South to Northern cities such as Chicago, and later incorporated the experience of black soldiers returning after World War II and the Vietnam War. In this way, the blues served to hold and document memories, create a sense of community, and provide a platform to share their visceral impact with others.

These population-wide experiences cannot be disentangled from horrific personal trauma and loss. The powerful lines in Charley Patton's 'High Water Everwhere' about the 1927 Mississippi river flood provide a clear example of how the early blues dealt with this kind of combined adversity:

> Oooh Lordy, women is groaning down.
> Oooh, women and children sinking down.
> Lord have mercy, I couldn't see nobody home,
> and was no one to be found.

The displacement and loss of life were so devastating that ultimately more than thirty blues artists were moved to sing about the flood; examples include Barbecue Bob's 'Mississippi Heavy Water Blues,' about the flood washing away his woman, and, most famously, Bessie Smith's 1927 recording of 'Back Water Blues.' Ralph Ellison's observation that 'the blues is an impulse to keep painful details and episodes of brutal experience alive in one's aching consciousness, to finger its jagged grain'[3] attests to the persistence of the disturbing narrative conveyed in blues lyrics and simultaneously reflects how both public and personal trauma become deeply etched in memory, perhaps accounting for the oft-made observation that the blues represents an alternative culture, the voice of an oppressed and alienated people.

The blues has always provided a unique way to 'find one's voice' and to attest to the hardships of life in a way that draws others in rather than turning them away. This ability of the blues to create a shared narrative and build mutual solidarity perhaps underlies John Lee Hooker's statement that 'it's a healer.'[4] This lamenting voice can be heard in many types of recording. Nehemiah 'Skip' Jones, son of a preacher from the Mississippi Delta, sang some of the most disturbing, heart-rending blues in the 1930s. His frantic anxiety-ridden guitar runs in minor keys had an eerie, ghostly sound. His songs, released during the Great Depression, overwhelmingly dealt with morbid themes, for example 'Calf Has Gone Die Blues,' 'Hard-Luck Child,' 'Hard Time Killin' Floor Blues,' and 'Devil Got My Woman.' Alabama blues artist Jaybird Coleman also wrote and performed dark music, including 'No More Good Water ('Cause the Pond is Dry)' and 'Trunk Busted-Suitcase Full of Holes.' Willard Thomas sang of hard times in 'No Job Blues,' 'Hard Dallas Blues,' and 'Poor Boy Blues.' The great Texas guitarist and blues singer Blind Lemon Jefferson sang about devastating poverty and homelessness with 'Broke and Hungry,' 'One Dime Blues,' and 'Tin Cup Blues.' In regard to a sense of hopelessness, blues lovers will be familiar with the following lyric from 'Driftin' and Driftin'':

> Well I'm driftin' and driftin',
> like a ship out on the sea.
> Well I'm driftin' and driftin',
> like a ship out on the sea.
> Well, I ain't got nobody in the world to care for me.

Early female blues singers sang about life on the streets, prostitution, and abusive men, with songs such as 'Walkin' the Street,' 'Black Hand Blues,' 'Wrong Doin' Daddy,' and 'Got Cut All to Pieces.' Death and prison, two prominent consequences of a lifetime of poverty and adversity, also appear frequently. Bumble Bee Slim sang about the death of his best friend in 'The Death of Leroy Carr.' The Reverend Robert Wilkens sang about the death of a loved one in 'I'll Go with Her Blues' and about confinement in 'Jail House Blues.' Ed Bell sang about crime and prison in 'My Crime Blues,' 'Big Rock Jail,' and 'Bad Boy.' But it was Blind Lemon Jefferson who wrote some of the most powerful blues about prison, including 'Blind Lemon's Penitentiary Blues,' ''Lectric Chair Blues,' 'Prison Cell Blues,' and 'Hangman's Blues,' ending his songwriting career with 'See That My Grave is Kept Clean.'

As described so poignantly by Little Hudson, the childhood and adolescence of many of the early blues artists were often characterized by harsh corporal punishment and extreme physical abuse. Hudson said of the death of his abusive stepfather, 'I went behind the chimney corner and if I didn't laugh awhile! I patted my hands, I was so glad I didn't know what to do! Cause he should have been gone a long time ago.'[5] As we know from studies of youth exposed to extreme familial violence, the abusive stepfather is seen as evil incarnate. But, importantly, clinical research has shown that experiencing an extreme desire for revenge and satisfaction at the death of a despised person can make emerging adults feel somehow that the devil has taken up inside them as they struggle with the wish to take justice and revenge into their own hands.[6]

Early blues artists also had to contend with a white-dominated social imprisonment that was, as Hudson said, 'so bad... If you stepped out of line – you didn't have to step out of line, just somebody said you did – they'd just as soon kill you or take you over there and beat you up.'[7] The early blues artists, mostly in the transition to young adulthood, were not just roving minstrels but also traveled the road of the blues toward social emancipation while communicating through their music and lyrics the dark personal history that they could not escape – a message that also resonated deeply with their audiences.

Even a cursory review of the plantation lives of sharecroppers during this era reveals the pervasive nature of traumatic bereavement in childhood, including loss of siblings; of early separation from parents and substituted extended family upbringing; of witnessing violent injury and death from natural and transportation disasters; and of human-perpetrated violence. Little Hudson sought to escape the violence of the South but, like other Delta blues artists who migrated to the big cities, he was forced to confront a radically unfamiliar ecology of urban violence in such cities as Memphis and Chicago. Even among the most successful blues artists, for example Muddy Waters, who sought a life dedicated to music free of violence, the lives of many blues musicians were punctuated by witnessing violent encounters and deaths of close friends and fellow artists. Son House attributed his sixteen-year absence from the music scene to his fear that he would die young, just as Charley Patton, Robert Johnson, and Blind Lemon Jefferson had.

Transforming Trauma, Loss, and Adversity

Blues songs have used a variety of techniques to artistically transform trauma, loss, and adversity. A great many of these transformation strategies correspond closely with ways that science, especially the fields of trauma psychology and psychiatry, has observed that traumatized individuals react to, attempt to recover from, and try to find meaning in the worst kinds of human experiences. One of the most common ways that traumatized individuals respond to overwhelming events involves putting the experience into words to better understand, find a new perspective on, and tolerate the experiences and reactions. In putting experiences and feelings into words, the blues also provides a platform to communicate to others for emotional release, comfort, and support; as Willie King once said of singing the blues, 'The spirit sent something down to the people to help ease a worried mind.'[8]

Dangerous experiences and traumatic bereavement, which evoke fear, helplessness, and extreme distress over separation, present more power-ful stimuli than the mind can comprehend and deal with at the moment of impact. In the aftermath, survivors commonly respond to such horrific experiences by repeatedly going over them in an effort to make sense of what happened. This allows time for the mind to review what was an overwhelming experience in order to better understand what occurred and, often, to determine whether action could have been undertaken to prevent the situation from happening or to avert any injurious consequences. Anyone who has had a difficult experience will be familiar with how the experience keeps coming back to mind in a highly intrusive way – in psychiatry termed 're-experiencing.' This attempt to process, understand, and accept the reality of what happened reflects an effort at continual rumination, which often takes the form of compulsive 'retelling.'

The use of the AAB format, typical of blues songs, where the first line presents an idea or issue and the second line repeats it, can be considered to be a representation in the blues of this powerful human need to retell the event, as if retelling might reduce its incomprehensibility. (Of note, the first line in the blues was originally stated four times, but this technique was dropped as blues music became more popular.) The repetition of an event represents one of the most basic and understand-able human responses to danger and helplessness, as human beings try to maintain vigilance in and navigate a world of ever-present threat and loss. In psychological treatment with traumatized individuals, the first step in therapy typically involves recreating the sense of safety and security needed to undertake construction of a 'trauma narrative.' This orderly recounting of the experience helps the survivor to better under-stand and accept the traumatic details and associated emotions, and to clarify any confusion, distortion, misunderstanding, or misappraisal – especially possible distortions in terms of excessive guilt or shame.

In addition to the function of recounting and ruminating, it is becoming increasingly clear that putting aversive experiences and reactions to those experiences into words alleviates the fear and anguish associated with the experiences; it is as if *repeating what happened and naming the emotion* – confronting it outright, as it were – dampens it. Lieberman and colleagues,[9] using functional magnetic resonance imaging, have demonstrated that verbal labeling serves a critical function in regulating fear and anger by dampening amygdala activity (the amygdala is an almond-shaped structure in the brain that has a primary role in the processing and memory of emotional experiences) through cortical inhibition, a process that matures over childhood, adolescence, and adulthood with increasing capacity for nuanced verbal differentiation of emotions.

As suggested above, another related aspect of the drive to recount the experience has its source in the fact that human beings take solace from one another. In this sense, communication of adverse experiences and distress can be seen as a natural response that elicits understanding and comfort from others, along with bonding and mutual support. The garnering of support from others is a well-documented way in which survivors deal with extreme experiences and emotions. In fact, research has shown that one of the most powerful recovery factors after trauma and loss is having good social support in the form of emotional comfort, reassurance, understanding, and connection with others. There is no doubt that the human impulse to recount difficult experiences and emotions – giving actual voice to them – and the need for social support play strong roles in the very existence, proliferation, healing power, and popularity of the blues.

The Blues as Living Oral History

The blues also serves as a platform from and venue in which to make a historical statement or lasting record of an event, and in so doing promote pro-social response and societal action for future prevention and protection. The historical record, and the trauma literature in particular, is replete with examples of how individuals and communities have preserved the memory of traumatic events in the form of memorials, monuments, and museums dedicated to preserving collective remembrance and promoting societal response. In this way, the blues may be seen as an aesthetic testimonial, something beautiful and enduring, with a significant social function. Many blues artists have specifically indicated that they intended to memorialize a catastrophic event in order to make a lasting historical statement. The creation of a magnificent oral history in the blues attests to the adaptive strength of blues musicians in

  ALAN M. STEINBERG, ROBERT S. PYNOOS, AND ROBERT ABRAMOVITZ

transcending the lack of opportunity and resources to send a powerful social message to their time and to the future.

Many images found in the blues have their roots in the history of trauma and loss among blues artists. While it is well known that the train can be used as a sexual image or as an image of escape, it is less well known that the widespread use of train imagery in the blues has its roots in the proliferation of both passenger and freight trains across the South and their association with deadly train wrecks, sometimes at crossroads where trains collided with wagons or killed unwary pedestrians. 'Sunnyland' Slim went a step further and actually took his name from the Sunnyland train, which he said 'was a fast train, run right out of Memphis to St. Louis on to Frisco. I started singing about it because, man it killed peoples.'[10] Another common image in the blues is that of rain and thunder, signs of a gathering storm that signal an impending flood (e.g., Elmore James' 'The Sky is Crying'). It is well known from the literature on trauma that these kinds of images, which are associated with threat and loss, serve as 'trauma reminders' that are central to ideas of post-traumatic stress reactions. Exquisite sensitivity to, and preoccupation with, trauma reminders is common among traumatized individuals, where exposure to reminders rekindles strong physical and psychological reactions. It is not surprising that trauma- and loss-related images, with such strong meaning and emotion, have been so pervasively used by blues artists.

In addition, a good deal of blues lyrics contain disguised references that served to express forbidden thoughts and emotions, such as anger and revenge. Willie King put it this way:

> Like when they were talking about women, but they were really talking about the boss man, you know, '*my baby so mean, she take all my money.*' You couldn't say that about him, they'd take you out and hang you.'[11]

Those who love the blues know well that blues lyrics often contain the most extraordinary humor and wordplay; for example, among so many great allusions, blues lyrics have included references to another mule kicking in my stall; wanting just a spoonful of your precious love; being tired of your jive; if you don't like my peaches, don't shake my tree; a red rooster on the prowl; a midnight rider; a back door man; wanting the key to your door; a crosscut saw; a jelly roll baker; a driving wheel; a king bee making honey; a black cat bone; a crawlin' king snake; evil going on; getting some help I don't really need; and having a hellhound on your trail.

These sorts of modified allusions, common among traumatized and bereaved individuals, can be seen as attempts to lighten what is being talked about in order to better tolerate the experience and manage ongoing emotions and reactions.

Transformation through Music

In his classic essays on aesthetics, Gorge Wilhelm Friedrich Hegel[12] characterized music as having a unique capacity to direct attention through sound toward complete absorption in one's inner life, an inner life that is made more aware of itself during the course of listening. The blues musician Taj Mahal described Charley Patton as someone who 'includes you way inside his mind.'[13] As with all great musicians, the complete absorption of a blues performer such as B. B. King in the emotion that he intends to convey to an audience is captured in the sublime intensity of his own immersion in his art. In his book, *This is Your Brain on Music*, Daniel Levitin surmised that 'although the studies haven't been performed yet, I'm willing to bet that when B. B. is playing the blues and when he is feeling the blues, the neural signatures are very similar.'[14] The point here is that the blues performer excites the audience to strong emotions that make unavoidable internal demands on them. Albert King, among others, is well known for playing a gut-wrenching lick on his guitar and shouting to the audience, 'can you feel it?!'

What makes the blues such a powerful exemplar of this phenomenon of combining disturbing feelings and emotions with excitement is its attempt to express and communicate the most intense negative emotions, expressed most forcefully through the exquisite timing of a blue note (a third, fifth, or seventh); this expression is the quintessential hallmark of the blues. The 'bending' and vibrating of notes to replace natural pure scale tones seems to be capable of activating an inner space in the audience that serves as a repository for disquieting emotions of loneliness, separation, abandonment, fear, and trepidation.

Now, unadulterated and unaddressed extreme negative emotions and raw, untransformed traumatic depictions can readily become intolerable for both musician and audience alike. The genius of the blues includes a complex armamentarium of musical techniques and lyrical strategies to turn these induced extreme emotions into musical excitement, and, in so doing, perform a transformation of traumatic material. This notion is in

  ALAN M. STEINBERG, ROBERT S. PYNOOS, AND ROBERT ABRAMOVITZ

keeping with the observations of Robert Stoller,[15] who described the role of aesthetic excitement in the artistic mitigation of unadorned extreme emotion. His insight was that excitement is created by a sense of uncertainty and anticipation. Sonny Boy Williamson II and Muddy Waters were renowned for one of the most revered techniques for mitigating blues emotions: through inducing excitement in the listener by the use of a well-placed delayed note or lyric. As Muddy Waters said, 'I'm a delay singer. I don't sing on the beat. I sing behind it, and people have to delay to play with me. They got to hang around, wait see what's going to happen next.'[16] Another excitement-inducing technique that blues lovers are familiar with is the buildup of tension before welcome relief is provided by the change from the tonic to subdominant chord, and the subsequent buildup and release of tension again in moving to the dominant and back to the tonic chord; a most stimulating, exciting, and, at the same time, extremely satisfying experience.

The current understanding of the inter-subjective world of mothers and infants is of interest in this regard. It suggests that mothers universally use a similar technique in singing to their young child by unexpectedly varying their tone and meter, especially through unexpected delays in their recitation of nursery songs and rhymes.[17] Muddy Waters has described his earliest forays as a three-year-old into singing, which consisted of creating a new sound by adding beat while humming his baby songs. The delayed notes of the blues do more than simply replicate this early mother/child phenomenon; via delay of an expected note or buildup and release of tension, the blues artist provides the audience with musical stimulation and consequent satisfaction through reunion with a seemingly abandoned musical necessity – a reunion that is represented in the blues but enormously longed for after real traumatic losses, separations, and abandonment.

Emotional Regulation in the Blues

The structure of blues lyrics also utilizes a major strategy common to efforts to master traumatic experiences and regulate associated emotions that it is feared will become overwhelming. The paradigm of blues lyrics is the AAB pattern of repetition in the first two lines of each twelve-bar structure. Within the narrative form, the repeated AA refrain often describes a situation or state of mind, with the response in B making the associated emotional distress explicit. The blues relies on this mechanism of emotional regulation, which prepares the audience for the content of the B response rather than immediately confronting them with emotionally charged content. A good example of this technique comes from LeRoy Carr in 'My Old Pal Blues':

> The day of his funeral,
> I hated to see LeRoy's face
> The day of his funeral,
> I hated to see LeRoy's face
> Because I know there is no one could ever take his place.

The B component can be understood as expressing another aspect of what is known about the human experience of, and response to, trauma and loss. An examination of B content reveals that it often expresses a range of common ways to take charge of a difficult emotion and threat. Content in B has included, among many other mechanisms, turning passive resignation into active response ('I'm gonna leave here runnin' 'cause walkin' is most too slow,' from 'Key to the Highway'); giving warning before a situation can accelerate into violence ('You better stop her from tickling me under my chin, cause if she don't stop tickling me, I'm gonna take that woman on in,' from 'You Better Stop Her'); and magical thinking ('I'm going down to Louisiana to get me a mojo hand, I'm gonna have all you women right here at my command,' from 'Mojo Hand').

The Creative Reverberation of Traumatic Loss

Through partnering and competing, listening and copying, and a strong relationship between protégé and mentor, blues music carries a genealogy of musicianship, in contrast to the disruption and loss of family genealogy produced by slavery and its aftermath. At the same time, personal lives were dramatically affected by violent, sudden loss, and themes of traumatic loss are prominent in the blues. In the study of children and adults, we have learned that unadjudicated violent loss of a family member or friend, where a perpetrator is not arrested or convicted, often produces intense preoccupations with fantasies of revenge. Perhaps there is no more literal infusion of this theme than in the music of the

  ALAN M. STEINBERG, ROBERT S. PYNOOS, AND ROBERT ABRAMOVITZ

seminal blues guitarist Robert Lockwood. Lockwood is quoted as having been devastated by the sudden loss of his mentor and stepfather, the great Robert Johnson, from whom he learned first-hand how to play the blues guitar:

> I didn't go near his funeral. I guess maybe I would never been able to play again if I had. As it was, it took me a year and a half before I could play in public. Everything I played would remind me of Robert, and whenever I tried to play, I would just come down in tears. That's really what inspired me to start writing my own material.[18]

Johnson – who, among his many contributions, gave us 'Me and the Devil Blues' – is reported to have suffered a horrific death, having been given poisoned whiskey after making a pass at a married woman. Lockwood's compositions in those first years after Johnson's death replaced Johnson's theme of distrust of women with that of the 'femme fatale,' as in 'Black Spider Blues' and 'Her Web's All Over Town.' He went on to substitute images of violent revenge for those merely of sexual prowess, as in 'Little Boy,' which includes the lyric 'I'm gonna take my dirk and stab her / You know I'm gonna turn it round and round.' Indeed, Johnson had once saved the younger Lockwood from the actual sudden thrust of a woman's knife. The much more well-tempered and restrained Lockwood could strike back in his lyrics against the terrible loss of his protector, while cooling down his emotional response through a new style of playing, 'taming Johnson's polyrhythmic ferocity.'[19]

The Blues as a Living, Evolving Legacy

The genius of the blues emerged like a phoenix out of what is often referred to as the nadir of African-American history, the years 1890–1920. At its roots was a young generation born after slavery and the Civil War, yet raised in a strange freedom epitomized by the brutal conditions of the sharecropping South, punctuated by lynching, and characterized by violent interpersonal lives. The blues represented an artistic triumph over the intense, unrelenting emotions of trauma and loss that permeated the lives of its originators, whose expression in music and lyrics resonated so deeply with their audiences, whether on the plantation, at the street corner, or in the juke joint. The interplay of blues music and lyrics not only created musical brilliance but also relied on artistic methods to transform traumatic material into aesthetic excitement and lyrical conquest. In so doing, blues artists entreat all of us to enter this raw world of emotions and emerge with a sense of triumphant reward.

In the capable hands of successive generations of blues artists, including many children of blues musicians,[20] the blues continues to serve as a living, evolving, cultural legacy of humanity's efforts to overcome trauma, loss, and adversity. It is a well-worn platitude that in order to make progress we must remember the past. Keeping the tradition of the blues alive, contemporary blues artists have expanded the old forms, both lyrically and musically, to address current issues and concerns. In addition, spectacular musical and lyrical improvisation over the initial song templates has given new life to the expression of trauma and loss, along with new transformative experiences. Just as the musician familiarizes himself with the song so that he can improvise over it, the audience can do the same with their own trauma and loss memories. Improvisation evokes the immediate present out of something already written and established, and this is a metaphor for how we negotiate our emotions and experiences over a lifetime. Traumatic events come to mean different things as time goes on, as the issues are confronted, and as later life experiences are interpreted through their prism, reframed with new meaning, and approached with more mature emotional regulation. The blues will continue to serve a reparative and transformative function in giving voice to harsh experiences and associated feelings rather than suppressing and avoiding them; continue to generate mutual understanding and support rather than isolation and withdrawal; continue to promote pro-social action rather than passivity, resignation, and revenge; and continue to be a creative mechanism to mitigate seemingly intolerable experiences and emotions.[21]

NOTES

1 Lawrence Cohn (Ed.), *Nothing But the Blues: The Music and the Musicians* (New York: Abbeville Press, 1993), p. 13.
2 Cohn, *Nothing But the Blues*, p. 322.
3 Ralph Ellison, *Shadow and Act* (New York: Random House, 1964).
4 Martin Scorsese (Dir.), *Martin Scorsese Presents the Blues – A Musical Journey* (United States: PBS, 2003).
5 Steve Cushing, *Blues Before Sunrise: The Radio Interviews* (Urbana/Chicago, IL: University of Illinois Press, 2010).

6   Robert S. Pynoos, Alan M. Steinberg, and Ruth Wraith, 'A developmental model of childhood traumatic stress.' In Dante Cicchetti and Donald J. Cohen (eds.), *Manual of Developmental Psychopathology* (New York: John Wiley & Sons, 1995), pp. 72–93.

7   Cushing, *Blues Before Sunrise.*

8   Scorsese, *Martin Scorsese Presents the Blues.*

9   Matthew D. Lieberman, Naomi I. Eisenberger, Molly J. Crokett, Sabrina M. Tom, Jennifer H. Pfeifer, and Baldwin M. Way. Putting feelings into words: Affect labeling disrupts amygdala activity to affective stimuli, *Psychological Science* 18 (2007), pp. 421–428.

10 Robert Palmer, *Deep Blues: A Musical and Cultural History, from the Mississippi Delta to Chicago's South Side, to the World* (New York: Penguin Books, 1982), p. 153.

11 Scorsese, *Martin Scorsese Presents the Blues.*

12 Gorge Wilhelm Friedrich Hegel, *Aesthetics: Lectures on Fine Art*, trans. T. M. Knox (Oxford, UK: Clarendon Press, 1975).

13 Scorsese, *Martin Scorsese Presents the Blues.*

14 Daniel J. Levitin, *This is Your Brain on Music: The Science of a Human Obsession* (London: Penguin Books, 2006), p. 210.

15 Robert J. Stoller, *Observing the Erotic Imagination* (New Haven, CT: Yale University Press, 1985).

16 Palmer, *Deep Blues*, p. 100.

17 Daniel N. Stem, Susan Spieker, Kyle Barnett, and Kristine MacKain. The prosody of maternal speech: Infant age and context related changes, *Journal of Child Language* 10 (1983), pp. 1–15.

18 Palmer, *Deep Blues*, p. 181.

19 Ibid.

20 Art Tipaldi, Children of the Blues: 49 Musicians Shaping a New Blues Tradition (San Fransisco, CA: Backbeat Books, 2002).

21 The authors would like to thank Danny Snedecor for assistance with research for this essay and helpful suggestions along the way.

DAVID C. DRAKE

CHAPTER 6

SADNESS AS BEAUTY

Why it Feels So Good to Feel So Blue

There is more to the emotional appeal of the blues than mere aesthetic appreciation of its basic musical elements, though this *is* important. There is also more to it than catharsis, though it *can* involve catharsis. There is something else present, something special that, although it is by no means unique to the blues, finds in the blues what could arguably be its most devoted expression. That something is this: the portrayal of *sadness as beauty*. Though never explicitly stated, this idea is subtly conveyed through every soulful lyric and every wail of the saxophone. And it is this remarkable idea – the bizarre equation of sadness with beauty – that draws out the listener's deepest emotional responses. By beautifying his sorrow, the musician beautifies his life story and, in so doing, beautifies himself. By relating to the musician's sorrow, the listener can also partake of that beauty, attaching it to her own sorrows, her own life story, her own self. Anyone of sufficient age and sophistication will be acquainted with sadness for one reason or another, so it is not difficult for this process to occur, whether consciously or subconsciously; and it is highly desirable to engage in this process, because doing so alleviates some of the pain usually associated with sadness, resulting in the seemingly paradoxical adoption of

Blues – Philosophy for Everyone: Thinking Deep About Feeling Low, First Edition.
Edited by Jesse R. Steinberg and Abrol Fairweather.
© 2012 John Wiley & Sons, Inc. Published 2012 by John Wiley & Sons, Inc.

a positive attitude toward one's sadness or even the transformation of some of one's sadness into happiness. But how is any of this possible?

The Nature of Beauty

Let's start with the concept of beauty. It's a difficult concept to define, for we tend to apply it to a wide variety of very different phenomena. We might see a musician and observe that he has a beautiful *appearance*, smell his cologne and observe it has a beautiful *fragrance*, then hear him sing and observe he has a beautiful *voice*. Is there really some single property called 'beauty' that can be shared by such disparate phenomena as sights, smells, and sounds? And what about other kinds of things: can a *feeling*, such as sadness, be beautiful? Can a person's *life* be beautiful? How do we distinguish beauty from ugliness, anyway? Are judgments of beauty subjective, objective, or a little of both? If I say that a particular blues song is beautiful, can I be wrong?

These questions place us squarely in the realm of aesthetics: the branch of philosophy concerned with the nature of art, taste, and, of course, beauty. Various theories of beauty have been proposed over the centuries and it continues to be an area of active debate. We'll take a look at a few of these theories and see how they might shed light on the appeal of the blues and, in particular, the phenomenon of sadness as beauty.

For starters, let's delve into the classical era. Plato, famed pupil of Socrates, believed that the three essential characteristics of any beautiful thing were (1) proportion, (2) harmony, and (3) unity among its parts. A beautiful human life should, on this account, have each of these elements, and this may actually *necessitate* a certain amount of sorrow. A life with no sorrow in the world as we know it would seem to lack proper proportion. When faced with heartbreak or another form of hardship, it is *right* to be sad: to feel otherwise would indicate a strange disharmony or lack of unity between the parts of oneself or one's life. Aristotle, the most influential of Plato's students, described the universal elements of beauty in a slightly different manner: (1) order, (2) symmetry, and (3) definiteness. Again, according to these criteria a beautiful life may necessitate some sadness. A life of nothing but happiness in a world such as ours would suggest a lack of order and symmetry. Thus we see that, according to Plato and Aristotle, a connection between sadness and beauty might have a sound philosophical foundation.

Fast-forward to the twenty-first century and we find the contemporary philosopher Denis Dutton attempting to delineate the fundamental features of all aesthetic activities: (1) expertise or virtuosity; (2) non-utilitarian pleasure; (3) style; (4) criticism; (5) imitation, in the sense of imitating life or the world; (6) special focus, as in being set apart from ordinary life; and, finally, (7) the experience of the activity as an imaginative experience for both producers and audiences.[1] This may or may not be right, but, regardless, it is interesting to see how the blues genre fits (or fails to fit) into it. It may sometimes fulfill each of the seven characteristics, but not always: (1) yes, we admire great blues musicians for both their natural and cultivated talents; (2) and yes, we generally enjoy the blues for its own sake and without any conscious practical motive in mind, but in its earliest phases it often had the purpose of helping African-American slaves cope with their hard life of forced labor and was sometimes even used by them to convey carefully hidden messages, such as describing in general terms where escaped slaves might go for assistance; (3) a blues song must satisfy certain loosely defined stylistic criteria, otherwise it just ain't the blues; (4) blues songs can be, and often are, critically judged and interpreted; (5) blues songs, whether with lyrics or without, are definitely attempts at 'imitating' life experiences in musical form; (6) blues music is generally in some sense set apart from everyday life and given dramatic focus, though it can also be enjoyed while engaging in mundane activities, and in fact, as has already been alluded to, the blues had as part of its origins the work songs and field hollers of slaves who presumably used their music as a way to find refuge from their extraordinarily difficult lives, even in the midst of performing their 'duties'; and (7) the experiences of composing, performing, and appreciating blues music surely all involve engagement of the imagination. It is this engagement of the imagination, coupled with the blues' unique imitation of the more melancholic side of life, that enables the poignant experience of sadness as beauty.

Speaking of imitation, if we go back to ancient philosophy for a moment we will find in Aristotle's *Poetics* the notion that Greek dramas involve imitation 'not of persons but of action and life, of happiness and misery.'[2] In other words, they imitate certain *ideal* or *abstract* concepts that are of great importance to their human audiences. Furthermore, Aristotle asserts that dramas – particularly tragedies – can be beneficial by inducing *catharsis*: a purging of the emotions through 'pity and fear.'[3] If blues music had been around in Aristotle's time, it's likely Aristotle would have described it in much the same way. Blues lyrics are generally full of idealized, non-specific references to one's life, one's lover, one's suffering,

DAVID C. DRAKE

and so forth. Even when specific people, places, and events are mentioned, the listener is still able to extract the abstract concepts involved. Furthermore, even in the absence of lyrics, blues music still has the remarkable ability to communicate emotions and ideas. As for catharsis, it seems clear that emotional purging is a major part of what draws people to blues music, and it is precisely the experience of sadness as beauty that facilitates this purging. Sadness without beauty is just depressing, but when coupled with beauty it becomes healthy, even therapeutic.

Judgments of beauty involve being able to discriminate between sensory experiences. According to Immanuel Kant, an extremely influential eighteenth-century philosopher, aesthetic experiences involve discerning a subjective yet *universal* truth. In other words, whether or not a certain song is beautiful is a matter of *fact* in spite of its also being a matter of subjective experience. On this account, if John Lee Hooker's 'Boogie Chillen" is beautiful, then *everyone* who understands beauty should agree that it is beautiful. That may seem strange, but to Kant beauty is more than something being enjoyable. He accepts that different people can find enjoyment in very different kinds of music, but that's just a matter of what he calls taste. But for something to actually be beautiful, part of the enjoyment must arise through reflection or contemplation. In other words, aesthetic judgments have sensory, emotional, *and* intellectual components. This is compatible with the experience of sadness as beauty through the blues, for the recognition of beauty in a musician's sadness requires reflecting on the words or emotions being expressed through her music, and to go further and see beauty in one's own sadness requires reflecting on how that message applies to oneself or compares with one's own life experiences.

Post-modernists have challenged the assumption that beauty is of primary importance in art and aesthetics and have focused instead on various other concepts, including the experience of the *sublime*. A sublime experience, in this context, refers to a mixture of pleasure and anxiety, such as a feeling of awe. As Jean-François Lyotard puts it, sublime art 'will please only by causing pain.'[4] Surely this is true of the blues, and a better expression of what is involved in perceiving sadness as beauty I would be hard pressed to find! In the feeling of one's sadness there is pain, but in the realization of one's beauty there is pleasure. Without the pain, this particular brand of pleasure would be unattainable. The blues could, therefore, be classified as a sublime form of music. It is sometimes claimed that experiences of the sublime elevate people in dignity or honor, and I believe this to be true of the blues, too. By revealing the beauty inherent in their sorrow, people are brought to see more clearly their personal dignity. Furthermore, when sorrow ought to be felt, there is honor in feeling it, and in recognizing the honorableness of one's sorrow the beauty of one's life experiences is made manifest.

A few other philosophers' views are worth mentioning before moving on to our next major topic. Alexander Gottlieb Baumgarten made the interesting claim that beauty is the most perfect knowledge that can be obtained through sense experience. If this is true, it would help explain why seeing beauty amid one's sadness can be such a pleasant experience: it is a source of *knowledge* that can make us feel better about ourselves and our lives. Arthur Schopenhauer, in a manner similar to the Greek Stoics as well as the Buddhists and other Indian philosophers, claimed that the cause of all human suffering was the *will*, by which he meant all forms of motivation, desire, and craving. The best way to alleviate suffering, according to him, is to stop willing, but this is difficult to accomplish. The next best option is to be temporarily distracted from the will by being caught up in aesthetic contemplation. This may be a significant factor in the therapeutic nature of perceiving sadness as beauty through the blues: not only does it cast a positive light on our suffering, but it temporarily distracts us from all our desires, including the desire for our suffering to end. Ironically, sometimes the only way to find relief is to cease desiring relief, and this may actually be promoted by seeing beauty in one's suffering: if the pain and sorrow in one's life are beautiful, why desire that they end?

Truth, Goodness, and Beauty

There is a long history of mentioning beauty alongside truth and goodness, so we should look into these concepts as well. Truth, goodness, and beauty have often been regarded as being not only of similar (if not equal) value but also tightly interrelated. For instance, it has sometimes been claimed that wherever one of them is, there also the other two will be. Some have even gone so far as to assert that these terms are somehow synonymous.

Thus we find in the poetry of John Keats the famous line, 'Beauty is truth, truth beauty.'[5] This thought is taken very seriously by many mathematicians, who see breathtaking beauty in the symmetry, simplicity, and order of mathematical truths.[6] It is also reflected in Occam's razor: the claim that simpler explanations are more likely to be true.[7]

DAVID C. DRAKE

Albert Einstein affirmed this principle when he said, 'It can scarcely be denied that the supreme goal of all theory is to make the irreducible basic elements as simple and as few as possible without having to surrender the adequate representation of a single datum of experience.'[8] Simpler theories and simpler proofs are often described as being more 'elegant,' and it is thought that this elegance is somehow related to their being superior statements of truth. There seems to be an underlying assumption that, although some facts are undeniably ugly, ultimate truth *must* be beautiful.

Can we find some evidence for a connection between truth and beauty in blues music? I would say so. Blues songs are beautiful to us in large part because they communicate fundamental *truths* about the human condition: about the perils of falling in love, the burden of poverty, and even, in the earliest days of the blues, the painfulness of slavery. Additionally, it seems critical to any serious blues performance that the musicians convey the feeling that they have *truly* experienced hardship and heartbreak in their lives. To illustrate this point, imagine knowing someone who had never experienced any difficulty or sadness in their life (a difficult thing to imagine, I know, but let's try). We would probably find it odd and even off-putting to hear them sing a blues song. Any beauty the song might have had would be lost as a result of our knowledge that the song was a *false* performance. Similarly, such a person could not understand the truth in someone else's blues performance, and consequently would not be beautified by it. Only true sadness can be made beautiful through the blues.

So much for beauty and truth. What about beauty and goodness? Well, first of all, it seems obvious that beauty is 'good' in the general sense of that word. That is to say, it has value. And so, when something is perceived to be beautiful it is necessarily also perceived to be valuable. Therefore, when one's life is perceived to be beautiful, even in its most sorrowful moments, one's life is simultaneously perceived to be 'good' or valuable. However, 'goodness' in this aesthetic sense is not the same as 'goodness' in a moral sense. Or is it?

Kant is one of several philosophers who have proposed that there is a close relationship between our aesthetic judgments and our moral feelings.[9] He suggested that appreciation of the beautiful and the sublime can prepare us for appreciation of moral goodness, and vice versa. Being drawn to beauty is a sign of 'a good soul,' he said: an indication of 'mental attunement favorable to moral feeling.'[10] Perhaps his most poetic expression of the subtle relationship between beauty and moral goodness may be found in the conclusion to his *Critique of Practical Reason*: 'Two things fill the mind with ever new and increasing admiration and awe, the more often and steadily reflection is occupied with them: the starry heaven above me and the moral law within me.'[11]

A more recent example of an attempt to describe the relation between beauty and goodness, *aesthetic ethics* is founded on the intriguing notion that human life should be governed by principles of beauty, or that goodness ought to be defined in terms of beauty. There does seem to be something to this: it seems right to regard a peaceful, orderly society as being not only morally superior but also more *beautiful* than a society consumed by violence and chaos. The human preoccupation with justice and fairness seems analogous to an aesthetic preference for balance and symmetry. In fact, as John Dewey once pointed out,[12] it is interesting that the English word 'fair' has two meanings: one ethical ('that's not fair!') and one aesthetic ('her face was very fair').

All of this aligns well with the perception of sadness as beauty that is encouraged by the blues. For one thing, it is often by recognizing that one has been morally wronged – or that one has morally wronged another – that one sees the appropriateness, and thus the beauty, of one's sorrow. An ugly 'imbalance' brought about through an unjust or unfair act may in some sense be 'balanced' by the sadness one feels in response to it, thus restoring at least some of the beauty and goodness that has been lost. Alternatively, it could be said that, by allowing oneself to feel keenly the injustices of life, one draws attention to one's sense of *what ought to be*, which is simultaneously a moral and an aesthetic sense, and arguably a truth-related sense, too. That one should even have such a sense suggests that one possesses at least some degree of truth, goodness, and beauty, and that is a comforting thought.

Friedrich Nietzsche once said, 'Whoever despises himself nonetheless respects himself as one who despises.'[13] This is related to the way sadness as beauty is conveyed by many blues songs. Blues lyrics often express derision for one's circumstances, one's life, one's actions, or even oneself, yet they can be enjoyable and therapeutic because they nonetheless imply respect for oneself as one who appropriately holds things in derision. Wisdom is required to discern what should be loved from what should be despised, so even as one despises oneself for being foolish one also respects oneself for having enough wisdom to recognize the truth of one's foolishness as well as the truth that such foolishness should be despised. In a similar way, when one is faced with the uncomfortable conclusion that one has made an immoral decision and thereby caused harm to others, at least some comfort can be found in the

DAVID C. DRAKE

knowledge that one still has a moral compass, that one still has the ability to recognize wrongdoing and feel remorse for it. Thus, even as a blues singer decries his misfortunes or his misdeeds (or, for that matter, the misdeeds of another), he is simultaneously glorifying himself, if only subconsciously or by implication, as one who properly decries that which is evil, in every sense of that word. Anyone who can do that has at least *some* degree of inner beauty. And so, this is a subtle way in which the blues conveys sadness as beauty: by revealing that one has wisdom in despising one's foolishness, goodness in despising one's wickedness, beauty in despising one's ugliness.

Beauty and the Blues

It is difficult to say exactly what lessons we should take away from this whirlwind tour of various philosophical eras and theories, but there are at least a few main points that stand out. We have examined ancient, modern, and post-modern theories of beauty and found that each may provide philosophical justification for the blues genre's ability to allow both performers and listeners to experience sadness as beauty, as well as for my claim that such experiences can be highly beneficial. We also discovered that all of this may be due in large part to a close relationship between truth, goodness, and beauty. However, philosophical theories in areas such as aesthetics may be nothing more than admirable attempts at using language to describe ultimately ineffable human experiences. In the final analysis, I suppose it's up to you to decide whether or not any of the ideas expressed in this essay coincide with your own subjective experiences when performing or listening to the blues. If at least most of them ring true for the majority of blues fans, as they do for me, then perhaps I am justified in the claims I made at the beginning, and perhaps art forms such as the blues indeed offer us a rare privilege: the opportunity to see the beauty that is in each of us not only when we're happy but also when we're blue.

NOTES

1 Denis Dutton, 'Aesthetic universals.' In Berys Gaut and Dominic McIver Lopes (Eds.), *The Routledge Companion to Aesthetics* (London: Routledge, 2001), pp. 203–214.
2 Aristotle, *Poetics* (New York: Hill and Wang, 1961), 1451b.

3   Aristotle, *Poetics*, 1449b.24.

4   Jean-Françoise Lyotard, *The Postmodern Condition* (Minneapolis, MN: University of Minnesota Press, 1984). See also Jean-Françoise Lyotard, 'Scriptures: Diffracted traces,' *Theory, Culture and Society* 21:1 (2004), p. 101.

5   John Keats, 'Ode to a Grecian urn.' In *Ode to a Grecian Urn and Other Poems* (New York: Kessinger Publishing, 2010).

6   For example, see Ian Stewart, *Why Beauty is Truth: The History of Symmetry* (New York: Basic Books, 2008).

7   This isn't really Occam's razor, but it is a common interpretation of it. Occam's razor is '*entia non sunt multiplicanda praeter necessitate,*' or 'entities must not be multiplied beyond necessity.' According to this principle, if two theories can adequately explain a phenomenon, but one of them posits more entities than the other, we should prefer the theory with fewer entities (because the one with more entities is apparently 'multiplying entities' beyond what is necessary with regard to explaining the phenomenon in question). As such, Occam's razor does seem to imply a connection between simplicity and truth, and, because simplicity is also widely regarded as a component of beauty, it may also imply a connection between truth and beauty.

8   Albert Einstein, 'On the method of theoretical physics,' *Philosophy of Science* 1:2 (1934), p. 165.

9   Immanuel Kant, *Critique of Judgment* (Oxford, UK: Oxford University Press, 2007).

10 Immanuel Kant, *Critique of Judgment*, §42, pp. 298–299.

11 Immanuel Kant, *Critique of Practical Reason* (New York: CreateSpace, 2010), §5, p. 161.

12 John Dewey, *The Collected Works of John Dewey, 1882–1953*, Jo-Ann Boydston (Ed.) (Carbondale, IL: Southern Illinois University Press, 1932), p. 275.

13 Friedrich Nietzsche, *Beyond Good and Evil* (New York: Tribeca, 2011), §4, p. 78.

CHAPTER 7

ANGUISHED ART

Coming Through the Dark to the Light the Hard Way

The musical mood and the lyrics – the content of blues – express feelings and memories of heartbreak, solitude, loss, betrayal, jealousy, and emotional and economic degradation. Assuming that the idiom of deep-throated wailing produces feelings in the listener similar to the feelings expressed by the artist, it makes sense to wonder what the appeal of experiencing pain and heartbreak is. Why would humans seek out, even pay money, to have bluesy experiences? Isn't there enough of this stuff in life already – real life, that is?

This is a similar question to one Aristotle asked in the *Poetics* about tragedy: Why would people wish to go to plays that tell horrible, heart-wrenching tales? How is it possible that people could prefer tragedy to comedy, to simple quotidian tales of ordinary folk life, or to drama where the good guys come out on top? Tragedy thrusts the ubiquity and ultimacy of defeat in our face. Blues music often does so too. Why would people want to experience vicariously the agony of defeat before their own turn to experience it in reality? It is generally puzzling why people seek out painful art – tragedy, classical requiems, operatic disasters, or, in our case, the blues. Here we try to say some helpful things about why

Blues – Philosophy for Everyone: Thinking Deep About Feeling Low, First Edition.
Edited by Jesse R. Steinberg and Abrol Fairweather.
© 2012 John Wiley & Sons, Inc. Published 2012 by John Wiley & Sons, Inc.

blues appeals and how it produces its interesting effects on our hearts and minds. Classical tragedy provides a useful but imperfect point of analogy.

Some say that anguished art, if it does appeal, appeals because we appreciate beauty in any and all forms, and that all excellent art is conveyed in a beautiful way. On this view good blues music is beautiful. No doubt some is beautiful – but there is more to it than that if, as seems plausible, the medium is the message, or part of it. The content, the lyrics of the blues as well as the soundscape, typically expresses, embodies, and exemplifies feelings and experiences of loss, solitude, and the sort of redemption that comes from being a survivor. And the question recurs as to why, among all the artistic forms that are beautiful, would one seek to listen to and experience feelings of those sorts. No sensible person would choose to eat dirt over chocolate, why would anyone choose to listen to blues over happy pop music?

Not all of the blues thrives on sentiments of heartbreak or trouble. There are, of course, examples of the blues journeying into lighthearted territory, with 'Hokum Blues,' 'Boogie Woogie,' and some other forms, which are often characterized by innuendo and a more upbeat musical aesthetic. It does seem though that the real heart of the blues is the music formed in the heart of America's Deep South and characterized by a voice that is filled with anguish, solitude, and, usually, an acknowledgment of subjugation and captivity. It is a medium of the pure expression of existential anxiety, but cast less in the voice of Kierkegaardian fear and trembling, sickness unto death, than in a sort of American 'I'm down, I was hurt, but I have survived, fuck 'em, fuck her' mode. In its purest form, the blues explores some dark and universal zones of human existence: love gained and lost, deep jealousy and betrayal, social and self-degradation at the hands of oppressors, and drugs and booze. The final notes are notes of survival but not typically of having emerged a winner, unscathed and on top of things – more as a survivor, ready to live another day, until as is likely the world gets to me, gets at me again.

The fact that the protagonist in blues (like the protagonist in related forms of Country music –'All my wives are in Texas, that's why I live in Tennessee') survives, indeed is a survivor, is one difference between blues and classical tragedy, where normally the action closes with everyone dead (or with death imminent). Antigone buries her brother despite the ruling of King Creon that no enemy warrior be buried. And, by the play's end everyone – Antigone, her fiancé, the King, as well as both her brothers – is dead. It is an unmitigated disaster. In the blues, Antigone might suffer all the same losses. Her life would be a disaster, a train wreck – but she would find a way to go on and to talk (sing) about it.

A constant theme in blues lyrics, like in tragedy, is one of love lost. Examples include Robert Johnson's 'Love in Vain,' in which the singer tells of saying goodbye to his love as she boards an outbound train:

> And I followed her to the station, with her suitcase in my hand.
> And I followed her to the station, with her suitcase in my hand.
> Well it's hard to tell, it's hard to tell when all your love is in vain. All my love is in vain.

Muddy Waters, also born in the Mississippi Delta, sings about the absurdities and short life of love that was meant to be forever in his iconic 'Five Long Years' (1952):

> Five long years, every Friday
> I come home with my pay.
> Have you ever been mistreated?
> You know what I'm talkin' about.
> I worked five long years for one woman.
> She had the nerve to put me out.

The sentiment in both songs is simple yet hits on the key existential absurdity of the human effort to seek love only to have that love simply disappear, like Sisyphus pushing the rock up the mountain only to have to start his journey again once he has reached the summit and his boulder has taken the plunge. Johnson and Waters sing here of the universal reality that, no matter how hard we work at something, we very well may fail. Moreover, our struggles in love, as in other facets of life, can be continuous. The giddy optimism and feeling of completion of early love yields to harm and hurt, often mutual, and to feelings of being broken, fucked up, fucked over. Classical Greek tragedy also involves loss of loved ones and convoluted love relations. But, unlike in blues, these are as often parent–child relations as love relations. Oedipus sleeps with his mother, Jocasta, by accident, and then blinds himself when he discovers what he has done; Agamemnon burns his daughter Iphigenia at the stake because his duty as king requires this (tragic) choice. Greek tragedy almost always involves familial death, murder, and mayhem. Romantic loss is a further, side casualty. Shakespeare's *Romeo and Juliet* marked the emergence of romantic love at the center of tragedy, although in that famous play it is family, specifically the Montagues and the Capulets, who destroy the lovers' bliss. In the blues, the protagonists get to mess up their love on their own, just by being normal flawed humans.

So far we have this: blues and tragedy are both, as we say, depressing. But there are two differences. First, whereas the tragic protagonist does not survive, the blues protagonist does survive, though often only barely. How many more cigarettes, shots of whiskey, and new lovers there are before the end is unclear. Second, although fate figures in both tragedy and the blues, the downfall of the tragic hero is embedded in deep structures of politics and the family, whereas the blues protagonist more or less gets to bring about his own undoing individually, by his unfortunate personal choices – wanderlust, the wrong chick, too much whiskey.

One possible answer to the question of why the blues appeals – what the audience gets out of bluesy experiences – is the one Aristotle gives in the *Poetics* about Greek tragedy when he asked: what is the appeal of seeing fellow human beings caught by their own fate, their own character, their own hubris in creating their own miserable undoing? His answer: Tragedy produces a catharsis, specifically a purgation of pity and fear by way of identification with the protagonist's plight. Perhaps this is also how the blues works, why it appeals. This notion of catharsis is complicated by the idea that classical tragedy usually works through the audience's identification with the downfall of royalty or something akin to royalty. If blues works through identification it is through identification with a working-class person. This is interesting and important. If tragedy works by way of me, as an audience member, identifying with the protagonist and experiencing fear because her plight could be mine, then tragedy requires suspension of my belief that I am plebian and these folk are patrician (even Romeo and Juliet are not commoners). Blues makes things easier since most of us are plebian and not patrician. I not only could be the guy who 'worked five long years for one woman' who 'had the nerve to put me out'; I am that guy or I am just the sort of guy to whom that kind of thing happens all the time, will happen, and so on. Imaginative identification is easier in blues than in tragedy.

A second possible answer, as we have said, lies in the fact that the downfall of the protagonist in the blues is, unlike in tragedy (Greek or Shakespearean), told in terms of a narrative of bad luck and bad personal choice and less in terms of the traps laid by being fated to fill a certain social role with its attendant duties, as when Agamemnon must save Helen from the Trojans and is told by a seer that the winds will not blow to take his navy to Troy unless he sacrifices his beloved daughter Iphigenia. There is nothing about kings and queens, real royalty, in the

BEN FLANAGAN AND OWEN FLANAGAN

blues, and not very much about role-related duties either, except the ordinary ones that come with sexual love, romance, and a perfectly ordinary job. What there are instead are gritty stories about ordinary members of the proletariat – some lower down than me, some where I am or have been, others where I see that I could easily go.

A third answer is that the emotions evoked in blues are broader than just pity and fear. Sexual jealousy, addiction, bad luck, poverty, betrayal, suffering, pride, loss of existential meaning, nostalgia/yearning for departed love and fortuitous times, solitude, salvation, God's presence or lack thereof, and emancipation are among many of the themes that are all repeatedly expressed within the blues.

Some say the greatest and most continuous appeal of classical tragedy has to do with the universality of its themes. But one might wonder whether this is right: choices between incompatible duties are the stuff of tragedy and frightening to imagine, but they are not so clearly the stuff of everyday life. The themes in the blues are more familiar to modern folk than problems of conflicting duties to one's state (do not bury enemy combatants) and to one's family (bury one's brother if he dies in war). These sorts of things are scary but rare. Losing your girl to your best friend after a debauched night out is scary and more common. It's both really fucked up, as we say, and really real. It happens a lot.

Freud offers an account related to Aristotle's of anxious, depressing art that captures better the more expansive set of emotions that are activated in the anguished arts, including the blues. If Aristotle's idea is one of purgation, Freud's is one of release. In his view, humans are governed initially by the pleasure principle – the insatiable desire to get exactly what we want. Reality is uncooperative and demands that we tame our desires, specifically our sexual and aggressive desires. Either we repress these desires, in which case they will gain release by deforming our nature in the form of neuroses, or we sublimate and release in a high-minded, socially acceptable way the frustration we experience at not always, indeed normally rarely, getting what we want. On this view, the deep troubles expressed in blues music allow us to sublimate, vicariously, rather than repress unsatisfied sexual and aggressive feelings, and to release sores in our being rather than having them fester inside, poisoning our souls.

Perhaps it is in this manner that the blues, like tragedy, produces something in the vicinity of catharsis, but something much more than just a release of pity and fear. The blues often works by asking the listener to identify with situations where there is romantic rejection (not love thwarted by externalities as in tragedy) or downfall brought on by or partly constituted by smoke, booze, and drugs (nothing the Greeks or Elizabethans abused as we gritty escapists do). The blues artist, and possibly the audience, get to release all sorts of ordinary everyday feelings from being pissed, feeling hurt, and wanting revenge, but always with the simultaneous expression of the gritty determination to go on, having learned whatever lessons the school of hard knocks offers. We might say that blues, unlike tragedy, is realistic. It seems obvious that feelings of solitude and psychic aloneness are universal, but even if such feelings are universal not every culture has developed art forms to express such feelings. The blues exemplifies these feelings in both its lyrical framework and its soundscape.

Whereas death, loss, and suffering are sturdy fixtures in both tragedy and the blues, the suffering that comes from the loss of love is the type that blues singers more consistently channel. It makes sense that the singer and the audience experience lost romantic love as an object of pity and fear, but the range of emotions released includes more than those two. The devil is in the details, so we need to know what it is about a specific play or song that activates which emotions. Fear of death, fear of loss of love or job, and fear of economic insecurity, even of indigence, are different fears or at least about different things, and these different fears affect different people at different times in different ways. One possibility is that the issues about winning and losing love born of individual choice, not because of one's social role, constitute a thoroughly modern problem, with its own set of absurdities.

Humans in each age live their lives by intersecting with spaces of meaning, such as politics, ethics, religion, science, technology, and art. For each space in a time there are rules of admission and permission that govern whether and how one interacts, as actor and audience, as producer and consumer, as participant and observer, and actively or passively. Indeed there have been periods in human history when being an actor as opposed to audience in many of these spaces of meaning required being a member of some elite. One could not be a politician or a priest in many places even recently (still in some places) unless one was born into the appropriate social status or male or white or some such. One could make a Ford car perhaps, but not own one, and so on. But in America, especially in the twentieth century, when both jazz and the blues and rap and hip-hop were born, all these spaces of meaning were democratized to varying degrees. In the case of art and music, there have been times when even being part of the audience – and thus participating in the space of meaning constituted by art – was highly restricted. This is still so for high art, high music, opera, and the like. In Athens it was free men only who attended and knew the content of classical tragedy. In classical China, Mozi lamented the fact that the proletariat were called upon to make musical instruments and that some were called upon to play them, but always at court performances, where ordinary people were not only not welcome, but neither invited or nor permitted. Many say that Mozi was against musical performance. This is false. He was against musical performance that restricted both participation and observation to the elite.

If one thinks that maximum opportunity to express, reveal, depict, avow, and honor one's form of life is both liberating and capable of producing catharsis, release, or just the simple relief that comes with happy or sad, or mixed, or bluesy expression, then we are lucky to live in a world in which more-proletarian, real musical forms such as blues (but also of course jazz and hip-hop) are both possible and actual. Attending the opera is expensive, as are concerts by big-time rock stars, but even the blues clubs on Bourbon Street in New Orleans and Beale Street in Memphis are, as we say, affordable. And, thanks to radio, blues – like jazz and hip-hop – has both a cadre of people who work at creating it for free and an audience of persons to appreciate it, learn from it, and have it do whatever artistic and psychic work it does, all for free.

One more idea is worth emphasizing. In both tragedy and the blues, things normally have gone badly recently, often because of the fickle finger of fact. But normally there has also been a bad choice, a way the protagonist has participated in his own downfall or undoing. Aristotle characterizes tragedy in the *Poetics* as a situation involving a dignified protagonist who experiences a reversal in fortune. For Aristotle, a proper tragedy will have this reversal in fortune brought on by *harmatia*, which refers not to a character flaw in the protagonist but to a mistake he could have anticipated but didn't. For the audience to identify positively with their protagonist, the latter must remain flawed, yet neither vicious nor malevolent: his folly must come from a place of ignorance or from being caught in a tragic situation from which there is no escape. Aristotle says that 'the change to bad fortune which he undergoes is not due to any moral defect or flaw, but a mistake of some kind.'[1] But what Aristotle calls a mistake is typically not what we would call a mistake so much as fate producing inescapable conflict between two duties. Your brother or the state? Your daughter or the state?

In the blues we see mistakes – *hamartia* – appear repeatedly but they are almost always of the 'I made a bad and/or stupid personal choice' sort, not usually of the completely passive 'I was screwed by fate' sort and never ever of the 'I was defeated by the requirement for me to satisfy incompatible moral duties' sort. Tragic heroes are never stupid, but they are often stubborn and they frequently, especially in Greek tragedy, have role duties (father and king) that are activated by fate in a rare form such that both cannot be satisfied.

In 'Baby Please Don't Go,' Muddy Waters tells of his stupid mistake – regrettably letting his love 'walk alone' when he should have been by her side. In this and many other blues songs the singer voices awareness that he has done something wrong but is unsure of the reason for such wrong-doing – both why he did it and why what he did, or didn't do, has gone so terribly wrong. Elmore James, in 'Done Somebody Wrong,' sings, 'The bell has tolled […] It was all my fault, I musta' done somebody wrong.' In classical tragedy, fate sets up the protagonist for his flaws to be revealed. In the blues, the ordinary flaws of everyday humans are revealed without much need for fate to assist. Human nature is enough to cause the universal problems that the blues depicts.

Existential struggles are seen in both mediums, often revolving around the subject of the rationality of going on as opposed to ending it all. In both the Greek tragedies and the blues, the protagonist wonders whether it is worth continuing – even if I am too pathetic to take my own life, at least I can look forward to the fact that one day the pathetic wretch I am will be gone, gone for good. Ray Charles laments in 'Hard Times,'

> Talkin' 'bout hard times
> Hard times
> Yeah yeah, who knows better than I?
> Lord, one of these days
> There'll be no more sorrow
> When I pass away.

But in blues, unlike tragedy, there is almost always satisfaction expressed – I am a survivor and I can and will go on.

While Aristotle believed that great tragedy must be artistically complex, the stories told in the blues manage to be wildly poignant while generally being quite simple in musical as well as in lyrical form. In all probability the familiarity – the commonality of the themes of the blues and the ease with which almost every post-pubescent soul can identify with the blues – is aided by this simple format. The key to the blues, and the immediate and visceral understanding and empathy that it brings out in the listener, may be the harnessing of this simplicity.

The upshot is this. We began with the puzzle of why people choose to listen to the blues. After all, the blues is depressing, or, if not that, it at least speaks of and expresses common kinds of pain. We suggested the following reasons. Good blues is like good tragedy, operatic disasters, sad poems, and so on. Each are beautiful, artful, and musically and lyrically pleasing. But, if tragedy works by prompting pity and fear, blues expresses and activates a much greater range of emotions. There are these emotions expressed and possibly activated that we have already discussed: loss of love, spirituality, loneliness, distress, anxiety, defeat, repression, death, and so on. In this way, the blues functions as a medium in which the performer expresses his suffering and in so doing perhaps either nullifies or activates (as appropriate to each individual) suffering in his or her audience and in that way provides emotional release. Either way there is beauty, release, and a feeling of shared and common humanity. The blues is not only important culturally but is an artistic medium that has true emotional and intellectual currency. It is anguished art that sheds light on some of the most difficult and most meaningful aspects of the human condition, as a result leading to something that is not only pleasant but also powerful, not just to the one with the guitar in his or her hand. Since the very first 'juke joints' of the early twentieth century in rural areas of the Deep South, people have been able to experience the blues together and undergo a symbiotic purging of worries and fears through music that is simple, emotive, and powerful. Why do most people with good taste prefer the blues to 'happy forever' pop music? It is more beautiful, but, more importantly, it is much more real. As Albert King sang,

> There ain't no need for me to be a wallflower
> 'Cause now I'm living on *blues power*.[2]

NOTES

1   Aristotle, *Poetics* (New York: Hill and Wang, 1961), § 1135b.
2   This is a famous lyric from the title song 'Blues power,' from Albert King's *Live Wire/Blues Power* album, recorded in 1968.

CHAPTER 8

BLUES AND CATHARSIS

 It is a cold winter night and two hundred tired and happy people are streaming out of the local roadhouse after an evening of socializing and dancing to the blues. I live in a small university town where, while town and gown relations are pretty good, the community as a whole doesn't regularly find itself sharing the same social spaces. So, even though I have helped contemporary practitioners of live blues for ten years now, one thing has never ceased to amaze me: the capacity of this primal music to enthrall and hence bring together audience members who are young and old, rich and poor, academic and blue-collar, black and white, with every possibility in between. What is it about this music that makes its charms so universal? Another way we can ask this question is: How did a music that originated in the suffering of a disenfranchised people go on to become the veritable backbone of popular American music? I propose to try and answer this question with Aristotle's help. In his discussion of musical education in the *Politics*, Aristotle insisted that catharsis is a central feature of musical performance. That is, he stated that music can help purge excessive accretions of emotion and

Blues – Philosophy for Everyone: Thinking Deep About Feeling Low, First Edition.
Edited by Jesse R. Steinberg and Abrol Fairweather.
© 2012 John Wiley & Sons, Inc. Published 2012 by John Wiley & Sons, Inc.

return the listener to a healthy psychological state. If Aristotle was right, we might see that the power of the blues lies in its ability to broadly bring about such emotional maintenance – what he calls 'catharsis.'

While it is not the purpose of this essay to delve deeply into the history of the blues, some context for the origins of the music and its role in African-American culture will help us to fully appreciate how this communal, highly rhythmic music evolved into its current form. This in turn will allow us to begin to understand the universal power of the blues.

The blues is thought to be the progeny of two distinct strains of music from West Africa (the original home of most of the slaves that were conveyed to North America): one from the Senegal-Gambia region and the other from the Congo-Angola region. Senegambian music tends to be rhythmically complex and shows traces of Arabic influence with its penchant for long, tortured melodies. The music of the Congo-Angola region tends to have less rhythmic complexity though the vocal poly-phonies are exceptionally refined and include a great deal of call-and-response singing. Both regions are nourished by the music of the griots, iterant musicians that play stringed instruments and sing about themes that have much in common with those in the blues, such as famine, love, injustice, and family. For both regions, music plays a communal, often dance-driven, role, with entire villages taking part in performances, be they for religious rituals, planting, harvesting, pounding grain, building dwellings, or just having a party. These musical traditions co-mingled with Western classical and folk traditions in times of slavery and would eventually evolve into the blues in the post-slavery era. These Western influences ranged from exposure to instruments such as the piano and the guitar to the music of the Church, especially in the form of Gospel music, which has had an enduring influence on the blues.[1]

Working and living conditions for African-Americans remained terrible in the post-slavery era; yet the creative originality of the blues, which makes it a quintessentially American music, probably received its impetus from Emancipation. Much of the freed African-American population in the South, and especially in Mississippi and Tennessee, worked as share-croppers on the same land on which they had worked as slaves. Sharecropping allowed former slaves to work the land that was still owned by the white man for a share of the harvest (usually cash crops such as cotton and tobacco). But, because much of what the sharecroppers needed to live and work – food, clothes, seed, fertilizer, and so on – had to be bought at the plantation owner's store or from a local merchant on credit, often at high interest rates, sharecropping ended up being little more than subsistence farming for the landless. What is worse is that sharecroppers often did not earn enough from their share of the crop proceeds to pay off their debts, which meant that they ended up being indentured to the former slave owners. But some things improved; at least musical instruments could be made and even bought, and individuals could perform music while at work or at play within and even outside their own communities with fewer restrictions than in the past. This music expressed the joys and sorrows of people's lives, helped the work day go quickly, and brought the people together in celebratory dance – we now know the music of such bluesmen as Charlie Patton, Tommy Johnson, and Son House to be some of earliest forms of the blues on record.[2] These early forms of blues showed substantial continuity with their African forbearers in terms of the complex rhythms and call-and-response patterns, which signaled the singers' communal connection to work and play. Yet this music was also new, not just because of the Western influences it absorbed but also because it expressed the suffering of a people whose trials and tribulations were far from over. These changes were also reflected in the dance styles, which shook off the more stylized and formal Victorian influences and became more rhythmic and fluid, more an expression of individuality, and distinctly more sexual.[3] It is important to see that the rhythmic, communal nature of the African and eventually the blues music probably reflects, first and foremost, the rhythmic nature of the work that the music accompanied. Music originates from different human experiences, and, as Aristotle pointed out, speaks to people differently depending on their experiences, which are often shaped by the work they do. Repetitive manual work, he suggested, requires a lively quality and a more 'vulgar' rhythm precisely because the music reflects the experience it speaks to.[4] How such 'speaking to' eventually results in catharsis we will see soon enough.

The difficult working conditions in the South, the Jim Crow laws, problems with crop infestations, and flooding eventually lead to mass African-American migration north to cities such as Chicago, St. Louis, and Detroit in the early to mid twentieth century. Such migrations were often fueled by economic booms and labor shortages in the North (e.g., because of the First World War) that allowed even those at the bottom of the socio-economic ladder to find decent work. But the African-American community was also the first to be hurt in difficult times, which often resulted in reverse migrations to the South, where conditions were no better – often worse. In all of this time, the blues continued to grow, evolve, and reflect the changing circumstances of its practitioners. While

ROOPEN MAJITHIA

the guitar remained the central instrument, it became electrified and was accompanied by other instruments such as the drum kit, the piano, the harmonica, and a variety of horns. In some places, the sounds became harsher and grittier to reflect the industrial landscape that was their new home. This was so, for instance, in the classic (Chicago) Chess recordings of Muddy Waters and Howlin' Wolf, both of whom were from Mississippi and both of whom started as acoustic Delta bluesmen in the tradition of Son House and Charlie Patton. In other music, such as that of Texan T-Bone Walker, the blues became smoother, more sophisticated and urbane, reflecting yet another aspect of city life. Many of the old themes of love and sex, of wanderlust, and of being hard done by persisted in the music. New themes such as dealing with leaving loved ones behind in the South (as in Albert King's 'Cadillac Assembly Line') and the desire to return to the warmer South (as in Muddy Water's 'Goin' Down to Florida') emerged. But, at its core, the music still persisted as essentially communal, essentially a form of highly rhythmic dance-driven music that spoke from and to the experiences of the African-American people.[5]

We are now in a position to look at Aristotle's analysis of musical catharsis and attempt to answer the question we set for ourselves at the outset: What makes the power of the blues universal? How can a music that speaks from and to the difficult experiences of a marginalized community speak to everybody else? Let me begin to respond by remembering that, if Aristotle is right, music has the capacity to speak to people, but different kinds of music reach different audiences. To capture his point in contemporary terms we might say, for instance, that classical music has the capacity to affect a refined audience. But Aristotle also recognized that music can reach a broader audience because it speaks to their common experience. Our first task, then, is to see how Aristotle understands this 'speaking to' in terms of catharsis, and our second is to show how the blues might broadly bring about such catharsis.

While we will focus Aristotle's discussion of musical catharsis in the *Politics*, it might be prudent first to give some background from the *Nicomachean Ethics* that will help us to understand Aristotle's views on catharsis.[6] In his account of moral development in the *Ethics*, Aristotle tells us that becoming any sort of person presupposes a process of habituation. So, to become a physically fit person over a lifetime, one needs to exercise regularly and eat in a healthy fashion (or eat poorly and not exercise at all to become a slothful one). It will not do to simply undergo bouts of enthusiasm at the gym or go on crash diets. But note that there is a relation between the acts of exercise and of eating and the kind of person that develops as a result. That is, to become a healthy person who has what Aristotle would call a healthy disposition requires that one act regularly or habitually in healthy ways even if one is not quite healthy yet. Once a person becomes healthy, she will continue to act in healthy ways, thereby maintaining her healthy disposition. So, there is an important connection between action and disposition that needs to be emphasized: healthy actions in training build healthy dispositions and healthy dispositions are the basis for truly healthy actions that in turn maintain these very same dispositions.[7]

If we apply this analysis to moral matters, we can deepen Aristotle's point further to highlight the role of emotions in relating actions to dispositions. In order to construct a moral disposition such as courage, a young person needs to be trained to act courageously in dangerous situations. Such habituation would involve learning to quickly perceive that one is in a dangerous situation, standing one's ground even though one is inclined to flee, rallying one's friends, and so on. By being habituated to act in such ways, a person can eventually develop a courageous disposition that can be the basis of truly courageous action. But how courageous action in training helps to construct a courageous disposition, whatever that means, is not as obvious as in the case of healthy actions being responsible for healthy dispositions. To see the connection, we have to understand the role of emotions here. If a person's natural inclination is to flee in the face of danger, this is because he feels fearful and is lacking in confidence. After all, it is natural for us to act on the basis of our feelings. Aristotle's powerful insight acknowledges this and adds that the relation also works in reverse: acting in certain ways makes us feel in certain ways.[8] Being habituated to stand one's ground after perceiving oneself to be in a dangerous situation eventually helps us to overcome excessive fear and lack of confidence. In fact, what it ultimately means for a person to have a courageous disposition is precisely that he feels the right amounts of fear and confidence in difficult situations.[9] Having a courageous disposition means having the basis to act courageously as the situation requires, whereby such action maintains the courageous disposition.[10] We now have as full a sense as we need of Aristotle's sense of the relation between actions, emotions, and dispositions to begin to understand his position on musical catharsis and eventually on the relation between catharsis and the blues.

In his discussion of the central role of music in educating the young, Aristotle tells us that music evokes an emotional response in us by simulating images of such dispositions such as courage. Courage for

  ROOPEN MAJITHIA

Aristotle, as we saw above, is nothing but a disposition or character to feel certain emotions in certain ways in certain circumstances. Thus, the courageous person feels a certain level of fearlessness and confidence that the coward lacks. So it should not be surprising that music for Aristotle 'supplies imitations of anger and gentleness, and also of courage and temperance, and of all the qualities of character, which hardly fall short of the actual emotions.'[11] Thus, music evokes feelings in us because it images these feelings realistically; we know the likeness to be fictional but it is real enough to evoke strong feelings in us nevertheless. Aristotle also insists that different modes (i.e., scales) of music evoke different feelings in us because they construe different kinds of images. Some modes are upbeat and make us happy; others are grave and evoke emotions ranging from sadness to fortitude.[12] Aristotle's contention that different music makes us feel in different ways is not surprising; we knew this already. What is important is *why* he thinks it does so: because the images music shapes are themselves emotional.

But, if this were all there is to the story, we would never listen to music – like some aspects of blues – that makes us feel sad or angry or anything other than happy. After all, most of us don't listen to music to feel badly. Aristotle responds to this challenge in the following way:

> In listening to the performances of others we may admit the modes of action and passion also. For feelings such as pity and fear, or, again, enthusiasm, exist very strongly in some souls, and have more or less influence over all. Some persons fall into a religious frenzy, whom we see as a result of the sacred melodies – when they have used the melodies that excite the soul to mystic frenzy – restored as though they had found healing and purgation (*catharsis*). Those who are influenced by pity or fear, and every emotional nature, must have a like experience, and others in so far as each is susceptible to such emotions, and all are in a manner purged and their souls lightened and delighted. The purgative melodies likewise give an innocent pleasure to mankind.[13]

Music's imitation of real emotions not only evokes these emotions in us but does so with a difference. We do not merely feel emotions such as fear and pity as we would in real-life situations; we feel them and in the process are purged of them. We listen to sad or angry music, in other words, not so that we can just wallow in such emotions, but so that we can be rid of them. Such purging or catharsis, it seems plausible, is pleasurable because it rids us of something that is inherently painful. Aristotle does not really explain why, but perhaps such emotional maintenance occurs because we recognize the fictional nature of images that music recreates in ways that are not afforded to us in our interactions with reality. More importantly, this restoration to a healthy psychological state means that we are no longer laden with excesses of negative emotion, which can otherwise result in misguided action, since feeling excessive emotion can often lead to excessive action. In fact, we shall see that catharsis also occurs because it involves action (in the form of dancing), as is suggested by the language of 'frenzy' above.

How, then, does this Aristotelian analysis apply to the blues? The blues, we saw, emerged in the post-slavery era in the United States. In its early incarnation, it is music about difficult times and terrible suffering whose intense and haunting power is captured in the recordings of such blues pioneers as Charlie Patton and Tommy Johnson. But it is also a music that adapted to and evolved alongside the changing (and often improving) circumstances of the African-American community, as the effects of Emancipation slowly filtered through the socioeconomic structures of America. It was this narrowing gap between the African-American community and mainstream American culture that allowed the evolving urban blues to be the bridge to a universal audience. What helped was that the blues has always been about universal themes: love and loss; trying to find strength in the face of misfortune; metaphoric, often comic, vignettes of sex; and so on – themes that increasingly occurred in the parlance of urban culture in ways that resonated with the experiences of people, cutting across race and gender. Hence, for example, T-Bone Walker's classic 'Stormy Monday Blues' celebrates the joys at the end of the work week and the difficulty of getting back to work on Monday, and Willie Dixon's 'Wang Dang Doodle' invites all the neighborhood for a romping party. Other essential ingredients in the universal success of the blues, in ways that eventually lead to rock 'n' roll and most other forms of popular American music, were electrical amplification of the instruments and the driving, sexual beat of the drum kit in the emerging urban blues of the forties and fifties. Good examples of this emerging transformation can be found in the music of Jimmy Reed, Elmore James, Little Walter, and Big Walter Horton, in addition to those mentioned above.

Music has always had the power to effect catharsis in conjunction with dancing. This was true of early African music as it was of European folk dancing. What made dancing to the blues unique – especially in its urban incarnation – was that its sexually charged rhythms captured the throb of urban life and the repetitive nature of industrial work, and portended the

ROOPEN MAJITHIA

coming of the broader sexual revolution in America in the sixties. This revolution was ushered in to the beat of rock 'n' roll, whose rhythmic ancestry can be easily traced to early urban blues. Thus, if Aristotle was right, the blues (and, to some extent, many forms of popular music that are influenced by it) effects catharsis universally because it musically recreates the emotional landscape of urban life and, in so doing, relieves us of our daily burdens. Moreover, the recreation and purging of the emotions of ordinary life by the blues are clearly aided by dancing. After all, as we have seen Aristotle say above, it is not just that feeling in certain ways can make us act in certain ways; it is also the case that acting in certain ways makes us feel in certain ways. Listening and dancing to the blues thus eliminates the excessive emotional buildup that seems to be endemic to urban life. It restores us and allows us to go about our business again until it is time for the next service call.

In closing, it might be fruitful to pursue the suggestion above that the blues recreates the emotional landscape of urban life. For one, it might help answer related questions concerning who can play the blues, where it is best heard, and so on. Since the early blues speaks from the terrible experiences of the African-American people, it has often been assumed that only African-Americans can play it with any authenticity. After all, it is not just the historical list of top-notch bluesmen and women that is substantially African-American, but any contemporary list of the new generation as well: Keb Mo, Corey Harris, Shemekia Copeland, Otis Taylor, Alvin Youngblood Hart, Guy Davis, and many, many more. But, if I am right, then modern electric blues, at least, goes beyond that. Not only does the music speak to urban people and their experiences, but it must, in order to do so, be based in such experiences. What would these experiences be? These are the common experiences of love and loss; of work that is often repetitive, inane, and not very intrinsically satisfying; of alienation and injustice in a fast-paced urban context; and so on. None of these are the particular province of African-American people, so on that front at least the music is not restricted exclusively to black performance. But, on a different front, the music might be more restrictive. Recall that the music originated from community experience of work and play in both the African and American contexts; note also that the African-American community remained a community even as it urbanized, if only because it was marginalized as a community (though this has hopefully been changing in recent years). Hence, the hallmark of this music is that it is still communal and intimate, and its best purveyors are communal creatures that have a particular capability to communicate their experiences, often by performing in intimate venues that allow for such communal interaction. Thus, witness the many fabulous non-African-American contemporary blues musicians: Tab Benoit, Marcia Ball, Moreland and Arbuckle, Watermelon Slim, Roomful of Blues, Coco Montoya, Debbie Davies, and many, many more. Not only do good blues musicians not have to be African-American, but it also follows that the best places to hear the blues are intimate spaces such as bars, and not the festivals and arenas that are more appropriate for the younger, more display-driven rock music that is a progeny of the blues. I trust that my suggestions go some distance toward explaining the phenomenon that I have regularly witnessed at the local roadhouse.

NOTES

1 For a concise and insightful discussion of the origins of the blues, see Robert Palmer, *Deep Blues* (New York: Viking Press, 1981), especially pp. 1–40. In what follows, my knowledgeable readers will see that, for brevity's sake, I will not be discussing the often symbiotic developments in the blues in places such as New Orleans and Texas.

2 Good examples from these early blues include Charlie Patton's 'Pony Blues,' Tommy Johnson's 'Slidin' Delta,' and Son House's 'Deathletter.'

3 For more on the history of dancing to the blues, see 'Blues dance' (n.d., http://en.wikipedia.org/wiki/Blues_dance).

4 Aristotle, *Politics*. In J. Barnes (Ed.), *The Complete Works of Aristotle: The Revised Oxford Translation*, vol. 2 (Princeton, NJ: Princeton University Press, 1995), VIII.5 (1340b1–10).

5 For a fuller understanding of the context of the blues, see Paul Oliver, *Blues Fell in the Morning: The Meaning of the Blues* (Cambridge, UK: Cambridge University Press, 1990). For a fuller treatment on the communal nature of the blues based on a distinction between folk and popular blues, see David Evan, *Big Road Blues: Tradition and Creativity in the Folk Blues* (Berkeley, CA: University of California Press, 1980).

6 There is a much-discussed parallel discussion of catharsis in the context of tragedy in the *Poetics*. But I will restrict myself to the more pertinent discussion of musical catharsis in the *Politics* in this essay.

7 Aristotle, *Nicomachean Ethics*. In J. Barnes (Ed.), *The Complete Works of Aristotle: The Revised Oxford Translation*, trans. W. D. Ross, revised by J. O. Urmson (Princeton, NJ: Princeton University Press, 1995), II.1.

8 For more on this issue, see Aryeh Kosman, 'Being properly affected: Virtues and feelings in Aristotle's ethics.' In Amelie Rorty (Ed.), *Essays on Aristotle's Ethics* (Berkeley and Los Angeles, CA: University of California Press, 1980), pp. 103–116.

9   For Aristotle, even the courageous person feels fear, for without it, we would have sheer recklessness, not courage. See Aristotle, *Nicomachean Ethics*, III.6–7.

10 See Aristotle, *Nicomachean Ethics*, II.4–6. Aristotle's analysis of virtuous action is much more complicated than I can present here. In addition, it involves an extensive discussion of the role of reason in wishing (*Nicomachean Ethics*, III.4), deliberating and choosing action (*Nicomachean Ethics*, III.2–3) in accordance with the mean (*Nicomachean Ethics*, II.6–9), and practical wisdom (*Nicomachean Ethics*, VI).

11 Aristotle, *Politics*, VIII.5 (1340a19–22).

12 Aristotle, *Politics*, VIII.5 (1340a39–1340b6).

13 Aristotle, *Politics*, VIII.7 (1342a3–16).

IF IT WEREN'T FOR BAD LUCK, I WOULDN'T HAVE NO LUCK AT ALL: BLUES AND THE HUMAN CONDITION

CHAPTER 9

WHY CAN'T WE BE SATISFIED?

Blues is Knowin' How to Cope

Introduction

A few years after the Rolling Stones' now classic if awkwardly titled '(I Can't Get No) Satisfaction' reached number one, Mick Jagger was asked whether he was any more satisfied. Jagger responded 'Sexually, d'you mean, or philosophically?' The answer of 'both' elicited 'Sexually – more satisfied; financially – dissatisfied; philosophically – trying.' The journalist followed with 'Are you sadder but wiser?' Jagger apparently heard 'or' instead of 'but' since he answered 'wiser.'[1]

I don't know why Jagger answered as he did. I would like to think it was because he had an unparalleled view of a question that confronts us all; namely, should you follow your emotions or reason? After all, Jagger was, and is, the frontman for the most popular blues band of all time. Many regarded him as thoughtful and introspective. Indeed, decades later, television's Gregory House, M. D. referred to 'the philosopher Jagger' on the eponymous show. With these credentials, it seems reasonable to assume that Jagger is profoundly aware of the tension between the emotions and

Blues – Philosophy for Everyone: Thinking Deep About Feeling Low, First Edition.
Edited by Jesse R. Steinberg and Abrol Fairweather.

reason. That's why he can discuss sex and money in terms of satisfaction and dissatisfaction, which are chiefly emotional terms, while his philosophical efforts involve mental activity – 'trying.' Jagger chose a particularly apt word since 'trying' also describes something that is difficult or hard to endure, as the project of being ruled by reason is. Lastly, Jagger's appreciation of the tension between emotions and reason explains his separation of sadness from wisdom, since to be wise means not to be sad.

Before working on this essay, this choice did not confront me as crisply as I am imagining it confronted Sir Jagger. Certainly there were isolated moments when I could sense a battle being waged between my emotions and reason. But I didn't fully appreciate the broader version of this question – the version that demands that one decides what force will rule one's life. Should this question seem merely academic, recall your worst choices and best moments. Chances are, they all involved the emotions. We tend to make poor choices when we're angry, hurt, or even madly in love, and our best moments are when we are happiest, or proudest, or when we feel most relieved or grateful. Even if one of your happiest memories is finally understanding how integral calculus works, or some such intellectual victory, you're probably remembering the feeling of mastery or relief or the satisfaction of your efforts paying off rather than the pure intellectual moment. These are all emotional responses. Keep your worst and best moments in mind for a little longer. Suppose you could all but eliminate the worst moments from your life. Would you? The catch is that the best must go, too. So you'd be trading life's vicissitudes for flatline stability. Would you do it?

This is not an idle question. You can actually choose to lead a life of tranquility or *apathia* (literally, freedom from emotion) by following the teachings of most philosophers, especially those known as the Stoics. To help you decide we will look at what such a life might be like. Since philosophers do not so much depict lives as raise objections, I will present two primary objections to the emotions. First we'll look at the Stoics' claim that the emotions indicate cognitive errors. Next we will examine the objection made by many philosophers, namely that the emotions represent a loss of self-control. Once we have an overview of the philosophic life, I will respond to the natural objection that such a life would be horrible. I will then approach the other option, that of an emotional life, using three popular Rolling Stones songs. To make the comparison as fair as I can, I have used various blues songs in my presentation of the philosophic life; otherwise, the two options would be incommensurable. Before doing any of that, however, let's turn to the objection that I am overlooking the best option, namely a rational life sprinkled with good emotions and generally free of bad ones. Sounds nice, right?

Why the Blues will Always be With Us

It may seem that the problem hasn't been articulated correctly. It shouldn't be reason versus the emotions. What people want is a happy life, so why can't we eliminate only the bad stuff?[2] After all, it seems that we can use reason to eliminate some negative emotions, such as anger. If that's true, we ought to be able to extirpate the negative emotions while keeping the positive, enjoyable emotions. Let me give two responses now, with a promissory note for another answer later.

First, it's important to note that anger management techniques are not purely rational. To be sure, they usually include suggestions such as 'think carefully before you say anything' and 'identify solutions to the situation.' Yet these techniques rarely eliminate an emotional response rationally. Instead they attempt to dissipate the feeling somatically. Thus, they suggest exercising, going away from the person with whom one is angry, and practicing relaxation techniques such as deep breathing.[3] While anger management is only one example of how reason might seem to be able to eliminate negative emotions, the same objection can be leveled against other techniques that aim at ameliorating the pain caused by undesirable emotions.

Since it would take too long to examine every psychological technique, let me give a second answer, this one from Plato. In his account of Socrates' last day, Plato reports that the prison guard undid the chains that had held Socrates around the ankles and wrists. Socrates rubbed his wrists and ankles and remarked how curious it is that pain and pleasure seem so tightly interconnected.[4] Had he not felt the pain of his shackles, he would not have felt the pleasure of their removal. And so it goes for much of life. Pains make us appreciate pleasures. The less positive concomitant is that the pleasures make us aware of pains. Sonny Boy Williamson makes this point in his 'So Sad to be Lonesome' (1958):

> So sad to be lonesome
> Too un-con-vin-yon to be alone
> But it makes a man feel so good
> When his baby come back home

The letters, telegrams, and phone calls from Williamson's lover make him momentarily happy but then draw his attention back to his loneliness. Implicit in both Plato's and Williamson's account of pleasure and pain is that pleasure is not merely a response to something external, and that it requires a change. We all know that soon Socrates' wrists and ankles will return to their normal state of not causing pleasure, and Williamson will no longer be alone but will not 'feel so good' for very long. Thus you cannot simply eliminate pain and leave pleasure intact.

What makes the choice between reason and the emotions so difficult is that the emotions are a mixed bag. It is tempting to think that we could improve the human condition by eliminating the unpleasant emotions while retaining the enjoyable ones. I have tried to show that, unfortunately, we will have to take the good with the bad, or eliminate them both. The reason for this is that what might look like instances of successful elimination of the bad do not eliminate negative emotions but attempt to redirect them. To be sure, it's better to run when you're angry than to punch a hole in a wall, but it would be better not to get angry at all. The elimination of anger and other pains requires the elimination of pleasures, as I hope I have shown in the all-too-brief discussion of Socrates and Williamson.

Having eliminated what would be the ideal solution – eliminate the bad and keep the good – let us examine what might be the best possible solution, namely eliminating the emotions.

Why Epictetus Never Sang the Blues

Philosophers have rarely lauded the emotions,[5] and it is not difficult to see why. The word 'philosophy' means literally 'love of wisdom.' Wisdom, in turn, involves having good judgment and acting on it. Most of us most of the time are not wise. Besides frequently displaying poor judgment, we often don't do what we believe is the right thing to do. According to many philosophers, the reason for our hypocrisy is the emotions. Reaching a good decision involves using reason and not the emotions, while the emotions excel at reaching poor decisions. You can demonstrate this to yourself. Recall some of your bad decisions. While some can be explained by ignorance, many probably resulted from your emotions making the decision instead of reason. Plato thought that any time the emotions directed one's actions one was essentially sick – deluded in much the same way as a fever might cause.

One group of philosophers, the Stoics, pursued this line of thought further than Plato did. Part of their legacy are the English words 'stoic' and 'stoical.'[6] We use these words to describe someone who isn't showing emotions, particular in a situation that would normally elicit a strong emotional response. Arguably the most thoroughgoing Stoic was Epictetus (AD 55–135). Epictetus was a slave in Rome until he gained his freedom. He then taught philosophy, for which he was exiled to Greece in AD 93, where he spent the rest of his life. For Epictetus philosophy was not another subject alongside biology, mathematics, and medicine.[7] Rather, it was a way of life.[8]

The Stoics opposed the emotions because they thought that emotions frequently stem from incorrect beliefs. The Stoics ask us to reflect on our bipartite reactions to events. Our first reaction is usually an emotional one. Whether it's the joy of finding money or the rage of discovering a lover in bed with another, our initial reaction is usually emotional. When the emotion has later quieted, our reaction becomes more thoughtful and more moderate. Yes, it was nice to find that twenty dollars, but it wasn't *that* nice. Yes, it was bad to find your lover with someone else, but maybe killing them both was not the best course of action. The emotions are not always bad, of course. If you happen to be the illicit lover, fear of being shot might save your life. As a rule, though, when you respond emotionally you almost certainly are motivated by a belief that isn't true – what philosophers call a false belief.

The Stoics believed that, along with holding specific false beliefs about mortality and the like, humans mistakenly apply the concepts of good and bad well beyond their appropriate sphere. Epictetus argues that the only things in the world that we may properly call good or bad are the things under our control – and there's not much under our control beyond our ability to judge events. Suppose you're stuck in traffic, and this makes you angry. According to Epictetus, gridlock per se is neither bad nor good because it's beyond your control. What is under your control is thinking that it's bad. Now, Epictetus is not suggesting that you think being stuck is good. For him, the proper attitude is that the gridlock simply is. He and other Stoics called this attitude *apatheia*, or freedom from emotion. To get a fuller picture of what a Stoic life might be like, let's see what Epictetus would say about three common themes of the blues: floods, death, and discovering that your woman is cheating on you.

Floods are a frequent and long-established theme in blues songs. 'When the Levee Breaks' was originally written shortly after the great Mississippi flood of 1927, although many people know it better from Led

Zeppelin's version. In both the original version by Memphis Minnie and Led Zeppelin's cover, there is one line Epictetus would endorse: 'Cryin' won't help you, prayin' won't do no good.' Why would you cry or pray? The world may not be as you want it but productive wanting requires control, and you don't control the weather.

After this good start, both versions veer from Epictetus' teaching. Memphis Minnie laments 'Mean old levee, cause me to weep and moan' while Robert Plant is more honest and takes responsibility for his sadness: 'All last night sat on the levee and moaned / Thinking about my baby and my happy home.'

Now you might be thinking that floods are horrible events, and that people die in floods and that's sad. This is where we get to the harshest part of Epictetus. To quote from his *Manual* (*Enchiridion*):

> Never say of anything, 'I lost it,' but say, 'I gave it back.' Has your child died? It was given back. Has your wife died? She was given back. Has your estate been taken from you? Was not this also given back? But you say, 'He who took it from me is wicked.' What does it matter to you through whom the giver asked it back? As long as he gives it you, take care of it, but not as your own; treat it as travelers treat an inn.[9]

Since we have been discussing Led Zeppelin, let me clarify that Epictetus does not mean that we should treat things as John Bonham treated hotel rooms, but that we should keep in mind the transitivity of things. You can see that it's a short leap from this passage to the cliché 'The Lord giveth and the Lord taketh away.'

The more general point that Epictetus makes, and here he's in line with other Stoics, is that the emotions do not give us access to the truth. Far more often than not, emotions stem from false beliefs. For example, Epictetus asks that you examine the beliefs that have caused you to feel grief. You may find that some of those beliefs are untrue. You might have assumed that the deceased would never die, or that people die only after leading full lives. You'd never state it that way, of course, but the fact that you're upset that a creature that you knew would die eventually did just that suggests that you have a mistaken belief. The twentieth-century German philosopher Martin Heidegger argues that most of us usually talk about death in such a way that when we say 'one dies' we mean 'nobody dies.'[10] His point differs from that of the Stoics, but his analysis helpfully shows how we can hold the false belief that people don't die.

If you eliminate this false belief you will become better able to face death, whether of a loved one or your own.

You might counter that what causes you to grieve is the deceased's absence from your life. In response, Epictetus would point out that you have imagined your future life and have decided what is important and how it is important. But your beliefs about the future failed to include the very real possibility that your spouse, or whoever the deceased was, would die before that future came to pass.

Given his views on the death of one's spouse, it is safe to assume that Epictetus would be unsympathetic to the quintessential blues theme, the cheating woman. Epictetus would have an easy time with the bluesmen concerning fidelity, since it is often the case that in the same song in which they complain about one woman cheating on them they mention another lover of their own. For example, in Robert Johnson's 'Terraplane Blues' he sings to his lover, whom he fears has allowed another man to drive his 'car': 'I'm goin' heist your hood, mama, mmm, I'm bound to check your oil.' But in the very next line he confesses – if that's the right word – 'I got a woman that I'm lovin', way down in Arkansas.' So Epictetus need only point out the bluesmen's beliefs about women include the belief that women never act the way men do, and that the bluesmen's multiple partners are faithful to them in a way that they do not reciprocate.

As mentioned before, Epictetus is the most anti-emotional of all philosophers. But this is not to say that philosophers have never been enthusiastic about the emotions. For example, Plato thought that some emotions, most notably anger and spiritedness, are acceptable provided that they do not usurp reason as a person's commanding faculty. His most famous student, Aristotle, made more room for the emotions, arguing that there is a correct amount of anger, for example.[11] But in both cases the emotions are largely at the service of reason and are connected to the truth. So, for example, anger can be a helpful motivator in fighting for the truth but there is nothing intrinsically valuable about the emotional experience itself.

Let's pull together these various examples into a Stoic life improvement process. According to the Stoics' view, emotional responses can be thought of as symptoms of intellectual problems that need to be resolved. As you work through your beliefs and correct the mistaken ones, especially those about the limits of your control, you will gradually experience fewer and fewer emotions.

Akrasia, or 'I can't help myself'

So far we've focused on what to do *after* experiencing an emotion. Philosophy's second objection to the emotions concerns what happens while you are experiencing one. The emotions can take over a person and render him or her animalistic. In philosophy this is often called 'incontinence,' or, because of that term's specific modern medical meaning, we often revert to the Greek *akrasia*. This is the all-too-familiar loss of control we have all experienced. It is frequently expressed in the blues as 'I can't help myself.'[12]

Sometimes the songs acknowledge the emotions' erroneous pull. For example, in 'Down Home Girl' the narrator reports that watching the down home girl dance takes his 'breath away' and forces him to both 'get down and pray' and 'go to Sunday mass.' I suppose these two religious references could mean that the woman is so stunning that the narrator feels compelled to thank the woman's creator, but I doubt it. It is more likely that her overt sexuality led to impure thoughts from which he now needs absolution. While we can rightfully challenge whether the woman has a causal role in the events, what's important here is that the narrator has lost control of himself and acts contrary to his own values. The extent to which he is no longer in control is emphasized by what he sees up close. The woman seems unerotic at best. Her dress is 'made out of fiberglass,' her perfume smells as if it were 'made out of turnip greens,' and while kissing her he notes that she 'tastes like pork and beans.' Someone unfamiliar with this song might initially see it as depicting the classic case of someone looking good at a distance but not so good up close, or perhaps as a 'what was I thinking?' post-break-up song. It is neither, however. All but the fiberglass dress aspersions occur in the first verse. The second verse is almost pure visual appreciation except for the observation about the dress. The third verse is entirely a visual appreciation, although this time it occurs in the singer's imagination. The song chronicles the narrator's complete loss of control. He fantasizes about a woman he does not find attractive because his emotions have usurped his reason.

Other blues songs display a more traditional weakness of will. For example, Junior Wells' version of 'Good Mornin' Lil' Schoolgirl' exhibits the tension he feels about a girl who is so 'young and pretty' but who 'love[s] somebody else' (1965):

> Lord, I love you baby, just can't help myself
> Don't care how you treat me, baby, I don't want nobody else

Good morning, little schoolgirl, hey hey hey!
Oohweeh, I'm gonna leave you baby, one of these old days
On account of how you treat me, baby, I'm gonna stay away

Sometimes the loss of control brought on by the emotions is acknowledged directly. One of the best examples of the negative power of the emotions comes from Blind Lemon Jefferson's 'Peach Orchard Mama.' He begins with these stage-setting remarks (1958):

Peach orchard mama, you swore that no one picked your fruit but me.
I found three kidmen shakin' down your peaches tree.

Stereotypically, a verse about a loaded gun or a southbound train would follow. Instead, Jefferson sings:

Went to the police station, begged them to put me in jail.
I didn't wanna kill you, mama, but I hate to see your peaches tree fail.

Apparently merely contemplating murder is not enough to have the jailer find you a room, so Jefferson tries to get his peach orchard mama to act right:

Peach orchard mama, don't treat your papa so mean.
Chase out all those kidmen and let me keep your orchard clean.

Both of these attempts were made because Jefferson knows what every philosopher knows:

Peach orchard mama, don't turn your papa down.
Because when I gets mad I acts just like a clown.

Philosophers don't want to act like clowns, and don't think any rational human wants to either. This means, roughly speaking, that we ought to control our emotions, or correct the erroneous beliefs that cause them.

Objections ('This Life Sounds Horrible!')

Now that you've seen the full range of emotions the Stoics want you to give up – from cutting loose on occasion to being laid low by natural disasters and death – you might be willing to accept the emotional life of the typical human being. The philosophic life sketched so far resembles the life of a robot, a Mr. Spock, or some other unfeeling monster. 'Better to have loved and lost than never to have loved at all,' you might think – or, more accurately, you might feel. These aren't objections but restatements of the alternative. Of course, we should expect as much coming from the emotions. Implicit in that response is the second answer to the earlier question of why you can't have both. How would you judge? Reason isn't going to let the emotions in, and the emotions aren't going to let reason in.

Now, you might object, that's too quick. The emotions have a purpose, and we can rationally evaluate that purpose. Fair enough. Many scientists now believe that emotions prod us into doing evolutionarily useful behavior.[13] For example, feeling gratitude moves us to do something nice to someone who helped us. That in turn rewards the helpful behavior. If this cycle is repeated, it reinforces the inclination to help others. But reason can motivate us, and perhaps do a better job since it can also ferret out others' attempts to manipulate us through our emotions. What we really need is a depiction of the alternative. Just as the Stoics gave us an idea of what the reason-dictated life would be like, the blues can give us an idea of the intrinsic value of the emotions.

I Can't Get No Satisfaction, and I Like it, I Like it, Yes I Do

To decide between reason and the emotions – between wisdom and sadness, philosophy and the blues – we need to appreciate the other option, of the emotional life. I can't do this side of the debate justice in words; it would be best for you to listen to three songs I've chosen for the purpose.[14] To make this easy, I've selected popular songs by the Rolling Stones: 'Jumping Jack Flash,' 'Monkey Man,' and the song we began with – '(I Can't Get No) Satisfaction.'

'Jumping Jack Flash' (1968) consists of three verses, each of which ends 'But it's all right now, in fact, it's a gas!' The song chronicles the singer's life, beginning with his birth 'in a cross-fire hurricane.' Given the optimistic if not cheery 'it's all right now,' you'd expect the next verse to describe how the singer overcame this ominous beginning. Instead, we learn that he 'was raised by a toothless, bearded hag' and 'schooled with a strap right across my back.' But 'it's all right now,' which might make you think this horrific childhood forged the sort of character necessary for later success. Alas, no. This is how the last third of the singer's life unfolded:

I was drowned, I was washed up and left for dead.
I fell down to my feet and I saw they bled.
I frowned at the crumbs of a crust of bread.
Yeah, yeah, yeah
I was crowned with a spike right thru my head.

But – you guessed it – it's all right now. We never learn why it's all right now, why it's a gas. There's no redeeming moment, no winning of the girl of his dreams, nothing but a strange admixture of Jesus Christ and Phineas Gage.[15]

To judge by my non-scientific Internet search, most people believe 'Monkey Man' is about drugs, maybe sex, and possibly drugs and sex. None of these interpretations seems correct. Since my claim, namely that the song attempts to depict the purely emotional life, is admittedly a stretch at first glance, let me begin by criticizing these interpretations.

That 'Monkey Man' is a song about sex is the most tenuous interpretation. The main piece of evidence for this claim is the line 'I could use a lemon squeezer.' This could be a use of the blues' classic double entendre but, even if it is, it leaves the rest of the song unexplained.[16] The drug, particularly heroin, interpretation fairs better, if only because the key piece of evidence – the word 'monkey,' as in 'monkey on my back,' as in 'drug habit' – is repeated throughout. According to this interpretation, the 'lemon squeezer' is to be taken literally, as the narrator needs some lemon juice to increase the solubility of the brown heroin he'd like to shoot with his newfound female junkie friend. The second line, 'All my friends are junkies,' ostensibly further supports the heroin interpretation, yet Jagger immediately follows this confession with 'That's not really true.' As was the case with the sexual interpretation, the drug interpretation leaves much of the song unexplained.

My own interpretation is that the song attempts to capture the rawness of emotional life, the antithesis of the hyper-rational life described by Epictetus.[17] Let's begin by surveying the song. As is often the case with blues songs, the singer imparts a feeling of victoriousness, or perhaps grim determination in the face of a brutal life. There is nothing good about the life described by this song. With the exception of the general claim 'We love to play the blues,' there is no positive emotion expressed, yet the song celebrates life itself.

The song not only avoid the easy depiction of the emotional life as hedonistic, it also steadfastly refuses logical interpretation. There is no narrative arc, no logical development of a thesis. Indeed, the song begins by putting the listener on guard. If someone tells you that what he just said is false, it's difficult to trust any later utterances. The narrator himself constantly changes form. First he's 'a fleabit peanut monkey,' then 'a cold Italian pizza,' then 'a monkey man,' then 'a sack of broken eggs,' and finally back to 'a monkey man.' Obviously the singer is not claiming to be a shapeshifting virtuoso. Rather, those phrases capture his emotional state. Indeed, this is highlighted by the very title, 'Monkey Man.' This is no hybrid but rather a hominoid shaped creature largely without reason.

Finally there's the Stones' ode to frustration, '(I Can't Get No) Satisfaction.' Although the song is often thought of as expressing sexual frustration, only a third at best of the song concerns Mick's unsuccessful attempts 'to make some girl.' The first two thirds of the song express dissatisfaction with commercialism. First, the announcer on the radio gives only 'useless information / Supposed to fire my imagination.' Presumably the reference is to advertisements, a theme more clearly addressed in the middle of the song:

> When I'm watchin' my TV
> And a man comes on to tell me
> How white my shirts can be
> But he can't be a man 'cause he doesn't smoke
> The same cigarettes as me

Unless Rod Serling once pitched laundry detergent, this is more likely a critique of Madison Avenue's failure to provide a unified picture of the happy life. By why would that failure leave Mick unsatisfied? Actually, the source of the dissatisfaction is identified at the outset:

> I can't get no satisfaction
> 'Cause I try and I try and I try and I try

It is the act of trying to be satisfied that causes the dissatisfaction. As noted in the introduction to this essay, 'trying' connotes an intellectual effort. So, before telling us how he has tried and failed to be satisfied, there's an acknowledgment that it's his own fault. Indeed, it's tempting to imagine Epictetus, if not most philosophers, agreeing with the lyrics because trying to be happy is usually a fool's errand. Happiness is serendipitous.

This song cannot be construed as a paean to Stoicism, however. Never does the singer suggest that he'll abandon the search for satisfaction.

Indeed, he never suggests any change at all. At one level, then, the song is a homage to the Sisyphean struggle against the failure of modern life to be satisfying. It also shows the failure of the rational to be satisfying. From the radio Mick gets 'useless information,' from the television an unintegrated account of the good life, and from the woman he tries to seduce a 'raincheck,' perhaps because she does not want to have sex while menstruating (i.e., she gives a reason for her rejection). Surrounded by failures, the Stones can only celebrate their existence as emotional beings by singing the blues.

In Place of a Conclusion

We've reached the point at which normally I wrap things up neatly by recapitulating my arguments for the superior side. I'd be lying if I said that I know which way to go. I love philosophy and I love the blues. I take comfort in an image that struck Nietzsche: in Socrates' death cell, the hyper-rational fine arts deprecating him made music.[18]

NOTES

1 Christopher Sandford, *Mick Jagger: Rebel Knight* (London: Omnibus, 2003), p. 172.
2 In this context, see Michael Ure, 'Nietzsche's free spirit trilogy and Stoic therapy,' *Journal of Nietzsche Studies* 38 (2010), pp. 60–84. Ure chronicles Nietzsche's attempt to be an emotional Stoic, if I can put it that way.
3 For one example see Mayo Clinic, 'Anger management: 10 tips to tame your temper' (n.d., http://www.mayoclinic.com/health/anger-management/MH00102).
4 Plato, *Phaedo*, 60b. The *Phaedo*, like the other ancient Greek texts I cite, is available online for free. One good source is MIT's Internet Classics Archive at http://classics.mit.edu/Plato/phaedo.html. The free translations are usually over a century old, and are never very good. It is worth locating more recently translated versions in your library or bookstore.
5 For a more nuanced account than I can give here, see Ronald de Sousa, 'Emotion.' In Edward N. Zalta (Ed.), *The Stanford Encyclopedia of Philosophy* (spring 2010 edition, http://plato.stanford.edu/archives/spr2010/entries/emotion). Among my favorite accounts is surely Martha Nussbaum's *The Therapy of Desire: Theory and Practice in Hellenistic Ethics* (Princeton, NJ: Princeton University Press,

1994). A chronological account that stops too soon (but understandably) is Simo Knuuttila, *Emotions in Ancient and Medieval Philosophy* (New York: Oxford University Press, 2004).

6　For an account of the Stoics' intellectual legacy, see Steven K. Strange and Jack Zupko (Eds.), *Stoicism Traditions and Transformations* (Cambridge, UK: Cambridge University Press, 2004).

7　A good source for beginning to learn more about Epictetus is Margaret Graver, 'Epictetus.' In *The Stanford Encyclopedia of Philosophy* (http://plato.stanford.edu/archives/spr2009/entries/epictetus).

8　Pierre Hadot, *Philosophy as a Way of Life: Spiritual Exercises from Socrates to Foucault* (Malden, MA: Blackwell, 1995).

9　Epictetus, *Manual*, §9. (*Manual* is sometimes transliterated as *Enchiridion*.)

10　Martin Heidegger, *Being and Time*, trans. John Macquarrie and Edward Robinson (New York: Harper & Row, 1962), P.298 (H. 253).

11　Aristotle, *Nicomachean Ethics*, II, 7 (http://classics.mit.edu/Aristotle/nicomachaen.2.ii.html) and IV, 5 (http://classics.mit.edu/Aristotle/nicomachaen.4.iv.html).

12　The classic is of course Sonny Boy Williamson's 'Good Morning Little School Girl' but other examples are John Lee Hooker's 'No More Doggin',' Billy Boy Arnold's 'I Wish You Would,' and Etta James' 'I've Gone Too Far.'

13　Richard Joyce, *The Evolution of Morality* (Cambridge, MA: MIT Press, 2006), pp. 94–101.

14　There is more than a passing parallel between the distinction I am making between the blues and philosophy and Nietzsche's distinction between pre-Socratic and post-Socratic tragedy. See his *The Birth of Tragedy Out of the Spirit of Music* in Walter Kauffman (Ed.), *Basic Writings of Nietzsche* (New York: Modern Library, 2000), especially §§ 10–13.

15　Phineas Gage was a nineteenth-century railroad construction foreman. In a freak accident, he had a tamping iron driven completely through his head. Like Jumping Jack, he survived.

16　The expression also does not have a fixed meaning. While the lemon is often the man and the squeezer the woman, in Sonny Boy Williamson's 'Until My Love Come Down' the roles are reversed.

17　In fairness to Epictetus, he was not the only hyper-rational philosopher. Nietzsche famously attacked Socrates' hyper-rationalism, but Descartes and Kant led lives of extreme rationality as well. See, for example, Desmond M. Clarke, *Descartes: A Biography* (New York: Cambridge University Press, 2006) and Manfred Kuehn, *Kant: A Biography* (New York: Cambridge University Press, 2001).

18　Stefan Lorenz Sorgner, 'Who is the "music-making Socrates"?' *Minerva – An Internet Journal of Philosophy* 8 (2004, http://www.ul.ie/~philos/vol8/socrates.html).

CHAPTER 10

DOUBT AND THE HUMAN CONDITION

Nobody Loves Me but my Momma…
and She Might be Jivin' Too

Doubt is a strikingly common theme in blues music. Albeit with a bit of humor, B. B. King expressed doubt about anyone loving him – even his momma! Otis Spann expressed doubt about his partner's fidelity when he worried about whether 'some other mule been kickin' in my stall.' For most of us, not only do doubts arise regarding trust in our relationships but we also commonly experience self-doubt. We have doubts about being able to overcome hardships. We have doubts about our capacity for self-control, for example in tempering our use of cigarettes, alcohol, and drugs. We have doubts about how we treat other people, for example when it's okay to lie to someone. Many of us are plagued with doubts about the numerous decisions, both major and minor, that we make in daily life. Blues music affords us a way of sharing this significant and rather pervasive part of our lives. It helps to know that others experience the same sorts of disturbing doubts that we experience. For many of us, it makes the struggle less difficult to know that others endure it too. However, even if it may be less agonizing to understand that doubt is part of the human condition and not some personal deficit,

Blues – Philosophy for Everyone: Thinking Deep About Feeling Low, First Edition.
Edited by Jesse R. Steinberg and Abrol Fairweather.
© 2012 John Wiley & Sons, Inc. Published 2012 by John Wiley & Sons, Inc.

knowing that we're not the only ones to suffer from such doubts, or that others can empathize with us and what we're going through, doesn't really solve the problem of doubt. Our doubts still remain.

Philosophers have had an awful lot to say about doubt and how it relates to the human condition. René Descartes, in particular, has had quite an impact on debates about *what we can know*. Descartes' famous book, *Meditations on First Philosophy*, was written in 1641, many centuries before a blues song was ever dreamed of, written, or sung. But Descartes wrestled with many of the same issues that make up this particular theme in blues music. He was concerned with what could be doubted and what was absolutely certain – that is, what could be known with certainty. He began by noting that there were a great many things that he had very confidently believed or thought that he knew, but that had turned out on careful inspection to be false. Much to our chagrin, we've all experienced this. Many of us have had loved ones betray us. Politicians have not lived up to the promises we thought they'd keep. We've all been fairly confident in believing that something would happen and then been disappointed by the way things actually turned out. *Appearance*, Descartes stressed, is often quite different from *reality*. This point is rather significant. According to Descartes, if we are to know something, then we must be absolutely certain of it. According to this view, in order for us to *really know* something, there must not be any room for the slightest doubt or any chance that we might be in error about what it is that we think that we know.

An example will help make his position clear. I think I know that my wife is faithful. I think I've got good evidence for this belief. We've vowed to be faithful to each other, she seems like a trustworthy person, and I haven't seen any evidence that would lead me to believe she's been messing around. But, as Descartes would point out, there is a chance or possibility that she's not being faithful. Some other mule might be kickin' in my stall. She (and that other mule) might just be very good at covering up their tracks. Until I can definitively prove that this isn't happening, Descartes would insist that I can't say that I *know* that she's not cheating on me. In other words, I cannot have knowledge until I can remove all shadow of doubt regarding her fidelity. According to Descartes, being really confident that she's not fooling around is not enough for knowledge. What I need is to be absolutely certain of it. But when are we absolutely certain of *anything*? Am I certain that my car is still in my garage right now as I sit here at my desk typing? It could have been stolen a few minutes ago. The same sort of thing can be said for just about anything regarding the world around us. In other words, for almost anything that I might claim to know about the world, there will always be a chance that I'm wrong.

Descartes posed this problem in the most cutting of ways. One rather powerful argument that he considered involves the possibility of *dreaming*. Descartes, thinking about sitting in his study, put it like this:

> I must nevertheless here consider that I am a man, and that, consequently, I am in the habit of sleeping, and representing to myself in dreams those same things, or even sometimes others less probable, which the insane think are presented to them in their waking moments. How often have I dreamt that I was in these familiar circumstances – that I was dressed, and occupied this place by the fire, when I was lying in bed?[1]

So Descartes would point out that you might think that you are awake and reading this book right now but it's certainly possible that you're snoring in your bed and are simply having a very vivid dream about reading a book about philosophy and the blues.

This is probably not what is actually happening, but you have to admit that it is *possible*. Recall that, in Descartes' view, to have knowledge is to be able to rule out all possible sources of doubt. And, since it's possible for you to doubt that you're reading a book right now – since you might be simply dreaming about doing it – you have to admit that you don't *really know* that you're reading this book right now. That is, in order for you to know that you're reading a book, you have to be able to prove that you're not simply dreaming that you're reading. We can spell out Descartes' argument more formally and clearly like this:

(1)   In order for me to know that X, I must be able to rule out that I am now simply dreaming that X when X is not really the case.
(2)   But I can't rule out that I am now dreaming.
(3)   Therefore, I do not really know that X.

Unfortunately, 'X' is a variable that ranges over an enormous variety of things! Not only does this argument seem to show that you don't know that you're reading a book right now, but also that you don't know that Muddy Waters was once a manish boy with a pompadour, that Lightnin' Hopkins was from Texas, that Albert King played a Flying V guitar, or that Little Walter played a mean harp. These (supposed) people might merely be a figment of your own private imagination – a product of a very vivid dream. These people might not have ever existed at all. But, if it is possible that you're simply dreaming that Little Walter existed, then you can't really *know* that he played a mean harp. The same can be said of other beliefs you have, like those regarding your date of birth, the name of your mother, the nature of your present vocation, or your appearance. You might, for example, be dreaming right now that you're a certain age when you're in fact quite a bit older, or you might be dreaming that you have a thick head of hair when you're really bald.

The upshot of all this is that it seems that Descartes has saddled us with a powerful argument for the conclusion that we hardly know anything at all. Because we can doubt so many of our beliefs, and because knowledge requires something that seems impossible – the ability to prove that we're not now dreaming – it appears that we lack a great deal of knowledge that we thought we had. This problem regarding our having any knowledge whatsoever about the world around us is what philosophers call the problem of 'external world skepticism.' The problem is that we cannot have true knowledge about the 'external' world – that is, the world around us – if knowledge requires absolute certainty.

How Does One Avoid Skepticism?

I've wrestled with this problem for many years and have talked quite a bit about it with family, friends, and, of course, my students. Many of these people have responded to this problem by saying that they simply don't care. Why, they ask, should we care if we don't know all those things? What does it really matter?! They often reply that, as long as it feels right and I'm content or satisfied, why should it matter to me whether I actually know all of those things? From these kinds of comments, it might appear that philosophers like Descartes and me have been worrying ourselves about a pseudo-problem, something that isn't really that big of a deal at all.

But blues artists have articulated rather clearly that *we do care* about knowledge. And many blues songs illustrate why *we should care* about what we really know. Junior Wells and Robert Johnson weren't worried about skepticism to the extent that many philosophers are, but they would have been able to point out that the way things *really are* matter to us. It's not just appearances that matter, but how things actually are that counts. B. B.'s 'sweet little angel' might appear to be as loving as ever, but if she's running around on him he certainly wants to know about it. Think about a person who you think is a good friend. I imagine that this person is usually kind to you and seems pretty supportive. But suppose that this person says terrible things about you whenever you leave the room and does all that he or she can to undermine your reputation and aspirations. So this 'friend' of yours seems affable to your face, but is your nemesis behind your back. Surely you care about how things really are and would not be content with how things merely appear to you. This point is highlighted in numerous blues songs. For example, Big Mama Thornton bemoans 'you ain't nothin' but a hound dog' when she discovers that her lover hasn't been acting as she thought he was. As she would likely stress, *ignorance is not bliss*. Other blues musicians have done a great job in articulating how much we care about the way things actually are. Consider these lyrics from Buddy Guy's 'I Smell a Rat':

> I think I smell a rat in my house, baby I believe you got just too late.
> Aw, I smell a rat, I smell a rat in my house, honey, I think you walkin'
> 'round too late.
> Sometime I think you're foolin' me baby, and I do believe it's just drivin'
> me around.
> Sometime I think you're foolin' me baby, honey I think you're just drivin'
> me around.
> Why don't you leave me alone woman, you know I think there's another
> woman I can go, I can be found.

When you listen to the tune, you can tell that Buddy's suspicions are agonizing. The doubt penetrates deep to his core.

A tune with a similarly lamenting theme is 'I Don't Know' by Rice Miller, also known as Sonny Boy Williamson:

> At eleven forty-five the phone began to ring.
> I heard someone say 'Sonny Boy.'
> And I know that was my name.
> Who call you?
> I don't know. I don't know.

As Sonny Boy would insist, we often have a profound desire for explanations of why things are a certain way and we yearn to know what exactly is going on in the world around us. So the sort of reply that many people make to the problem of external world skepticism that I mentioned above – the 'I just don't care' response – is deeply mistaken. This is because we do care when we get things wrong. Most of us care very deeply when we are the victims of deception or are in gross error about the nature of reality. What most of us seem to really want is a guarantee out of life. But, as many painfully surmise, there don't seem to be any guarantees.

The Experience Machine

A philosopher named Robert Nozick made an argument that will shed some light on this point.[2] Nozick was deeply concerned about a view called 'hedonism.' This is the view that pleasure is all that really matters to us. The response to skepticism that my friends and students often give is a kind of hedonistic one in the sense that it depends upon the assumption that all that really matters is how things feel to us. According to their reply to skepticism, it doesn't matter how things actually are, since this really doesn't make a difference regarding how pleasurable my life is. So this kind of reply to skepticism involves making the assumption that all that really matters is just how things feel or appear. And, since this kind of reply to skepticism depends upon hedonism, if we can show that hedonism is wrong, then we've shown that this sort of reply to skepticism just won't fly. I think Nozick has made a good case against hedonism and in favor of the view that we care about more than just pleasure.

Nozick asks us to imagine a machine that can give us whatever pleasurable experiences we could want. As Nozick describes it, 'super-duper-neuropsychologists' have figured out a way to stimulate human brains to induce pleasurable experiences using a complex system of computers and wires that attach to one's brain. So we can plug into this machine and it 'feeds' us blissful experiences. Our experiences feel as if they are perfectly real even though what we are experiencing is a computer-generated illusion. Envision a tank like in the movie *The Matrix* that you can rest in while the machine you are plugged into provides you with an imaginary world filled with pleasure. In this fictitious world, you can be a professional blues musician or have any other vocation you want. You can look however you want to look, do whatever you want to do, and so on. The sort of life you would lead in the machine would be more pleasurable than the one you would have in the real world. Would you choose to enter the experience machine? Oh, did I mention that once you entered the machine all your previous memories,

JESSE R. STEINBERG

including regarding the fact that you are in the machine, would be erased. So your experiences from then on would all seem real to you, even though they would be a product and total fabrication of the machine. So, would you choose the illusory but pleasurable life in the machine or would you choose a real but less pleasurable life outside it?

Nozick argues that, overwhelmingly, people would prefer not to enter the machine. He thinks that we would rather have a necessarily less pleasurable life in the real world than a more pleasurable one in the machine, where it would only appear that our lives are real. If, in the machine, I was married to a beautiful and kind woman (who, mind you, would simply be part of an elaborate computer program manipulating my mind), you couldn't say that my relationship with her was genuine or authentic. She'd merely be part of a computer simulation and so our 'relationship' would be missing something that I think I've got with my real wife. Nozick also points out that I would want to feel that I am accomplishing things and that I am playing an active role in how my life unfolds. But if I went into the machine I would simply be a puppet being manipulated by the computer software/the neuropsychologists. Therefore, my 'accomplishments' would simply be a product of some-one else and so not really accomplishments at all. Even though life in the machine would be pleasurable, it would miss something that is quite significant.

Nozick seems to have shown, then, that hedonism is false. He makes a strong case for the fact that other things matter besides pleasure and appearance. If he is right, then skepticism is a problem that can't be so easily dismissed by simply saying 'I don't care – all that really matters is how things feel and seem to me.' This is because we *should care* about such significant things as whether we are living authentic lives, whether our relationships are as they appear, and whether we are the sort of people that we think we are. And not only *should* we care about such things but many of us *do care very deeply* about them. We care about what we know and whether we might be in error. The blues is a great expression of this concern (and, often enough, turmoil) that we experience regarding what we believe and what we think we know. All this goes to show that skepticism is a genuine problem. Blues music affords us an expression of the significance, pervasiveness, and profoundness of the source of this problem: doubt. But, as I said in the opening paragraph, knowing that we're not the only ones that suffer from doubt or that others can empathize with us may give us some comfort, but it doesn't really solve the problem. Our doubts persist.

Contextualism

A fairly new attempt at solving the problem of skepticism is called 'knowledge contextualism.' This is a view about the nature of our language, especially about words such as 'know.' According to the contextualist, whether we know something depends upon the context we're in and what salient or relevant features there are of that context. Contextualists usually offer examples to help illustrate their position. Consider the sentence 'Tomorrow is Saturday.' I can say this sentence at a variety of different times, but it's only true if I say it on a Friday. So the word 'tomorrow' is what philosophers call 'indexical.' The reference or meaning of the word changes from context to context. Whether my sentence 'Tomorrow is Saturday' is true depends upon when I utter it. This might also apply to the word 'sturdy.' A certain table might be aptly called sturdy in a certain context. I might be looking for a place to put my drink and the table might be sturdy enough for this purpose. But the table might not be sturdy enough for other purposes. That is, in other contexts where other details are pertinent, that table might not correctly be called sturdy. So, if I'm looking for a place for my huge Fender amplifier, the very same table wouldn't be sturdy in that context. Again, the table is appropriately called sturdy in some contexts, but not in others.

The contextualist about knowledge claims that the word 'know' is indexical and that whether a person knows something depends upon a variety of features related to contexts. The idea is that knowledge isn't an all-or-nothing affair – it's not like you either have it all the time or you don't. Instead, the contextualist thinks that you can have knowledge in some contexts and not have it in others in much the same way that 'Tomorrow is Saturday' is true in some contexts and false in others.

So what should we make of the contextualists' attempt to resolve the problem of skepticism? It would require too long a book to delve deeply into the various objections to contextualism, but there are a few quick replies that are worth considering. First, it doesn't really seem like the word 'know' is indexical and it doesn't appear that knowledge is really context-sensitive in the above way. If the contextualist is right, then it seems that I would know, for example, that my wife is faithful and that my car is in my garage in a variety of contexts – indeed most contexts. But then in other contexts, like when I'm writing a chapter for a book on skepticism or I'm lecturing about Descartes in a class, I do *not* know such things. Since the context has shifted and certain possibilities are salient, the contextualist claims that I now don't know these things. But this is a

JESSE R. STEINBERG

strange view indeed! It doesn't seem that my sitting here thinking about these things has changed anything about my wife or my car. My evidence for these beliefs hasn't changed in the least. All that have changed are the nature of the topic of conversation or the kinds of things that I'm wondering about. But these aren't the sorts of things that could alter *what I know*. Another way to make this point is that it seems bizarre to hold the view that two people could have exactly the same evidence for the same belief and yet one person has knowledge and the other lacks it because of the different contexts in which these two people find themselves. But the contextualist has to say that this happens often to us. So, some philosophers see contextualism as a case of throwing the baby out with the bathwater, since contextualism is an attempt to get around skepticism at the cost of having a view of knowledge that is, quite frankly, rather bizarre. It's worth adding that contextualism doesn't really solve the problem of skepticism. Even if contextualism were true, I would not *now* know that my wife is faithful or that my car is in my garage, since I'm *now* in the right sort of context to rule out my having this knowledge. So, even if the contextualist can preserve my having some knowledge in some contexts, what I really want when I'm looking for a reply to skepticism is my having knowledge more than just *some* of the time under some limited set of conditions. And I particularly want to be able to have knowledge even in philosophical contexts in which skepticism appears irrefutable.

My Take on Skepticism

I don't see any plausible way out of the problem of skepticism. This doesn't mean that I've got a mind to give up living (and, like B. B. King, go shopping for a tombstone instead). It's a serious philosophical problem, but even an external world skeptic can be practical. What I have really come to think is that we should just not worry about being certain of things. Instead, we should settle for having strong justification for our beliefs. Rather than trying to rule out every possible doubt, all we can strive for is having a great deal of evidence for what we believe and a lack of counterevidence for it. I can be rather sure that my wife is faithful even if I'm not certain of it. As I said, she really seems trustworthy and I don't see any evidence of the existence of some other mule. So, I might not *know* that she's faithful, but I'm justified in believing that she is. I have to admit, of course, that this isn't a good philosophical reply to skepticism. I've basically just admitted that I don't know much at all. But I find solace in this approach to my beliefs. I am relatively content to abandon all hope of being absolutely certain of how things really are in the external world. And I'm prepared to settle for what I can have strong justification in believing. Indeed, I think this is all that any of us can do, given this predicament about knowledge.

And this sort of view, dating back to Socrates, Plato, and Aristotle, is in keeping with a long-standing philosophical tradition of the importance of living an examined life guided by reflection and reason. In the *Apology*, Socrates is reported by Plato to have said that 'the unexamined life is not worth living.' Man – and woman – is a rational animal, and, as such, we have been endowed with the capacity to base judgments on experience and logic. Using these tools we can use experimentation and inductive reasoning to advance our understanding of the world. All this is to say that we do possess the intellectual capacity to evaluate our beliefs for the sake of guiding our judgments and behavior. In this regard, we are not totally unequipped to meet the challenge of understanding the world around us and determining, as best we can, how things are and what to do about them. And, if this is the best we can do, so be it.

That being said, blues music does provide a window into this pervasive part of the human condition. I've said a few times in this essay that it can help to know that others experience the same sorts of disturbing doubts that we experience. Somehow it is comforting for us to know that others are plagued by doubts too. However, knowing that we're not the only ones that suffer, or that others empathize with us and what we're going through, doesn't change the human condition. Our doubts are still there, dammit! But the blues represents a sour and sassy way of coping with this fate. We can find solace in the whining groans and pulsating rhythms that artistically express the ultimate uncertainty of life. In the end, we can philosophically agree with Charley Patton when he sang in Future Blues, 'Can't tell my future / Can't tell my past.' But we don't have to agree that we can't make reasonable judgments about either.

NOTES

1 Rene Descartes, *Meditations on First Philosophy*. In *Descartes: Philosophical Classics*, trans. Elizabeth S. Haldane and G. R. T. Ross (Mineola, NY: Dover Publications, 2003), p. 68.
2 Nozick's description of the experience machine can be found in his *Anarchy, State, and Utopia* (New York: Basic Books, 1974), p. 42.

ROBERT D. STOLOROW AND
BENJAMIN A. STOLOROW

CHAPTER 11

BLUES AND EMOTIONAL TRAUMA

Blues as Musical Therapy

*Music as Schopenhauer conceived it [speaks] [...]
directly out of the 'abyss' as its most authentic,
elemental, nonderivative revelation.*
(Friedrich Nietzsche)[1]

With roots in African music, the blues was born
in the Mississippi Delta as a distinctively African-
American musical genre in response to the dehum-
anizing traumas of slavery and its aftermath. It has
origins in spirituals, work songs, field hollers, and
so on, all of which are types of music associated
with enslaved people attempting to deal with their painful situation.
Although blues is a uniquely African-American music, it has a distinctively
universal appeal. There is something in the blues, and in music with
qualities that derive from the blues, that people can relate to. What are
these qualities? Irrespective of whether people who relate to the blues are
truly able to relate to the collective historical trauma of African-Americans,
there seems to be something expressed in the music that strikes an
emotional chord in people from a wide range of ethnic and cultural
backgrounds. What is this something? And why is the blues universally

Blues – Philosophy for Everyone: Thinking Deep About Feeling Low, First Edition.
Edited by Jesse R. Steinberg and Abrol Fairweather.
© 2012 John Wiley & Sons, Inc. Published 2012 by John Wiley & Sons, Inc.

compelling? That is the mystery – that people of many different cultures respond to the blues and to the 'bluesy feeling' prevalent in other music.

In this essay, we try to show that there is something about the blues that allows us to come face to face with universally traumatizing dimensions of human existence. Indeed, the music itself may be seen as a process of working through such trauma (musicians use the phrase 'working it out'). How does the blues put us in touch with the universally traumatizing aspects of the human condition? We will look for answers both in the blues' lyrical aspects (such as themes of irony, the absurdity and burdensomeness of existence, and hopelessness with hope) and its musical qualities (rhythm, pitch-bending, and the bluesy sound produced by shifts and ambiguities between major and minor keys). First, however, we must explore the nature of emotional trauma itself.

Emotional Trauma

Emotional trauma is an experience of unendurable emotional pain. Robert Stolorow in his book *Trauma and Human Existence*[2] has claimed that the unbearability of emotional suffering cannot be explained solely, or even primarily, on the basis of the intensity of the painful feelings evoked by an injurious event. Emotional pain is not pathology – it is inherent in the human condition (we will have more to say about this in later paragraphs). Painful emotional states become unbearable when they cannot find a 'relational home' – that is, a context of human understanding – in which they can be shared and held. Severe emotional pain that has to be experienced alone becomes lastingly traumatic and usually succumbs to some form of emotional numbing. This numbing flight from unendurable emotional pain is vividly illustrated by some verses of a bluesy song, 'Numb,' written by Stephanie Stolorow and performed by her and her brother Benjamin Stolorow under the name 'Stoli Rose.'

> How do I get numb?
> How do I get numb?
> Because I can't stand all this feeling
> Anymore
> Lord hand me a gun
> Lord hand me a gun
> Because I can't stand all this feeling
> Anymore

In contrast, painful feelings that are held in a context of human understanding gradually become more bearable and can eventually be included in one's sense of whom one experiences oneself as being.

Consider the following clinical illustration – a fictionalized composite. A young woman who had been repeatedly sexually abused by her father when she was a child began an analysis with a female analyst-in-training whom Robert Stolorow was supervising. Early in the treatment, whenever the patient began to remember and describe the sexual abuse, she would display emotional reactions that consisted of two distinct parts, both of which were entirely bodily. One was a trembling in her arms and upper torso, which sometimes escalated into violent shaking. The other was an intense flushing of her face. On these occasions, the analyst was quite alarmed by her patient's shaking and wanted to find some way to calm her.

Robert had a hunch that the shaking was a bodily manifestation of a traumatized state and that the flushing was a bodily form of the patient's shame about exposing this state to her analyst, so he suggested to his supervisee that she focus her inquiries on the flushing rather than the shaking. As a result of this shift in focus, the patient began to speak about how she believed her analyst viewed her when she was trembling or shaking: Surely her analyst must be secretly regarding her with disdain, seeing her as a damaged mess of a human being. As this belief was repeatedly disconfirmed by her analyst's understanding, rather than contemptuous, responses, both the flushing and the shaking diminished in intensity. The traumatized states actually underwent a process of transformation from being exclusively bodily states into ones in which the bodily sensations came to be united with words. Instead of only shaking, the patient began to speak about her terror of annihilating intrusion.

On the one and only occasion the patient had attempted to speak to her mother about the sexual abuse, her mother shamed her severely, declaring her to be a wicked little girl for making up such lies about her father. Both the flushing of the patient's face and the restriction of her experience of terror to its nameless bodily aspect were heir to her mother's shaming. Only with a shift in the patient's perception of her analyst as potentially shaming like the mother had been to accepting and understanding could the patient's emotional experience of her traumatized states shift from an exclusively bodily form to an experience that could be felt and named as terror.

How the process of bringing bodily forms of emotional pain into linguistic dialogue is crucial to the working through of emotional trauma, and how this process is uniquely facilitated by the blues, is the focus of later sections.

The Therapeutic Power of the Blues

Having discussed emotional trauma in terms of its context-embeddedness, we turn now to its existential significance – how it is implicated in the human condition in general. Robert Stolorow has proposed in his book that the existential meaning of emotional trauma lies in the shattering of what he calls the 'absolutisms of everyday life' – the system of illusory beliefs that allow us to function in the world, experienced as stable, predictable, and safe. Such shattering is a massive loss of innocence, exposing the inescapable dependence of our existence on a universe that is unstable and unpredictable and in which no safety or continuity of being can be assured. Emotional trauma brings us face to face with our existential vulnerability – to suffering, injury, illness, death, and loss. These are possibilities that define our existence and that loom as constant threats. Because we are limited, finite, mortal beings, trauma is a necessary and universal feature of our all-too-human condition.

In our clinical vignette, we alluded to the role played by the process of bringing the visceral, bodily aspect of emotional experience into language in working through painful emotional states. Such visceral-linguistic unities – of bodily sensations with words, of 'gut' feelings with names – are achieved in a dialogue of emotional understanding, and it is in such dialogue that experiences of emotional trauma can be held and transformed into endurable and namable painful feelings. The blues is a wonderful example of such dialogue. The lyrics, of course, provide the words that name the particular experience of trauma. The more formal aspects of the music seem universally to evoke the visceral dimension of emotional pain. In the unifying experience of the blues, songwriter, performers, and listeners are joined in a visceral-linguistic conversation in which universally traumatizing aspects of human existence can be communally held and borne. In experiencing the blues, we are joined together as 'brothers and sisters in the same dark night.'[3]

ROBERT D. STOLOROW AND BENJAMIN A. STOLOROW

Three 'Clinical' Illustrations – The Role of Lyrics

We have claimed that emotional trauma puts us in touch with our mortality – we all know that we will die, but we don't know when. These facts about our existence evoke conflicting feelings, and such ambivalence about our mortality often plays a central part in the lyrics of the blues. Consider the following illustration from an untitled song by an unknown songwriter:

> I'm goin' to lay my head on some
> lonesome railroad track
> I'm goin' to lay my head on some
> lonesome railroad track
> and when the train come along, I'll
> snatch my damn head back.

A first impression might be that the songwriter/singer is expressing a conflict about escaping from suffering through suicide. But we think a deeper interpretation is also possible – that traumatic suffering has put the songwriter/singer in touch with his or her mortality and with the existential fact that he will certainly die, but at an unknown time. Suicide can be a way of ending the anguish of not knowing, by taking control of one's death and making it happen voluntarily. The agonizing uncertainty of when death will occur is thereby replaced by certainty. But the above lyrics reflect the songwriter's/singer's ambivalence about such a solution – he wants to end the dreadful uncertainty, but he does not really want to die! This ambivalence or paradox expressed in the lyrics gives the song a quality of tragic irony, a quality often conveyed by the blues. Our existence is revealed as absurd – too painful for us to bear, but too precious to us to end.

Here is a more extensive illustration from a song by Louisiana Red, a.k.a. Iverson Minte, called 'Too Poor to Die' (2009):

> Last night I had a dream
> I dream I died
> The undertaker came
> To carry me for the ride
> I couldn't afford a coffin
> Embalmin' kinda high

> I jumped off my deathbed
> Cause I too poor to die
> I dream at the cemetery
> I couldn't afford enough
> To pay the gravediggers
> To cover me up
> It cost a lot of money
> Cause they was union men

The absurdity of our finite, mortal existence is clearly captured in these lyrics. Louisiana Red, obviously traumatized by the suffering of poverty, anticipates his death in his dreams. But the poverty that traumatizes him renders him, later in the song, 'too poor to go lay down and die' – he can't afford a coffin, embalming, gravediggers, or (in a later verse) to grease the devil's palm – so he jumps off his deathbed and evades death. In a twist of tragic irony, the very same poverty that puts him in touch with his mortality provides him with the means for escaping it, and simultaneously it becomes the focus of his lament.

The heavy burdensomeness of finite human existing is captured in a song written by Willie Dixon with the title 'One More Mile to Go' (1994):

> It's been a hard desert journey
> And I don't have to cry no mo'
> Baby keep yo' light a-burnin'
> So your man will know the score
> I did wrong when I took a gamble
> You know I bet my money wrong
> I was bettin' on my baby
> And my baby wasn't at home

These lyrics contain a rich interweaving of the existential themes we have been discussing. First, there is a longing to find relief from the burdensomeness and painfulness of human existing – from the 'hard desert journey.' Toward the end of the song there is a line, 'One mo' mile to go,' that is reminiscent of the similar mournful lament 'All my trials, Lord, soon be over,' from a well-known bluesy folk song. Second, the lyrics point to a basic aspect of our existential vulnerability: we need connections to other people – people who keep a 'light a-burnin'' for us to help us find our way in life. But the others with whom we are deeply connected are also finite, mortal beings, and so we are constantly threatened with the possibilities of traumatic disappointments, rejections, and losses. Third, the lyrics point to a central dimension of our human limitedness – we can never forecast in advance the outcome of the life decisions we make: 'I was bettin' on my baby / And my baby wasn't at home.' Because of the limitedness of our ability to know and predict the future with certainty, human existence is always a 'gamble'; we are always at risk.

Musical Characteristics of the Blues

The blues also has musical qualities that communicate the visceral aspects of emotional trauma. In music, one of the most important expressive devices is the use of tension and release. The tension and subsequent release can be melodic, harmonic, or rhythmic. Emotionally expressive music tends to have a greater degree of musical tension, which makes the release more effective. One of the ways in which tension is created in the blues is called 'pitch-bending.'

The blues started out as a mainly vocal music. Thus, in instrumental blues the musician will try to imitate the sound of the human voice on his or her instrument. Pitch-bending is a technique that is used by both vocalists and instrumental musicians. It plays on our ear being accustomed to hearing melodies composed of pitches, or notes, that relate to a key. A key comprises a series of usually seven adjacent notes (as in the major scale) that are fixed. Blues musicians slide up or down in between pitches of a key, thus 'bending' the notes and creating tension.

Pitch-bending gives rise to an ambiguity between major and minor keys. Traditional Western harmony has rules that provide clarity as to whether a piece or tune is in a major or minor key. This clarity is built on the certainty that pitches will more or less be in tune. Blues musicians intentionally sing or play around the pitches of the key to create tension. Then, at just the right moment the musician resolves the tension created by the pitch being out of tune by sliding up or down to the note that is in the 'correct' key. It is easy to get a sense of pitch-bending by watching a great guitar player play the blues. The guitarist slides his or her finger up and down the fingerboard while keeping the vibrating string depressed. The shortening or lengthening of the vibrating portion of the string alters the pitch. A skilled player can use this technique to approach the notes that are in the 'correct' key by sliding into them. Tension is created because, en route to the note that is in this key, the pitch that is actually heard is in between notes in the key. During this 'in-between time,' there is a build-up of tension, which is then released when the target note is reached. Piano players, too, can create the feeling of pitch-bending by sliding from a black key to a white key. Pitch-bending can be an enormously effective expressive musical device.

Because of the ambiguity in the blues between major and minor keys, it can be said that the music is not really in either a major or minor key in the traditional sense. We suggest that this ambiguity is one of the elements of the music that gives it its power to capture viscerally the emotionally traumatizing quality of human existence. This is so because we typically associate music in a major key with happy or joyful emotions and music in a minor key with sad or painful feelings. Blues music gives us both at the same time, paralleling the way the lyrics can convey the tragic irony and absurdity of our existence, as we discussed earlier.

Blues musicians also use rhythm as an expressive tool. As with pitch-bending, timing of musical tension and release plays a key role. To create a bluesy feeling, the lead musician may sing or play something that is 'out of time,' meaning that he or she will intentionally dance around the beat that is being kept steady by the band. The lead musician, the one who is playing with the rhythm, is also hearing where the beat is while playing out of time, and is probably also keeping an internal sense of the time as well. When the musician is ready to release the tension created by his or her rhythmic play, he or she will 'snap' back to the beat and lock in with the band. The use of this rhythmic play helps to create a rhythmic looseness that is an essential component of the 'bluesy feeling.' This rhythmic looseness has an emotional quality that parallels that of the ambiguity between major and minor keys, with both components being able viscerally to capture the paradoxical, enigmatic, traumatizing quality of finite human existence. Additionally, the out-of-time feature of blues rhythm points to the disturbing impact of trauma on our 'normal' experience of lived time.

The classic blues is a twelve-measure form consisting of three four-measure phrases. For many blues songs the first phrase is sung in the major key. The second phrase is often the same as the first phrase but with a 'minor third' instead of a 'major third.' (The third is the note of the scale that determines whether the key will be major or minor.) The last phrase is usually the 'punchline' – in other words, some kind of ironic answer to the first two phrases. A great blues song will make a statement about the painful way things are; that statement will be repeated in the minor key; and then the punch line will usually be an ironic expression of resignation. Contradiction and irony are built into the structure of

ROBERT D. STOLOROW AND BENJAMIN A. STOLOROW

both the music and the lyrics of the blues, just as they are built into the structure of our existence. These are just a few of the essential, emotion-laden musical qualities of the blues. There are many other subtleties that can be felt and appreciated through repeated listening and exposure to the music.

Concluding Remarks

We have tried to show that, in the unities of its music and its lyrics, the blues provides a therapeutic, visceral-linguistic conversation in which universally traumatizing aspects of human existence can be communally held and lived through. Therein, we have suggested, lies the blues' universal appeal. But, to grasp the profundity of the blues, we must return to its origins in African-American history and in the traumas of slavery.

Why was the need for such a visceral-linguistic conversation especially powerful in *this* context – so powerful as to give rise to a musical genre with such universal appeal? LeRoi Jones suggests in his book *Blues People*[4] that the birth of the blues was linked to the circumstances of newly freed African slaves having to establish their identity as African-Americans. Having endured generations of brutal enslavement, these former Africans were faced with having to figure out their identity in a land where they and their ancestors were forcibly brought to work, and to do so amid the bleak conditions of post-slavery and post-Civil-War America. They needed a form of dialogue through which the devastating nature of their experience in America could be conveyed and shared in *their* English and, at the same time, that could capture viscerally the traumatic suffering entailed in that experience. It was in this context, claims Jones, that the blues came into being.

In the blues there is a quality of acceptance of the way things are, however miserable. The conditions under which the creators of the blues brought this profound music into being show a remarkable resilience of spirit. These resilient and expressive people were forced to endure a dreadful plight, and we think it was in part through their music that they tried to regain the human dignity that had been brutally stripped from them and sought to rebuild their traumatically shattered world. We owe an incalculable debt of gratitude to the creators of the blues, who endured unimaginable suffering while bringing forth this powerful music that continues to help people face, own up to, and cope with the human condition.

In his song 'Imagine,' John Lennon offered his vision of a Utopian future. We close our essay with some similar musings. Imagine a world in which providing deep understanding of others' existential vulnerability and pain – that is, of the potentially traumatizing emotional impact of our finiteness – has become a shared ethical principle. In such a world, human beings would be much more capable of living in their existential vulnerability, rather than having to revert to the defensive, destructive evasions of it that have been so characteristic of human history. A new form of individual identity would become possible, based on owning rather than covering up our existential vulnerability. Vulnerability that finds a hospitable and understanding home could be seamlessly woven into the fabric of whom we experience ourselves as being. A new form of human solidarity would also become possible, rooted not in shared ideological illusion but in mutual recognition of and respect for our common human limitedness. If we can help one another bear the darkness rather than evade it, perhaps one day we will be able to see the light – as finite human beings, finitely bonded to one another. We contend that the creators of the blues have brought us a significant step closer to the attainment of such a world.

NOTES

1 Friedrich Nietzsche, *On the Genealogy of Morals*, trans. Walter Kaufmann (New York: Vintage Books, 1887), p. 367.
2 Robert Stolorow, *Trauma and Human Existence: Autobiographical, Psychoanalytic and Philosophical Reflections* (New York: Analytic Press, 2007).
3 Lawrence Vogel, *The Fragile "We": Ethical Implications of Heidegger's Being and Time* (Evanston, IL: Northwestern University Press, 1994).
4 LeRois Jones, *Blues People: Negro Music in White America* (New York: Harper Perennial, 1999).

CHAPTER 12

SUFFERING, SPIRITUALITY, AND SENSUALITY

Religion and the Blues

I was brought up in a white Baptist church in Virginia. We sang hymns, but church music never moved me in any way. The music seemed stiff and disembodied. In my adolescence, I abandoned the sacred music of the church for rock, and through rock and roll I discovered blues music. Admittedly, I was looking for the roots of the rock music I had come to love. But the blues captured my imagination and my heart. It was the blues, I thought, that made rock and roll so good, so powerful. I wanted to play licks like B. B. King and sing like John Lee Hooker. I had no idea that this wonderful emotional music had anything to do with gospel music or religion. I just loved the blues. When I first saw John Lee Hooker perform, I was convinced I was on holy ground. As far as I was concerned, John Lee Hooker's voice just was the voice of God. Quickly I began to absorb blues music of all kinds – Muddy Waters, Lightning Hopkins, Howlin' Wolf, Mississippi John Hurt, anything I could get my hands on. Then I discovered the bluesy sounds of black gospel music while listening to a blues radio show, and soon attended a

Blues – Philosophy for Everyone: Thinking Deep About Feeling Low, First Edition.
Edited by Jesse R. Steinberg and Abrol Fairweather.
© 2012 John Wiley & Sons, Inc. Published 2012 by John Wiley & Sons, Inc.

black gospel music service. I remember thinking that, if the music in my church had been like that, I might still be attending church today. Still it struck me that there seems to be an apparent tension between the bawdy themes raised in blues music and the spiritual ideals expressed in hymns and gospel music. Is the blues sort of an apostate religious music? To my ears, the line between black gospel and blues music was very thin both in sound and content. On the Internet I found the following account of the blues, which explicitly mentions its religious roots:

> (1) The Blues... It's [sic] 12-bar, bent-note melody is the anthem of a race bonding itself together with cries of shared self victimization. Bad luck and trouble are always present, and always the result of others, pressing upon unfortunate and down trodden poor souls, yearning to be free from lifes' responsibilities. Never ending beats repeat the chants of sorrow, and the pity of a lost soul many times over. These are the Blues.

> (2) Found under the blazing sun of the Northern Mississippi cotton fields, it's father, the old African tribal call and response, and it's mother, the Gospel sounds which bellowed from the church choirs.

> (3) A lead worker would chant the opening lines, and the chorus of workers would answer, falling into a regular pattern to match the task at hand. This ancient African call and response chant is the core of the Blues, found both in African-American church pulpits (an elevated platform or high reading desk used in preaching or conducting a worship service), and antebellum (existing before the Civil War) plantations.[1]

So, I wondered whether the connection between blues and gospel was merely a superficial historical connection or if there was something deeper.

No one performer better illustrates both the connections and the contraction between gospel and blues than the great Son House. Some of his songs, such as 'John the Revelator,' express vague apocalyptic thoughts in ways that might have found a comfortable audience in my old stodgy Baptist church. Even that gospel-like song could not have really passed muster because the sound was too much like rock and roll. Still, the lyrics are acceptable from an Evangelical or Fundamentalist perspective. But much of Son House's music expresses an uncomfortable relationship with faith. In the first version of his 'Preaching Blues,' Son House sings a gospel-like tune that seems to express his desire for faith and to be a preacher. But the lyrics tell a different story:

JOSEPH J. LYNCH

Oh, I'm gonna get me a religion, I'm gonna join the Baptist Church
[...]
I'm gonna be a Baptist preacher, and I sure won't have to work
Oh, I went in my room, I bowed down to pray
[...]
Till the blues come along, and they blowed my spirit away
Oh, I'd-a had religion, Lord, this every day
[...]
But the womens and whiskey, well, they would not set me free
Oh, I wish I had me a heaven of my own
[spoken] Great God almighty!
Hey, a heaven of my own
Till I'd give all my women a long, long, happy home

Notice that, in the very first stanza, Son House contrasts being a Baptist preacher with having to work. Now, admittedly, this is coming from the perspective of someone doing time. If you're slaving away on a prison chain gang, preaching for a living is bound to look pretty attractive. So, becoming a Baptist preacher represents a kind of liberation from having to work at all, and liberation from the imprisonment of 'womens and whiskey' as well. While getting religion and preaching are put forward as a kind of salvation, there does also seem to be an implicit critique of institutional religion or at least professional religion. Perhaps preachers are preachers simply because they wish to avoid work like the rest of us. So, it appears that in part religion can be a vehicle for our salvation from unpleasant labor and vices, while at the same time perhaps the motives of the clergy are less than pure.

It is important to note that in the above lyrics Son House does not say he's going to preach the *gospel*. He says he's going to preach the *blues*. We can see in this one song a portion of Son House's resolution of the tension between the typical values expressed by most versions of Christianity and those values generally expressed in blues music. In the blues there are countless references to sexuality, drunkenness, and even violence. In some Delta blues these are indeed described as sins of the flesh, as in Robert Johnson's 'Drunken Hearted Man':

Now, I'm the drunken hearted man and sin was the cause of it all
[spoken] Oh, play 'em now
I'm a drunken hearted man, and sin was the cause of it all
And the day that you get weak for no-good women, that's the day that
   you bound to fall

SUFFERING, SPIRITUALITY, AND SENSUALITY 133

But at the same time Johnson has songs that refer to young attractive women as biscuits and men, if they are good lovers, as 'biscuit rollers.' Muddy Waters famously bragged of sexual prowess in 'Hoochie Coochie Man' as well as 'Mannish Boy.' In the various versions of John Lee Hooker's 'I'm Mad Again,' the singer describes how he kills his former friend execution-style. No hint of spirituality there, to be sure.

But Son House had a particular notion of just what the blues is and how it arose. Here is his brief remark on the origin of the blues:

> We were always singing in the fields. Not real singing, you know, just hollerin', but we made up our songs about things that was happening to us at the time, and I think that's where the blues started.[2]

For Son House, the principle ingredient in the blues was not the content, but the heart. The blues is born of suffering and is the expression of that suffering. I think that what Son House might be trying to say is that the expression of the suffering is the liberation from the suffering. Let me offer a few different readings of what this might amount to. I want to say something about each of Marx, the Buddha, and Kierkegaard that I think might throw some light on the apparent contradictions evident between the blues and religion. This is not, of course, the place to go into detail about any of these thinkers. But I do think these perspectives clarify what might be a resolution to the conflict between preaching the gospel and preaching the blues.

Marx Sings the Revolutionary Blues

Karl Marx was clearly critical of religion. After all, he's the guy who said that religion is the opium of the masses. Now this remark *seems* to suggest that religion is an opiate in the sense that it is delusional. And, in light of other things that Marx says, this certainly makes sense. After all, for him religion is a part of the superstructure of a society that comprises various ideologies that reinforce relations of production, for example the institution of slavery or the exploitation of the working class. So, religion helps to keep the workers slaving away in what is suggested to them is their rightful place, whether fields or factory floors, with the promise of an afterlife in which their suffering will be rewarded. But, prior to making his remark about the opium of the people, Marx called religion 'the heart of a heartless world.' In full, he said:

> Religious suffering is, at one and the same time, the expression of real suffering and a protest against real suffering. Religion is the sigh of the oppressed creature, the heart of a heartless world, and the soul of soulless conditions. It is the opium of the people.[3]

From a Marxist perspective, the blues is like religion. It articulates the cries of those who suffer and helps ease their pain.

Religion, according to Marx's view, is the natural expression of oppressed people. It is an opiate not just in that it obscures the reality of class relations and power but also in that it can ease the pain of the oppressed. It is not just the promise of an easy afterlife that draws people to religion, but also the sense of belonging, community, and meaning. And, while Marx might well roll over in his grave at this proposition, his own views can be seen in a religious way. After all, he identifies the basic problem of the human condition as the problem of alienation; for him, this means alienated labor. His vision is that the natural expression of the alienation of the working class through revolution would lead to their liberation. Religion expresses the broken heart of the oppressed, but Marxism expresses it better, and heals it as well. And, a more contemporary form of Christian theology, known as 'liberation theology,' has appropriated some Marxist themes in its understanding of the nature of the Christian message.

What is the connection then between Marx and Son House's version of the Blues? Marx is both sympathetic and scathingly critical of religion. His own analysis seems to produce something that is itself a kind of new religion, with a different sort of salvation story. It is religion reinvented. Similarly, Son House is at least implicitly critical of religion and perhaps also implicitly critical of the blues. Perhaps preachers are those who can benefit from the fact that those they preach to must labor while they do not. At the same time Son House, along with many other blues performers, see the blues as arising out the suffering that comes from labor. The labor of the slave and other disenfranchised workers is, from Marx's point of view, alienated labor by definition. The laborer suffers and generates profit for others. Just as Marx may be seen as describing a kind of Materialist-workers religion as a path to liberation, Son House expresses liberation in the blues itself. And, as he sees himself as *preaching* the blues, he is preaching a new kind of gospel. The oppressed and the enslaved liberate themselves through the very expression of their suffering.

Did the Buddha Have the Blues?

The prince Gautama, who became the Buddha, is the last person you'd expect to have had the blues, at least according to the standard stories. He was born into the lap of luxury but found it unsatisfying. Even though he could avail himself of any pleasure he wished, he knew he could not escape aging, illness, and eventually death. While it is certainly true that Gautama was not oppressed in the more obvious ways, since he was a prince, he nevertheless did take on the life of an ascetic for a while and genuinely suffered quite a bit. The person who became the Buddha definitely had the blues. And perhaps the Buddha can be seen as a kind of bluesman himself. In fact, when he was finally enlightened and told others about his experience, he did a little preaching of his own. The Four Noble Truths are usually described as the Buddha's Deer Park Sermon.[4]

The first of the Four Noble Truths is the truth of suffering. Christianity sees sin as the fundamental problem with the human experience and for Marx it's alienated labor, but for the Buddha it's just suffering. The Pali word *dukkha* (translated as 'suffering') has a very broad meaning; it certainly does refer to ordinary pain and distress, but also struggle and a general sense of the unsatisfactory character of human existence, which is what Gautama experienced when he had wealth and power. Indeed, much of the suffering in blues music has to do with matters of the heart. In 'No Substitute,' John Lee Hooker sings,

> When your woman gone,
> there's nothing can,
> can take her place.
> But there's no substitute, substitute for love.

For the Buddha, the spiritual path begins when one is made aware that life is characterized by suffering. It is not that there aren't enjoyable experiences; on the contrary. But rather, nothing in ordinary human experience seems to provide a lasting sense of satisfaction. This is because, according to the Buddha, everything we experience is impermanent.

This impermanence was one of the key ideas for the Buddha. The Buddha's path for overcoming the blues is really a matter of embracing it. That is, the recognition of impermanence, the experiential awareness of suffering, is part of the path to liberation. The Buddha thought that it was craving for substantiality and permanence that just aren't there that perpetuates our suffering. The direct awareness of impermanence can help us to let go of the craving that leads to our suffering.

Obviously, there's much more to the teaching of the Buddha and Buddhism than this, just as there's much more to Marx and Marxism than I discussed above. Still, it strikes me that the message of Buddhism in part draws attention to the human condition in a bluesy sort of way. There's a powerful sense in which fully embracing suffering is the path to liberation. Of course, there may be a striking difference. According to the Buddha, the main cause of suffering is craving. This is in fact the second noble truth. And the expression of craving seems to be at the heart of many blues songs, for example the emptiness conveyed in Robert Johnson's 'Love in Vain,' in which the singer expresses his hunger for his love, who must leave him. Or the countless blues songs about economic and physical struggles that contain an overwhelming craving for these to cease – a fairly contemporary example is 'Hard Times' by Ray Charles and Eric Clapton:

> My mother told me
> 'Fore she passed away
> Said son when I'm gone
> Don't forget to pray
> 'Cause there'll be hard times
> Lord those hard times
> Who knows better than I?
> Well I soon found out
> Just what she meant
> When I had to pawn my clothes
> Just to pay the rent
> Talkin' 'bout hard times
> Lord those hard times
> Who knows better than I?

Conversely, the blues can be seen as a kind of meditation on craving and suffering. The Buddha wasn't advocating suppression of desire but release and freedom. Aside from that, it's worth noting that, in addition to the mindfulness meditation techniques of Buddhism that directly focus on suffering and its causes, as Buddhism developed there emerged certain schools that draw attention to some seeming contradictions between a spiritual and a not-so-spiritual life. In India and later in Tibet, forms of Buddhism used the techniques of tantra, eventually mainly as visualizations but initially as a deliberate way to ritually violate certain taboos to do with sexual practices and the consumption of alcohol and meat. There was a powerful sense in which the profane was embraced as a vehicle for liberation – under the appropriate guidance, of course. In tantra one uses the passions to overcome the passions.[5]

I have to admit that it's hard to reconcile the quiet mindfulness practice of the Buddha and Buddhists with the wailing of a blues singer such as Howlin' Wolf. But it can be argued that the blues is, precisely, deliberate and melodic mindfulness on human suffering. The way in which the Buddha had the blues was in the recognition of the suffering of the human condition and in the practice of liberating oneself from the suffering by being mindful of it. I think that the preaching of Son House is something like this. His gospel, and the 'gospel' of the blues, generally express the manifold suffering of the human condition, especially the oppression of African-Americans. But the music itself *is* the liberation. In the same moment, it draws attention to the pain and provides freedom from it.

So far I have tried to show that what Marx did with religion looks a lot like what the blues does, and that the Buddha similarly directly addresses the theme of suffering. In both cases, embracing suffering can be seen as a vehicle for liberation from suffering. But, as examples such as ancient Buddhist tantric practices suggest, there still seems to be a contradiction inherent in a life simultaneously both spiritual and given over to the appetites of the flesh. The struggle here, it seems to me, is that religion seeks both transcendence and immanence. Human beings may want meaning, but they also want embodiment. Religion is often the quest for the spiritual in the realm of the senses. And, when one tries to express what this means, it just might sound contradictory. But, let's face it, there never has been a Buddhist blues singer, and probably for good reason. And I certainly don't know of a Marxist one either. Buddhists generally aim to be released from passions, and Marxists would probably use passions to struggle for revolution. The blues must be felt and felt passionately. Now, most blues performers come from a Christian background, so they would be likely to see life a bit differently from the Buddha or Marx. But there was a Christian philosopher who directly faced the contradictory nature and the deeply felt passion of religious faith in a blues-like way. His name was Søren Kierkegaard.

Kierkegaard's Passion and the Passion of the Blues

Kierkegaard was no bluesman. But he believed in passion. For him, faith (in God) was the highest human virtue, not reason. While he had deep faith in God, Kierkegaard rejected what he called the 'God of the philosophers,' the sort of God that you could 'prove' with rational arguments. The classic arguments for the existence of God from Anselm, Aquinas, and other philosophers were not even desirable to Kierkegaard because rational proofs will never yield the absolute passion of deeply felt faith. In a strange way Kierkegaard's diminished view of reason was reminiscent of that of Hume. Hume thought that reason was and ought to be the servant of the passions, whereas Kierkegaard held that reason ought to be the servant of the passion of faith. You can't have faith if you have proof. Faith is an intense passion, which proof and reason generally destroy.[6] When I remember my childhood faith at the Baptist Church, I don't remember any passion at all. We had a sincere sense of inner certitude. We had neither passionate faith nor proof. And the dreary drones of the hymns we sang contrast very sharply with the bluesy exaltations of the black gospel choirs.

Kierkegaard compared the passion of faith to the passion of a love affair. Falling in love involves risks. Your lover might not be faithful, might not stay in love with you, and so on (and how many blues songs have been written about just that?), and this riskiness is precisely where the passion of being in love comes from. And it is that passion that makes being in love so deeply satisfying. If relationships are formed on cool rational analyses, they are not likely to be such a satisfying experience. And one potential reason that love relationships can be satisfying is the risk involved – you could get it wrong, after all. Like Muddy Waters begging his woman 'baby please don't go,' it could all end horribly. And, in the song of that name, it does.

For Kierkegaard, if we rely on reason, we will arrive at the conclusion that life has no meaning. In this way, faith, like the blues, is born from the womb of despair. As Wittgenstein once remarked, 'To say that God exists is to say that life has a meaning.'[7] Since genuine faith requires intense passion, and intense passion requires that the objective probability of truth is very low, genuine faith requires belief in what is improbable. Here, of course, Kierkegaard is very unlike Hume. This means of course that faith requires doubt. Not just the sort of doubt you might have about a love relationship, but *serious* doubt. Without doubt there can be no faith at all. And so here is the central element of the Christian faith: that God became a man. The infinite becomes finite. This is, for Kierkegaard, the ultimate absurdity, and a wonderful absurdity that is the proper object of true passionate faith. Unlike the theologians and philosophers who have tried to defend the concept of the incarnation, Kierkegaard agrees with those skeptics who claim that it is senseless and absurd – this is why Christianity requires the leap of faith. For the blues singers the release from pain and suffering is the embracing of pain and suffering through singing the blues. In the Elmore James and Junior Wells tune 'It Hurts Me Too,' the singer sympathizes with the plight of his unfaithful wife because she will be hurt. And this will hurt him too. He is passionately hurt by her and passionately feels pain for her. There is no promise of future resolution, no rational explanation or reason to hope. The expression of the pain, in this case, love, is all the resolution there is.

If thinkers like Kierkegaard are right, Christianity at least, and perhaps religion generally, require passionate faith, which comes from both doubt and despair. The tension between faith and reason, the sacred and the profane, is built into religion already. Without the requisite tension, faith just won't be satisfying. Now, of course, not everyone has or even wants the sort of faith that Kierkegaard is talking about. But I think his approach elucidates the work of blues 'preachers' such as Son House. For Kierkegaard, the very idea that God could become a finite human being – the unity of creator and creature, God as embodied – inspires passionate faith. Unlike certain approaches to spirituality, where the sensual is denigrated and in some cases abandoned, from this perspective to be spiritual is to be embodied. The spiritual is the sensual. Kierkegaard's approach contrasts sharply with that of Plato, who urged the purification of the soul *from* the body and was leery of the power of music generally.[8] But for Kierkegaard the infinite, the spiritual, is also finite and a human being. It is as marvelous as it is senseless. Kierkegaard didn't try to figure it out – he didn't think it could be figured out at all. The tension between the sacred and secular is not going to go away. The blues honestly embraces sensuality, the love for boogie-chillin' and other things, in ways that can't be done within the official context of the Christian church. But one might say that the blues reaches into all dimensions of human suffering, does not try to limit itself in themes or theology, and is a more honest expression of religious faith than religions can normally provide. Robert Johnson and Son House didn't try to figure it out. They not only embraced the suffering that birthed the blues but openly embraced the contradiction of faith. That passion is what gives the blues its seemingly transcendent power. The blues and the blues singers and writers capture that passion of faith.

NOTES

1 'Blues language' (December 17, 2000, http://blueslyrics.tripod.com/blueslanguage.htm#creper). Extract transcribed exactly as it appears in the original.
2 Eddie James, 'Son House' (n.d., http://blueslyrics.tripod.com/artistswithsongs/son_house_1.htm).
3 Karl Marx, 'Contribution to the critique of Hegel's theory of right' (1844, http://bearspace.baylor.edu/Scott_Moore/www/texts/Marx_Contr_Crit.html).
4 There are many good sources detailing the life of the Buddha and his teachings about suffering and ending suffering. One of the best introductions is Donald Mitchell, *Buddhism: Introducing the Buddhist Experience* (New York: Oxford University Press, 2008).
5 Also, in Zen Buddhism very ordinary activities become themselves spiritual. This sort of Buddhism even influenced training in the fighting arts, which it might seem counterintuitive for a Buddhist to practice.
6 Soren Kierkegaard, 'Subjectivity is truth.' In Louis Pojman (Ed.), *Concluding Unscientific Postscript to the Philosophical Fragments*, trans. Louis Pojman (Princeton, NJ: Wadsworth, 1994).
7 Ludwig Wittgenstein, 'Lecture on ethics' (n.d., http://www.galilean-library.org/manuscript.php?postid=43866).
8 See Plato's *Phaedo* for the purification of the soul, and especially the *Republic* for his thoughts on music.

CHAPTER 13

WORRYING THE LINE

Blues as Story, Song, and Prayer

The Blues tell the story of life's difficulties, and if you think for a moment, you will realize that they take the hardest realities of life and put them into music, only to come out with some new hope or sense of triumph. This is triumphant music.
(Martin Luther King, Jr., Opening Address to the Berlin Jazz Festival, 1964)[1]

Story

For Mother's Day this year my typically recalcitrant and cynical teenage son displayed a welcome moment of human engagement when he chose to give me a powerful collection of 'raw and rare and otherworldly' African-American gospel music (spanning the years 1944–2007). *Fire in My Bones* was issued by Tompkins Square, a small label dedicated to drawing attention to neglected treasures of American music and, in this case, raising funds for the New Orleans Musicians Relief Fund. Across eighty songs spanning six decades, the collection ranges from scratchy field recordings to intricate vocal harmonies to snappy adaptations of rock 'n' roll rhythms. This is gospel music as it has been sung and

Blues – Philosophy for Everyone: Thinking Deep About Feeling Low, First Edition.
Edited by Jesse R. Steinberg and Abrol Fairweather.
© 2012 John Wiley & Sons, Inc. Published 2012 by John Wiley & Sons, Inc.

performed in tiny storefronts and large sanctuaries, from rural Georgia to urban Los Angeles. It is clearly among the most vibrant, playful, beautiful, and emotionally charged music in the world – and it sounds just like the blues. What is apparent from all the recordings is that the spirit of the Lord is rooted in the spirit of the blues.

You don't have to be twice born to feel the inspirational power of a Holy Ghost working its mojo through music. Communing with some greater force, regardless of its theological bent, is something music lovers seek every day. Whether from God or some other cosmic source – 'From on high he has sent fire into my bones, and it has overcome them' (Lamentations 1:13) – the painful reality of life is always with us. The great genius of the blues is to show us how to handle it and how to come out the other side with, as Martin Luther King, Jr. announced, 'some new hope or sense of triumph.'[2]

That a collection of gospel music would evoke the blues makes perfect sense, considering the mythic origins of the most legendary blues musician – Robert Johnson. Ever since somebody told somebody who told somebody about Robert Johnson making a deal with the devil at the crossroads, the blues and religion have been inextricably bound. Undisputed facts about Johnson's life are few and far between. All we know for certain is that Johnson lived in Mississippi from 1911 to 1938 and left us twenty-nine songs recorded over two sessions. But in between those years his proficiency and personality gave rise to rumor, mystery, and eventually a legend so compelling that it took on mythic proportions. The story about the birth of the blues became as important as the songs themselves to understanding the philosophical dimensions of African-American life.

As recounted in Johnson's composition, 'Crossroad Blues,' the musician 'Went down to the crossroad / Fell down on my knees,' deliberately choosing a place associated with power in African and diaspora religions. Whether met by St. Peter guarding the gates of Christian heaven or Legba, the trickster Vodun deity, the musician knew that at the crossroads he would meet a holy being that had Ashe or Amen: the power to make things happen. Although the song does not particularize a desire to perform the blues, it does articulate the conditions that would drive a man to want to play the blues – loneliness, despair, and helplessness.

Somewhere along the chain of narrators and performers, the protagonist of the song became Robert Johnson and the myth took on the potency of scripture. Johnson became, in Victor Turner's formulation, a lead actor in the social drama that is American life – a bluesman who so desperately longed for fame and fortune and who was so dissatisfied with his own musical abilities that he made a momentous decision.³ At the stroke of midnight, he walked down to the windswept crossroads at the junction of highways in Mississippi and invoked a deity who in this case turned out to be Satan. In exchange for Johnson's immortal soul, the devil tuned his guitar, thereby giving him the abilities he so desired. From then on, the young bluesman played his instrument with an unearthly style, his fingers dancing over the strings. His voice moaned and wailed, expressing the deepest sorrows of a condemned sinner. Or so the story goes.

The relationship between religion and the blues is not a through line. Indeed, very little in African-American cultural production or philosophical thought follows a straight trajectory, but it is all connected at the source and by the existential effort to create meaning out of life. A more appropriate image would be a circle, which is foundational to African philosophical sensibilities that view life in terms of what Mircea Eliade called the myth of eternal return.⁴ In African cosmology as it came to America with people who would be enslaved, there is no distinction between sacred and profane. Secular problems have spiritual answers and spiritual remedies offer practical results.

This relationship was established early and was articulated by Frederick Douglass in his first narrative. Describing the spirituals he clearly identifies the paradoxical existential state that engenders such music that is both the 'prayer and complaint' of a people and expresses the 'highest joy and deepest sadness [...] the most pathetic sentiment in the most rapturous tone.'⁵ In creation and performance, the spirituals first established the terms of an African-American philosophical perspective that would later become the blues. This perspective promotes the story of paradox as the condition of life, endorses song as a means of recording life experience, and advocates prayer in improvisatory, fragmented, and signifying ways to negotiate the contingencies of life.

A secularized version of the spirituals, the blues establishes continuity between the emergence of an African American culture and the present times and provides a similar philosophical guide to life. The blues unifies people over time and space, offers functional advice for living, creates opportunities for and an analysis of society, engages political energies, and reinforces theological and spiritual values. The blues, however, does so in a unique way that brings an aesthetic dimension to the process of making meaning out of the harsh contingencies of life. What the blues depicts is not factual information as such but rather the life of human feeling, and therein the connection to a religious impulse also resides. For all the lure of the real there is also the blur of the real that shapes a

KIMBERLY R. CONNOR

narrative to mythic proportions – as in the case of Robert Johnson at the crossroads – in order to make it meaningful and useful.

This process is neatly described by Richard Wright, who defended his fictionalization of his autobiography in the following way:

> I've used what I lived and observed and felt, and I used my imagination to whip it into shape to appeal to the emotions and imaginations of other people, for I believe that only the writing that has to do with the basic issues of human living, moral, political, or whatever you call it, has any meaning. I think the importance of any writing lies in how much felt life is in it: It gets its value from that.[6]

As story, the blues is an inseparable and fluid balance of the sacred and the secular, of art and religion, of God and the Devil, set forth as myth, recalled in ritual, memorialized in symbol, generating a transcendent experience led by a chosen griot who conjures the incantatory magic of words and invokes the obligation to name things as he feels them. In the heroism of telling his tale, the bluesman prepares himself, and others, to live another day.

Song

A story doesn't do any good unless it is told, and singing is how the blues story is told. When sung, the blues offer a ritualistic way to affirm the essential worth of human existence. After facing the indignities of life, one can release the pain and frustration by stomping the blues, knowing full well that the expression is temporary and most likely ineffectual in terms of changing anything in a fundamental way. The stomp lasts Saturday night, and then you get up Sunday, go to church and repent, and start the cycle all over again. The blues, therefore, acknowledges that there is more to trouble and suffering than simply being in a bad mood or having a lousy string of luck; rather, these conditions are simply the structure of existence, for which the blues provides a kind of cathartic metaphysic, identifying what is real but in terms that are concrete, not abstract, and encompassing a full range of human expression.

According to Albert Murray – a preeminent practitioner, promoter, and priest of the blues – the music 'extends, elaborates, and refines'[7] the philosophical impulse to make meaning out of experience and creates the opportunity to develop and demonstrate the capacity to endure existence through transcendence as a strategy for survival and eventual – if temporary – triumph. The blues, like spirituals, is typically composed and sung not to answer the problem of evil – it is not a theodicy – but to describe the reality of a situation in which evil is present. It is functional in the most essential way because the blues converts experience and renews existence by embracing life in all its aspects: sorrow becomes joy, work becomes play.

Indeed, therapeutic and playful dimensions of the blues are often overlooked by two concerns that often dominate any discussion of the blues: a focus on the misery the blues describe and debates about the criteria for authenticity. Both issues, however, can lead to a corruption of the technique of 'worrying the line.' For blues musicians, 'worrying the line' is the technique of breaking up a phrase by changing pitch, adding a shout, or repeating words in order to emphasize, clarify, or subvert a moment in a song. In a broader sense worrying the line can describe the ongoing musical attempts that humans create to fashion a relevant philosophical response to a particular event or setting. If the nature and function of art are the means by which raw materials of experience are processed and stylized into statement, then the blues, Albert Murray argues, is the ultimate extension, elaboration, and refinement of rituals that represent the basic and definitive survival philosophy of a people in a given time and place.[8]

Linked to improvisation, the ability to worry the line is a powerful resource for living in an unpredictable world. The sampling, mixing, and mashups of contemporary hip-hop are the most recent extensions of the blues impulse to worry the line. Neither race, gender, class, ethnicity, nor age limit this power. The blues, Murray repeatedly insists, is an Omni-American response that influences the dominant culture in significant ways. The blues is not proprietary but imitative and contagious, shaped by procedure and custom but primarily by improvisations. The blues provides a context for transforming a miserable existence into a heroic life. Just as worrying the line is really a matter of innovation and improvisation, the blues isn't about staying blue but about moving beyond the tragic and pathological dimensions of life through a brave confrontation and affirmation of what remains possible. The blues is art as celebration, an act of stylizing a particular existential condition into significance.

Like the paradoxical trajectory of human experience that it describes, the blues functions in a paradoxical way – as a highly pragmatic yet playful device for existential affirmation yet also as a strategy for acknowledging the fact that life is a low-down dirty shame, and also as a means for improvising or riffing on the exigencies of that predicament. As Albert Murray observes,

KIMBERLY R. CONNOR

I don't know of a more valid, reliable, comprehensive or sophisticated frame of reference for defining and recounting heroic action than is provided by the blues idiom which enables the creator to deal with tragedy, comedy, melodrama, and farce simultaneously.[9]

Hence philosophy (and in this case its twin, theology) is a more adequate and sufficient tool than social science to capture the richness of the blues experience and to characterize what Murray describes as the 'incontestably mulatto'[10] character of the Omni-American. There isn't a white blues or a black blues or a norm from which one contrasts deviations because the particulars of what causes the blues may be individual but the solution of stomping is shared. Taken to a higher level, the community becomes that of the Omni-Americans, a term that resolves, in some measure, the double consciousness that Du Bois describes in *The Souls of Black Folk*.[11] Black and white Americans are partners, willing or unwilling, in a single enterprise of living in the hyphen: the space between African and American, sorrow and joy, work and play, and heaven and hell. 'For all their traditional antagonisms and obvious differences, the so-called black and so-called white people of the United States resemble nobody else in the world so much as they resemble each other.'[12] Hope, therefore, is not an optimistic abstraction but a discipline to be practiced in a ritual way that makes community possible.

Prayer

One is seldom alone in stomping the blues. As described by Murray in his swinging prose, the Omni-American bluesman is, fundamentally, not a just a metaphysician but an ethicist:

> Extemporizing in response to the exigencies of the situation in which he finds himself, he is confronting, acknowledging, and contending with the infernal absurdities and ever-impending frustrations inherent in the nature of all existence by playing with the possibilities that are also there.[13]

As a 'humanizer of chaos,'[14] the blues reveals a sense of connection to a philosophy, a way of negotiating the world from which blues people are alienated that does not concede existential power to the dominant class. The blues humanizes the chaos of life by, among other things, retaining, in the midst of suffering, togetherness as a sense of cultural being and finding ways to use the blues idiom as prayer, as an agent of change.

The hope beneath the despair of the blues is what Martin Luther King, Jr. heard, and his success as a reformer is due, in part, to his appreciation of the blues. His strategy of direct action through non-violent resistance was an elegant example of the signifying – the practice in African American culture, involving a verbal strategy of indirection that exploited the gap between the denotative and figurative meanings of words – that goes on in the blues. He turned a passive act into an active one, emphasizing the discipline and skill required to remain pacifist in the midst of violence by rearranging the terms of the action and adding a negative prefix: 'non.' Choosing not to fight became, therefore, a new way of worrying the line and in the estimation of Henry Louis Gates Jr was 'one of the most magnificent things anybody ever invented in the civil rights movement.'[15]

The blues is seldom associated with Martin Luther King, Jr. but its idiom was foundational to his life and career. In an opening address to the 1964 Berlin Jazz Festival, King offered remarks that give us insights that, in true blues fashion, circle back to where we began by considering the relationship between the blues and religious faith. Indeed, King began by identifying the blues as originating from a divine source:

God has wrought many things out of oppression. He has endowed his creatures with the capacity to create – and from this capacity has flowed the sweet songs of sorrow and joy that have allowed man to cope with his environment and many different situations [...] The Blues tell the story of life's difficulties, and if you think for a moment, you will realize that they take the hardest realities of life and put them into music, only to come out with some new hope or sense of triumph. This is triumphant music.

He went on to worry the line, to suggest that jazz

has continued in this tradition, singing the songs of a more complicated urban existence. When life itself offers no order and meaning, the musician creates an order and meaning from the sounds of the earth which flow through his instrument.

He continued his brief comments by crediting musicians as the leaders in the American search for identity and the inspiration behind his movement:

Long before the modern essayists and scholars wrote of racial identity as a problem for a multiracial world, musicians were returning to their roots to affirm that which was stirring within their souls. Much of the power of our Freedom Movement in the United States has come from this music. It has strengthened us with its sweet rhythms when courage began to fail. It has calmed us with its rich harmonies when spirits were down.

Certainly aware of the ironies of speaking in Berlin before the wall came down, King concluded by lifting his comments out of the particular and in to the universal:

> For in the particular struggle of the Negro in America there is something akin to the universal struggle of modern man. Everybody has the Blues. Everybody longs for meaning. Everybody needs to love and be loved. Everybody needs to clap hands and be happy. Everybody longs for faith. In music, especially this broad category called Jazz, there is a stepping-stone toward all of these.[16]

King's comments are echoed by Cornel West, who cites the blues as the most effective strategy for dealing with the lingering and catastrophic effects of an 'empire in decline, a democracy in decay, and a civilization that is wobbling and wavering.' The problems society faces go beyond the mere 'problematic' and require 'fundamental transformation,' West pronounces, that can be found in the blues, 'an autobiographical chronicle of personal catastrophe expressed lyrically [...] with grace and dignity.'[17]

What makes the blues effective as an agent for social change is its ability to show us how to live with integrity while accepting the contingencies of radical disappointment and profound disenchantment. The blues gives one the context and method for organizing and mobilizing around common concerns while at the same time providing the opportunity for the individual, so often lost in the mass of human need, to have a moment of single recognition and identity as the author of her own song, her own struggles, her own blues. To stick to one's calling as a blues person, however, requires support and, according to West, 'a courageous few who are leavening a loaf'[18] by bearing witness to the truth of our circumstances. Martin Luther King, Jr. was one such bluesman who offered a model for how to live a sanctified life.

That King was and West is Christian presents no existential conflict. Indeed, philosophy and theology are two sides of the same coin, a feature apparent in the ways one bluesman adopted King's cause as a subject for his music. 'Alabama Bus,' a blues song by Brother Will Hairston, illustrates the dualistic role of the blues: providing relief through its religious sensibilities and signifying to criticize society. Like the civil rights movement itself, which advanced a secular cause of justice motivated by spiritual indignation, 'Alabama Bus' rides the road on which both the spirituals and the blues travel. The song tells the story of the Montgomery bus boycott, beginning with a chorus that is a repetitive protest against the system that discriminated against African-Americans: 'Stop that Alabama bus / I don't wanna ride.' The mythic narrative sung by the bluesman who tells of a 'bus that don't have no load' punctuates the collective chorus. The song continues with an account of a particular individual's experience of discrimination.

A black man boards an empty bus and pays his fare. However, he is not allowed to sit where he wants. The bus driver acknowledges the fact of payment but threatens to fine the man if he doesn't take his 'proper' place. The existential condition of the passenger, of course, transcends the circumstances of the bus and, as the song progresses, Brother Hairston redefines what 'proper' can be, transforming the dominant racist culture's depiction of an African-American's place at the back of the bus. In this brief account delivered as a blues composition, Brother Hairston illustrates the social challenges faced by African-Americans and gives voice to the indignities discrimination generates. But the blues lament is imbued with religious elements, particularly the invocation of Reverend Martin Luther King, 'the man God sent out in the world.' Drawing directly from the historical foundations of black spirituality, God is identified as one who intervenes in history, just as God sent Moses, also referenced by Brother Hairston and compared to King.

If we compare the present circumstances with the biblical past, the bluesman not only elevates the actions of the resisting passenger but gives him a role to play in a grand and sacred drama. Just as God delivered the Israelites in Egypt by anointing Moses to lead them out of slavery, African-Americans will find their collective deliverance by following their ordained leader, King, who will lead them from the back of the bus. King's lament in the song to 'treat us right' resonates with his response to the criticism of eight white clergymen as set forth in the 'Letter from Birmingham Jail.' The clergy had stated that King had no business in Alabama because he wasn't a resident there; they also urged the blacks in Alabama to withdraw their support of King and other civil rights leaders. King, however, affirmed his right to be in Alabama because 'injustice anywhere is a threat to justice everywhere.' Furthermore, he established the difference between just laws 'rooted in eternal law and natural law' that uplift, and unjust laws, such as the black codes of segregation, that degrade. King declared that it was humanity's obligation to defy any laws that were not just.[19]

As the song continues, it reaffirms the fact that African-Americans were being denied privileges despite their contributions to the general welfare of the nation. Brother Hairston makes a classic blues maneuver and particularizes the cultural struggle by citing his own father, left blind by World War II but unable to reap the benefits of that war. Finally the song returns to King's story of imprisonment and pays tribute to him and his followers who substitute the pain of segregation for walking 'along the streets until their feets was sore.' Throughout the song there is a cry for recognition of humanity – 'Lord, there comes a bus don't have no load / You know, they tell me that a human being stepped on board' – that culminates in a classic blues statement Hairston attributes to King: 'a man ain't nothing but a man.'

There will always be a reason to sing the blues. But sometimes, when the song is sung, it tells a story that makes you want to pray along with Dr King that 'the deep fog of misunderstanding will be lifted from our fear-drenched communities and in some not too distant tomorrow the radiant stars of love and brotherhood will shine over our great nation with all their scintillating beauty.'[20]

NOTES

1 Martin Luther King Jr., 'On the importance of jazz: Opening address to the 1964 Berlin Jazz Festival,' (1964, http://www.hartford-hwp.com/archives/45a/626.html).

2 Ibid.

3 Victor Turner, *Dramas, Fields, and Metaphors: Symbolic Action in Human Society* (Ithaca, NY: Cornell University Press, 1974).

4 Mircea Eliade, *Cosmos and History: The Myth of the Eternal Return*, trans. Willard R. Trask (New York: Harper & Row, 1959).

5 Frederick Douglass, *Narrative of the Life of Frederick Douglass, An American Slave* (New York: Penguin Books, 1981), pp. 57–58.

6 Keneth Kinnamon and Michel Fabre (Eds.), *Conversations with Richard Wright* (Jackson, MS: University of Mississippi Press, 1993), p. 4.

7 Albert Murray, *The Hero and the Blues* (Columbia, MO: University of Missouri Press, 1973), p. 33.

8 Murray, *The Omni-Americans* (New York: Outerbridge and Dienstfrey, 1970).

9 Albert Murray, *The Hero and the Blues*, p. 33.

10 Murray, *The Omni-Americans*, p. 58.

11 W. E. B. DuBois, 'The souls of black folk.' In *Writings* (New York: Literary Classics of the United States, 1986), pp. 364–365.

12 Murray, *The Omni-Americans*, p. 22.

13 Murray, *The Omni-Americans*, p. 58.

14 Murray, *The Omni-Americans*, p. 63.

15 Henry Louis Gates, Jr., 'The king of cats,' *The New Yorker* (April 8, 1996), p. 73.

16 This and the three preceding quotes are from David Kyuman Kim, 'Democracy, the catastrophic, and courage: An conversation with Cornel West and David Kyuman Kim,' *Theory and Event* 12:4 (2009).

17 Kim, 'Democracy, the catastrophic, and courage.'

18 Kim, 'Democracy, the catastrophic, and courage.'

19 Martin Luther King Jr., 'Letter from Birmingham Jail.' In James M. Washington (Ed.), *Testament of Hope: The Essential Writings of Martin Luther King Jr.* (New York: Harper and Row, 1986), p. 293.

20 Ibid., p. 302.

THE BLUE LIGHT WAS MY BABY AND THE RED LIGHT WAS MY MIND: RELIGION AND GENDER IN THE BLUES

CHAPTER 14

LADY SINGS THE BLUES

A Woman's Perspective on Authenticity

White people have no business playing the blues ever, at all, under any circumstances. What the fuck do white people have to be blue about? Banana Republic ran out of khakis?

(George Carlin)[1]

What, indeed, do white people have to be blue about? The position that Carlin's clever remark sketches for us – that blues performance belongs exclusively to one group of people – can be reformulated as follows:

(1) In order for a person or group of persons legitimately to sing the blues, they must suffer, or have suffered, in the relevant way.

(2) White people do not suffer, or have not suffered, in the relevant way.

(3) Therefore, white people 'have no business' singing the blues.

The argument above captures a few related objections to white people performing the blues. Some blues purists object for largely aesthetic reasons – the blues just doesn't ring true somehow when

Blues – Philosophy for Everyone: Thinking Deep About Feeling Low, First Edition.
Edited by Jesse R. Steinberg and Abrol Fairweather.
© 2012 John Wiley & Sons, Inc. Published 2012 by John Wiley & Sons, Inc.

interpreted and performed by whites. Others suggest that, in addition to this aesthetic problem, there are good *moral* reasons for white musicians to abstain from adopting – and profiting from – the blues style. These objections invoke the idea of ownership, and of these what amounts to cultural theft is the most serious charge. We'll look briefly at a couple of these arguments later. Though there may be reasons in favor of rejecting the first premise of the argument altogether, let's assume for the sake of discussion that there is a certain kind of lived experience that may be vital to blues performance – for both artist and audience. Absent this experience, blues musicians offend at best aesthetically and at worst morally. For the most part, it will be the second premise with which I take issue in this essay; I will argue that at least some white people suffer in the right sort of way and that it is very much their business to sing the blues.

I'm going to try to show that, at the very least, women – whether black or white – are entitled to sing the blues, and they ought to be encouraged to do so. From Ma Rainey and Bessie Smith to Bettye Lavette and Bonnie Raitt, the history of the blues is backed by a chorus of powerful female voices. I hope I can persuade you that the importance of the blues for women's expression crosses racial and ethnic boundaries, and that the social frustrations faced by women – from sexual politics to unfairness in the work world – provide a compelling answer to the challenge of inauthenticity. The blues has been and continues to be an important medium for the promotion of women's sexuality and independence. The blues can be performed authentically by women of any race or ethnicity, owing to their shared experiences of oppression.

So it was, out of oppression, that one of the most influential musical and lyrical styles in history was born and, although the effects of oppression tend to be silencing, there's nothing silent about the blues. We can't help but listen, and we can't help but respond. It's no accident that the blues has the emotional power it does – it's a dialogue between the artist and her instrument, her band, and the audience that harkens back to the call-and-response field hollers, work songs, and reinterpreted spirituals of the eighteenth century and before. The form of the blues is, without question, an African-American creation, and possesses a unique ability to communicate the full range and depth of emotional experience. Much early, and some contemporary, blues satirizes and provides escape from the oppressed conditions experienced by its black authors and originators.

MEGHAN WINSBY

Why so Blue?

So what does it mean to 'suffer' in the way that's relevant to the blues experience? The objection that white blues is inauthentic because white people don't get the blues assumes that the kind of feeling required to perform the blues convincingly is acquired through group affiliation. Blues purists of this sort claim that white people lack some crucial experience that is key to the blues aesthetic, and so the very fact that they are members of the white cultural majority detracts from the performance. It takes away from the *believability* of the performance, and this is crucial to the blues experience for both artist and audience. And so purists like Carlin can mock 'white blues' because white people, they contend, have nothing to be blue about.

In the very early days of the blues and its roots, the black population of the United States under slavery comprised a group that suffered under the full weight of oppression. Despite the depth of time and tremendous social change since slavery's end, discrimination, marginalization, and acts of violence and intolerance have continued to be a part of the lived experience of many African-Americans. The blues as creation, response, and catharsis, then, arose out of the enduring condition of an oppressed people. Black oppression did not vanish with the abolition of slavery.

The late political and feminist philosopher Iris Marion Young offered a philosophical treatment of oppression that will be useful, I think, for this discussion. All oppressed people, she said, 'suffer some inhibition of their ability to develop and exercise their capacities and express their needs, thoughts, and feelings.'[2] So, what unites oppressed social groups – blacks, women, gays and lesbians, the disabled, and the elderly, to name a few – is that their members face this condition under which their goals and preferences may be chosen for them and their own voices silenced.

Though it gives us a starting point, this paints a pretty broad picture of oppression. One might say, for example, that anyone can look at this characterization of what it means to be oppressed and fit herself into it somehow. Also, the oppressive circumstances facing women must surely differ in cause, degree, and expression from those facing blacks. Furthermore (though somewhat obviously), it is important to point out that there is overlap between these and other groups. Does this mean black women are *doubly* oppressed? There is considerable sociological, feminist, activist, and philosophical literature devoted to elucidating the complexities involved in this question, and, without a doubt, on this view oppression admits of degrees. That is, it is certainly possible to be *more* or *less* oppressed. However, quantifying oppression – as one might imagine – is exceedingly difficult. There is no quick and dirty oppression meter.

Young went on to talk about 'five faces' of oppression. These faces name five conditions that variously influence the social lives of oppressed groups; namely, exploitation, marginalization, powerlessness, cultural imperialism, and violence. So, in order to make sense of a given social group's experience of oppression, we need to consider the effects that these forces have on the lives of its members. Under slavery, it is safe to say, blacks experienced fully every one of these forces. Slavery is paradigmatically the most oppressive circumstance under which a human being can live. However, it is important to bear in mind that our concept of oppression here is not as simple as the domination of one identifiable group over another. As we use the term today, 'oppression' is much more complex and refers to various social groups in contemporary liberal democratic societies. Oppression in the sense we are considering exists as a state of *imbalance* among the power relations between classes, races, genders, and ages. It can be conscious and/or unconscious, subtle, and self-perpetuating. Viewing social conditions in this way, Young said, 'makes sense of much of our social experience.'[3]

It is not news that women share in the history, as well as in the present experience, of being oppressed. Women's oppression, in particular, cuts across divisions of race, class, age, ability, and so on, and constitutes – along with race and class – one of the most basic structures of oppression. Women continue to struggle with discrimination, sexual objectification and abuse, domestic violence, and gender norms that tend to reinforce these conditions. Despite many positive social changes over the last century, they also experience exploitation of their labor both privately and professionally. On this Young wrote:

> women undergo specific forms of gender exploitation in which their energies and power are expended, often unnoticed and unacknowledged, usually to benefit men by releasing them for more important and creative work, enhancing their status or the environment around them, or providing them with sexual or emotional service.[4]

So, bringing us back to Carlin's question as to what it is white people have to be blue about, it would seem that we have a candidate subgroup of non-blacks – namely, women – who share in the sort of experience that

MEGHAN WINSBY

frustrates personal autonomy, self-expression, and social mobility in a way that lends a key component of believability to a blues performance.

Women and the Blues

The emergence of the blues into mainstream music followed and coincided to some extent with the expansion of women into the sphere of professional musicians (from the 1870 into the 1900s). Prior to the late nineteenth century, opportunities for women to become career musicians – with the exception of pianists – were pretty limited.[5] Like all steps forward for women's participation in social and professional life, the growing number of women pursuing musical careers was met with controversy and derision. Some detractors even went so far as to mark it the 'degeneracy' of the art. By 1900, however, music as a profession was a common choice for more and more women entering the world of work.

At the outset of this trend, English art critic John Ruskin had this to offer women seeking to find work as musicians:

> Advice to young women: In music especially you will soon find what personal benefit there is in being serviceable [...] Get your voice disciplined and clear, and think only of accuracy; never of effect or expression: if you have any soul worth ex-pressing, it will show itself in your singing; but most likely there are very few feelings in you, at present, needing any particular expression; and the one thing you have to do is make a clear-voiced little instrument of yourself, which other people can depend upon for the note wanted.[6]

It is significant, then, that among the first to record the blues were black women. The first vocal blues recording by an African-American, in 1920, was Mamie Smith's 'Crazy Blues.' The recording became widely popular, and paved the way for a generation of successful female blues singers. These included Ma Rainey (1886–1939), Ida Cox (1896–1967), Alberta Hunter (1895–1984), and Bessie Smith (1894–1937), to name a few. Though there were fewer women musicians of the older, country blues form, women were at the forefront of the more commercial urban blues – the 'classic' female blues of the twenties. This popularity of women's blues among blacks as well as among whites is telling, considering the prevailing attitude toward women generally and toward women as musicians. The idea of a female blues singer who embodied strength, independence, and some degree of sexual freedom was *novel*, though less so to her black audience.[7] It signified the beginning of a mainstream cultural shift toward stronger voices for women in public and political life – marked most vividly in 1920, when women's right to vote was universally recognized in the United States. Against the backdrop of a patriarchal, white, middle-class social order, early blueswomen defied convention and demonstrated that in fact there *were* a few feelings women needed to express.

When Lucille Bogan cried out for her 'sweet black angel,' loving 'the way he spreads his wings,' she was participating openly in a dialogue steeped in explicit sexual reference and metaphor – stepping out from the prescribed sphere of appropriate female behavior, where women were expected to be demure, subservient, and 'ladylike.'[8] Moreover, she did so, for the most part, in an environment of public acceptance. Blueswomen were icons within as well as outside the black community of the time. It is in this sense that the history of the blues as a black form and its history as a women's form are bound together.

The structures and language of the blues have afforded women a safe forum in which to acknowledge and celebrate their sexuality since the early days of the genre, when African-American blueswomen challenged the status quo by objectifying their male objectifiers. Women urban and country blues artists asserted their sexuality alongside male performers. Though the early blueswomen, with their provocative and sometimes downright raunchy lyrics, may not have been consciously furthering feminist concerns or knowingly opening feminist dialogue, the lack of censorship and the encouragement of defiant, sexually aggressive lyrics allowed women to express themselves openly and equally with men. Examples of this expression vary as to how overt they are. So, Memphis Minnie sang in 'If you see my Rooster' (2008),

> If you see my rooster, please run him back on home
> If you see my rooster, please run him back on home
> I haven't found no eggs in my basket, since my rooster been gone.

And, more blatantly, Dorthea Trowbridge and Stump Johnson's 'Steady Grinding' has the lyric (1933),

> Ain't but the one thing that makes me sore
> When you grind me one time and just won't do it no more.

  MEGHAN WINSBY

The blues not only facilitates the expression of female sexuality, but has historically given voice – literally and figuratively – to women musicians wishing to confront the social, political, and material conditions of their lives. Themes of role reversal, independence, and protest against physical abuse permeate the lyrical content of women's blues. This was true of early blueswomen; for example, here are some lyrics from Bessie Smith's 'Young Woman's Blues' (1929):

> I'm as good as any woman in your town
> I ain't no high yella, I'm a deep killer brown
> I ain't gonna marry, ain't gonna settle down
> I'm gonna drink good moonshine and run these browns down

And the same is true for contemporary blueswomen. Here are some lyrics from Bonnie Raitt's 'Hell to Pay' (1994):

> Hey Mister, we want you to know
> We think you've taken this about as far as it can go
> It's about to Blow
> You got nowhere to run, why don't you sit back and watch the show?
> You used to drop your little darlin' off at Sunday School
> Family values while you're getting some behind the pool
> She's nobody's fool
> So don't be actin' surprised when your daughter wants it bad as you

Despite the talent, strength, and charismatic personalities of its popular female performers, the blues itself has been a male-dominated genre for most of its history.[9] The initial popularity of women's blues in the twenties wound down toward the end of the decade. The association of blues music with the bluesman – the solo guitarist/vocalist – has relevance to our present question. The question 'can, or should, white *men* play the blues?' is far too commonly posed to be ignored.[10] Though I am confident that women – black and non-black – have a case when it comes to the experiential element to authentic blues performance, I don't know that I have a straightforward response to Carlin's question for white, middle-class men. Let's take another look at Carlin's stern treatment of white blues performers, via his elaboration:

> White people ought to understand that it's their job to *give* people the blues, not to get them. And certainly not to sing or play them. I'll tell you

a little secret about the blues, folks: it's not enough to know which notes to play, you need to know *why* they need to be played.[11]

My answer to Carlin is that women, as a group, have suffered the silencing effects of oppressive cultural practices and attitudes. Many women blues musicians know exactly *why* they need to sing and play the notes they do. The blues helped many of them find their voice, as the early blueswomen brought the conditions not only of black experience but also of women's experience to public notice. The experience of being systematically unheard – of having one's frustrations ignored – by a male, white, middle-class majority is the kind of suffering that delivers the blues. And playing the blues delivers us *from* that experience.

Stealing the Blues

It is important, I think, to turn now by way of acknowledgment to the moral arguments against white people playing the blues. In addition to the specific, experiential element of authentic blues performance we've been looking at so far, there are other arguments leveled against the acceptability of white blues. Those who take offense at white blues performance may do so for a variety of reasons: maybe white people just can't effectively imitate the style; perhaps, as some critics have argued, the blues as a whole has become 'diluted'[12] under the influence of its white consumers and performers; or – as we've been discussing – perhaps non-black performers can't really *feel* the blues. However, these are largely aesthetic criticisms.

The more serious objections to white people performing the blues include charges of inauthenticity, but go further and suggest that white people who adopt the blues style are engaging in harmful cultural appropriation. This objection has a *moral* as well as an aesthetic dimension, so that merely calling attention to successful and talented white blues musicians such as Johnny Winter or Susan Tedeschi in the hopes of settling the issue of whether white people can play the blues just won't do. The sense of 'can' here has nothing to do with whether they are able to play and instead refers to whether they ought to play. Pointing to blues music we like that is performed by white artists who display great skill – or effective imitation of the blues style – would be too dismissive. The fact that white artists *can* and *do* play the blues will not satisfy those who believe the artists don't have the right kind of relationship to the blues. It will not count in favor of whether white musicians *should* adopt the style.

Cultural appropriation

Behind allegations of cultural appropriation lies a sort of rights-based moral objection to the use of the blues style by non-blacks. The charge is that, owing to its history and cultural importance, the blues *belongs* to blacks. Essentially, cultural appropriation (or *mis*appropriation) amounts to the theft of this cultural property. As James Young explains, cultural appropriation is a species of the broader phenomenon of 'voice appropriation' and is an issue that extends beyond the case of the blues. It 'can arise in the context of any multicultural society.'[13] In addition to the worry of a sort of theft taking place is the concern that the adoption of a minority culture's unique symbols, stories, and linguistic and other style elements has the potential to cause harm to this culture by misrepresenting them to members of the majority.

Familiar examples of this kind of misrepresentation can be found in portrayals of Native Americans in the movies and on television, which often feature ceremonial dress and references to 'the Great Spirit' and to other spiritual beliefs and practices that are out of context. Whether portrayed as the 'Noble Savage' or the blood-thirsty Indian, many portrayals of Native Americans in pop culture represent a distortion; one that has arisen from a long history of misunderstanding and misrepresentation of Native culture on the part of the white cultural majority. A further worry, in terms of propagating negative cultural stereotypes, is that the minority group itself (and, in particular, its younger members) is faced with mixed representations, and some degree of misunderstanding of their *own* culture and group identity can result.

The blues style is, in a sense, a living artifact of African-Americans' cultural heritage and identity. So, when Bonnie Raitt belts out a verse and Eric Clapton bends a blue note, they are participating in a style – in a sense, adopting a language – that they can only ever understand from the outside, in virtue of their membership in majority culture. The blues form, to continue the metaphor, can only ever be their *second* language.

Appropriation of audience

Another side to this ownership argument addresses the appropriation of *audiences*. When members of the white majority produce blues music, the objection goes, they are limiting the audience for black blues musicians.

The suggestion is that audiences can only consume so much blues and will be faithful to a limited number of artists. Hence, the more white blues there is, the less room there is for black blues artists to find an audience for their music.[14]

A perusal of the music/guitar magazine stand will confirm the disproportionate audience reception of white blues. Why, for example, do women such as Bonnie Raitt and Susan Tedeschi (somewhat rare as female blues singers/guitar players) get more press – why are they featured in more music magazines and better publicized – than black women blues singers/guitarists such as Debora Coleman and Beverly 'Guitar' Watkins? Critics of white blues have pointed to this issue and to the unfairness inherent in white performers enjoying more success than black performers of equal skill and experience.

Even if it were the case that without white-biased blues journalism black women artists would be more popular than at present, it seems that this does not speak to the credibility – or lack thereof – of the blues performances themselves. Does blame for the harm here rest with the artists themselves or is it rather an expression of the deeper fact that racism and white-bias still persist in mainstream culture more generally? The fact that racism persists is certainly undesirable, and it may be that we can encourage important changes through certain kinds of social interventions. However, it is difficult to see how calling for white blues players to abstain from playing would address this problem in any positive way. One would think, intuitively, that discouraging young musicians who are not black from playing the blues – because the blues belongs to somebody else – may serve only to drive the racial wedge in further.

The question of how to go about respecting the cultural property rights of African-American blues musicians presents us with a whole host of interesting – and important – further questions about the borrowing, covering, sampling, flat-out plagiarizing, and other forms of adoption of the blues form by artists who are not African-American. For example, are the concerns different – or more/less worrisome – when a white artist is covering a particular blues song written by an African-American, rather than performing an original blues composition? How do we determine the body of blues compositions to which blacks have these cultural property rights, especially in light of the genre's nearly immeasurable influence on rock 'n' roll, soul/R&B, and country? At the very least, do the artists have an obligation to address these social issues in their music?

Whether or not you think it makes sense to talk about the blues as though certain groups of people have – or don't have – ownership and performance 'rights' to the art form, we can say for now that these concerns at the very least give us reason to tread carefully. The blues as an art form has an important cultural history, and in particular has special significance to black history and culture. The suggestion that the use of the blues style by non-blacks may under some circumstances misappropriate an important expression of cultural identity for African-Americans has a great deal of weight.

Conclusion

To summarize, my modest aim in this essay has been to meet the aesthetic challenge that white people lack the experience of the blues necessary to perform convincingly. I hope to have shown that at least some white people – women – share with other oppressed groups a history and experience of social frustration and silencing that brings with it the emotional center of the blues aesthetic. Those of us who are not black musicians but nonetheless adopt the blues style must be careful which elements of the blues and its language we emphasize, so as not to engage in the kind of bad imitation and misrepresentation that results in harmful caricature. However, those who still object that there is something aesthetically suspect about whites performing the blues – ever, at all, under any circumstances – should be just as careful not to cartoon their targets. As a white woman I frequently have the blues, occasionally sing the blues, and, if Banana Republic were to run out of khakis, I'd be the last to know.

NOTES

1 George Carlin, *You are All Diseased* (United States: MPI Studios, 2003).
2 Iris Marion Young, *Justice and the Politics of Difference* (Princeton, NJ: Princeton University Press, 1990), p. 40.
3 Young, *Justice and the Politics of Difference*, p. 39.
4 Ibid., p. 51.
5 See Judith Tisk, 'Women as professional musicians in the United States,' *Anuario Interamericano de Investigacion Musical* 9 (1973), pp. 95–133; also Adrienne Fried Block and Nancy Stewart, 'Women in American Music, 1800–1918' In Karen Pendle (Ed.), *Women and Music: A History* (Bloomington and Indianapolis, IN: Indiana University Press, 1991), pp. 142–172.

6   John Ruskin, preface to the 1871 edition of *Sesame and Lilies*, as cited in Tisk, 'Women as professional musicians in the United States,' p. 96.

7   See Michael J. Budds 'African-American women in blues and jazz.' In Karen Pendle (Ed.), *Women and Music: A History* (Bloomington and Indianapolis, IN: Indiana University Press, 1991): pp. 282–297. Women have a long history of participation in African-American music, and songs celebrating the powers and commanding personalities of the 'voodoo queens'/priestess figures influenced the stage personae of early blueswomen.

8   This is from 'Black Angel Blues,' one of Bogan's tamer compositions.

9   This is particularly true of female electric guitar players (see Maria V. Johnson, 'Electric guitarists, blues, and authenticity.' In *Black Women and Music* (Urbana and Chicago, IL: University of Illinois Press, 2007)), though there are several notable exceptions, such as Memphis Minnie, Deborah Coleman, Bonnie Raitt, and Susan Tedesci.

10 See, for example, Ralph J. Gleason, 'Can the white man sing the blues?' *Jazz and Pop* (1968), pp. 28–29 and, as a more recent example, James O. Young, 'Should white men play the blues?' *Journal of Value Inquiry* 28 (1994), pp. 415–424.

11 Carlin, *You Are All Diseased.*

12 See Paul Garon, *Blues and the Poetic Spirit* (London: Eddison Press, 1975).

13 Voice appropriation involves adopting the perspective of a member of another social/cultural group as a means of artistic expression. As well as borrowing cultural elements, voice appropriation can include adopting the perspective of a member of a different sex, sexual orientation, and so on from which to create a work of art. See James O. Young, 'Should white men play the blues?' p. 416.

14 Ibid.

CHAPTER 15

EVEN WHITE FOLKS GET THE BLUES

It is a commonplace belief among many people that only black musicians can play the blues. Almost by definition, the belief goes, a white (or Hispanic or Asian) musician cannot really be a blues musician. This is not a belief shared by many of the most important blues musicians.

In his introduction to *Moanin' at Midnight*, B. B. King's very interesting biography of his friend Howlin' Wolf, King writes:

He was fifteen years older than I was, but I found out he and I listened to a lot of the same blues singers when we were coming up. Like me, he loved Blind Lemon Jefferson, a bluesman who came from Texas, not the Mississippi Delta. Like me, he sang along to the records of Jimmie Rodgers, the Father of Country Music, who was really a blues singer who happened to be white.[1]

Thus, B. B. King, whose credentials as one of the pre-eminent blues performers in the world cannot be questioned, regards Jimmie Rodgers as a blues musician. His whiteness is a matter of indifference.

Blues – Philosophy for Everyone: Thinking Deep About Feeling Low, First Edition.
Edited by Jesse R. Steinberg and Abrol Fairweather.
© 2012 John Wiley & Sons, Inc. Published 2012 by John Wiley & Sons, Inc.

Howlin' Wolf himself also took a color-blind approach to the blues:

A lot of poor white folks come out of the South playing good music, y'know what I mean? You see, the peoples that come up the hard way – that come up sufferin' – they can play that music, and they can sing them songs, them old songs [...] We got some white players play good music that come out of the South. Now you take these white kids in the North, y'know, they don't know what it means. They're just playing. They just want to be out there under the blue lights [...] Now you take the white peoples way back, they used to play that long-haired music. You'd get tired and brood over it over the night. But they'd done had a plenty, them rich folk, and they haven't had no ups and downs back there like the poor white man. The poor white man come out of Arkansas, Mississippi, and Alabama [...] them guys could play some music [...] They come along on that same track that I fall on.[2]

Howlin' Wolf ignores a musician's color and looks to the details of his life to see whether he is a blues player. If a person experiences the ups and downs, the hard knocks he himself experienced, he is ready to call that person a blues musician. Without the right type of experience, a musician is 'just playing.'[3] Given what B. B. King says about Howlin' Wolf's development, it seems clear that Howlin' Wolf regarded Jimmie Rodgers as a blues musician even though he was white.

Perhaps the most succinct summary of the views of many blues artists about whether white musicians can play the blues was expressed by a black blues player interviewed in 1981 by a local Boston television station: 'Even white folks get the blues.' His statement is a rich source for thinking about who can play the blues and for understanding why it is claimed that only black musicians can play the blues. The term 'get' can be used in many different ways. It can, for example, be used to talk about having experiences. We say that people 'get excited about music,' and we often say that one 'gets sick' or 'gets religion.' Let us call this the 'experiential' sense of 'get.' 'To get the blues' in the experiential sense of 'get' is to have the blues; that is, it is to experience a type of profound sadness. This experiential sense of 'get' is used by many to say that only black musicians can play the blues by arguing that, in order to get the blues in the experiential sense, one has to live the life of life characterized by deprivation and misery that middle-class Americans and Europeans do not live. (Howlin' Wolf in the quotation above seems to be thinking about the blues somewhat in these terms.)

Another sense of 'get' is found in expressions such as 'I just don't get these instructions' and 'I just don't get why you did that.' It is the 'get' of understanding or comprehension. We do not get instructions when we do not understand them; we do not get people's actions when we cannot make sense of them. The 'get' of comprehension involved in the blues is really two different types. First of all, there is the understanding of the lyrics and the meaning(s) behind them. Many people link the understanding of the lyrics of the blues with a narrow view about the experiential sense of 'get' and say that without living a life of deprivation and misery one cannot comprehend the lyrics of the blues.

But there is a second type of comprehension. It is the 'getting' (understanding) of the music of the blues. While many people overlook this aspect of the blues – perhaps because it is technical – it is crucial, for without the music of the blues there would be no blues. If we think only about the comprehensive 'getting' of the music of the blues, it seems fairly clear that a variety of musicians get the blues. The basic blues song is a twelve-bar song whose music and lyrics follow an AAB pattern. Howlin' Wolf's 'I've Been Abused' (1999) follows this pattern:

> All my life I've caught it hard.
> All my life I've caught it hard.
> I've been abused and I've been scorned.
> I feel so bad; this ain't gonna last.
> I feel so bad; this ain't gonna last.
> I've been scorned and I've been kicked out.

The AAB pattern is not, however, an absolute requirement. For example, Howlin' Wolf's famous 'Smokestack Lightnin'' (1956) does not follow this pattern:

> Ah, oh, smokestack lightning
> Shinin', just like gold
> Why don't ya hear me cryin'?
> Ah, whoo hoo, ooh...
> Whoo...
> Whoa, oh, tell me, baby
> What's the matter with you?
> Why don't ya hear me cryin'?
> Whoo hoo, whoo hoo
> Whoo...

Usually, blues music contains only three or four basic chords repeated in various permutations. The basic framework for the lyrics is twelve bars in a 4/4 time signature. To understand this basic framework and to see how lyrics interact with the music, we can look at a specific example: Robert Johnson's recording of 'Sweet Home Chicago.' This is a very good example of a twelve-bar blues song. It starts out with a progression of notes called the 'turnaround,' which is repeated with some variation throughout the song and indicates a repetition. At the end of the progression, the first verse, 'Oh, baby don't you want to go,' is sung over an E chord for the word 'Oh' and an A chord for 'baby don't you want to go.' Johnson's singing is backed by a shuffle rhythm, which is a common blues (and later rock 'n' roll) rhythm that consists of two eighth notes that are played together repeatedly in a rhythm that can be vocalized as '*dow*-da *dow*-da *dow*-da *dow*-da.' For the second verse, when Johnson repeats the phrase 'Oh, baby don't you want to go,' the A chord is continued. There is then a change to a B7 chord and Johnson sings 'from the land of California.' After this line, he suggests a chord change back to A by bending a note at the seventh and eighth frets, emitting a very voice-like effect. Bending notes produces microtones, which are essentially the notes between the keys on a piano keyboard. (Microtonal variation has been used in many various styles of music, including Indian, Arabic, and even Asian music.) Over this section Johnson sings the lyrics 'To my sweet home Chicago.' Following this line the turnaround mentioned above occurs again, leading to a repetition of the structure just outlined.

There are many instrumental techniques that have been associated with blues music. One of the most notable examples is the use of a slide for ornamentation. The use of a slide on a stringed instrument to produce a voice-like effect has been associated with nearly every culture. It is believed that the idea of using a slide in blues music came from Hawaiian lap slide players, who used a metal bar to produce a variation in pitch. In Hawaiian culture, the instrument is placed on the lap instead of being held in the regular manner. In blues, most slide playing is done holding the guitar in the standard playing position, though the playing styles of The Black Ace and Oscar 'Buddy' Woods are notable exceptions. A slide can be made out of a variety of materials. The top of a glass bottle is often used as a slide, as is the smooth side of a pocket knife blade. Delta blues musician Mississippi Fred McDowell talks on his album *I Don't Play No Rock and Roll* about fashioning his slide out of a beef bone. A good example of a slide ornamentation in a blues song is Blind Willie Johnson's slide piece 'Dark was the Night (Cold was the Ground).' In this piece, Johnson plays a melody that is accompanied solely by his own wordless moaning. This piece is also notable because it is not a standard twelve-bar, three-chord piece; it consists entirely of one chord with no changes. The rhythm that is played also has a free rhythmic feel throughout.

Another technique that has long been associated with blues music is pitch-bending. This technique is in many ways very similar to the technique of the slide; it also produces microtones, again with a very vocal effect. The technique of pitch-bending is also very common in many musical cultures. Much of B. B. King's unique guitar style relies heavily on this technique (for a good example listen to his single-note beginning to the classic 'The Thrill is Gone,' with its extremely vocal quality). King admitted that he developed his bending technique while spending time with his cousin, Bukka White, who was a notable bluesman and slide player. King stated that, since he himself could not use a slide, he wanted to develop a technique that could emulate the voice-like tones of a slide player. The technique of pitch-bending is not, however, exclusive to B. B. King. Bent notes are used by nearly every blues guitarist. Especially notable are the early single-note styles of Lonnie Johnson and Eddie Lang. These two musicians were among the earliest blues players to incorporate a single-note style into their playing.

A number of blues musicians play in a finger-picking style. This style involves the use of a bass line played by the thumb as well as a melody line that is played using the fingers, all on the same guitar. Among the best of the musicians who use this style are Mississippi John Hurt, Blind Blake, and the Reverend Gary Davis. The style is generally associated with the blues of the Piedmont Region, but is also used within the Delta blues tradition as well in the Texas blues tradition.

Early blues music was acoustic since its practitioners often lived without electricity. When blues musicians moved from rural to more urban areas, they incorporated the electric guitar. Several musicians who learned acoustic blues adapted to electric instruments, for example B. B. King, Howlin' Wolf, Muddy Waters, and Albert King. Today, the use of electric instruments is widespread, even in Delta areas long dominated by acoustic blues. R. L. Burnside is an example of a Delta blues musician who has adopted electric instruments.

Various regions of the United States have their own unique sound. Already mentioned is Delta blues. The hallmarks of this type of blues are a more percussive musical attack and the use of a slide to outline the melody of the song. Another attribute of this style is the use of multiple rhythms during the same song. For an example of this style listen to Charley Patton's 'Screaming and Crying.' Other styles include Texas blues (which often contains a strong monotonic bass line under a finger-picked melody as well as a strong adherence to twelve-bar structure) and Chicago blues (marked by the use of electric instruments: usually using microphones to amplify instruments such as harmonicas, drums, and other ensemble instruments).

Although the blues has been historically thought of as a black art form, there have been many performers who are not black. Mike Bloomfield, who achieved fame playing with such bands as The Electric Flag, and Paul Butterfield (of the Paul Butterfield Blues Band) are good examples of important blues musicians who were not black. Another notable example of a white blues musician was Texas blues/rock guitarist Stevie Ray Vaughan, who greatly helped renew interest in the blues during his heyday in the 1980s. Today, such musicians as Scott Ainsley and Steve James help to keep the art of acoustic country blues alive by actively touring and releasing records. Roy Bookbinder, who studied and toured with the Reverend Gary Davis, is a white blues musician in the 'Piedmont' or 'East Coast' blues style. Chris Smither, equally at home in the folk tradition and the blues, continues the finger-picking blues style so common to several styles of the blues.

It is clear, then, that if we focus on the music of the blues – the technique of playing the music of the blues – different types of musicians can play the blues. It really is a matter of the skill and desire of the musician. Of course, going back to the quotation from Howlin' Wolf at the beginning of the essay, one can wonder whether playing the music is what he called 'just playing' without 'knowing what it means.' In order to really 'get' the blues, shouldn't one need to understand the lyrics of the blues? And, in order to understand the lyrics, doesn't one need to have a certain life story that only American blacks have had and can have?

How tied are a person's experiences to their understanding of words? Surely they are related, but how closely? It is clear that the experiences of black sharecroppers at the end of the nineteenth century (when the roots of the blues were formed) were different from the experiences of urban blacks of the 1940s and 1950s. The challenges and the ups and downs experienced by sharecroppers differed considerably from those of an urban black person. If we think that the blues comes from the share-croppers of the late nineteenth century and that their experiences are required to 'get' the blues, urban blacks such as Freddie King and Hubert Sumlin are not blues musicians. Even Muddy Waters and B. B. King, whose early years were spent among Southern black sharecroppers, would fail to qualify, for their most significant work took place far removed from the fields of the South. So, one should not link the ability to 'get' the blues with too narrow a historical period. Is there, however, a general culture that black musicians can participate in that other races cannot

DOUGLAS LANGSTON AND NATHANIEL LANGSTON

and that gives black musicians the ability to 'get' the blues? If there is such a general culture, is it truly unavailable to other racial groups?

Some recent analytical philosophers have investigated issues that shed some light on these questions in their discussions of the 'incommensurability of conceptual schemes.' In brief, one's conceptual scheme is that system of beliefs and assumptions through which one encounters and makes sense of the world. By and large, an individual's conceptual scheme is molded by the conceptual scheme of the culture the person is part of. It has been argued by Alasdair MacIntyre, for example, that the conceptual scheme of the early Middle Ages (Augustine and his followers) is incommensurable with the conceptual scheme of the ancient world (Aristotle and his followers).[4] The traditions are incommensurable because they disagree about the adequacy of the human mind to know its objects, about the nature of truth, and about the existence and nature of the will.[5] Other examples of incommensurable conceptual schemes include Aristotelian science and Newtonian science, and the incommensurability between such 'primitive' cultures as the indigenous cultures of Africa and the cultures of the European colonists of the nineteenth century. The general claim about these incommensurabilities is that the people in one culture or tradition live such different lives and make such different assumptions about the nature of reality and how to relate to it than the people of another culture that the people of the two cultures cannot really understand each other. It is as if they live in two completely different worlds and have no common basis for communication.

Philosophers such as Donald Davidson dismiss such incommensurabilites.[6] They argue that even radically diverse cultures have points of agreement that provide a basis for translating the language of one culture into the language of the other. But does translatability really equal commensurability? Many of us are familiar with travelling to a foreign country and using the appropriate foreign language phrase book.[7] When we want to find a bus or purchase a meal, we can look up the relevant phrase. The test of success is a pragmatic one: we catch the bus or we don't; we enjoy our desired meal or are served something completely unwanted. Being able to use a phrase book is not to be confused with knowing the appropriate language. To know a language is to be part of a network of associations and even non-linguistic actions and gestures that allows one to be linguistically creative in situations that a phrase book cannot anticipate.

Even speakers of roughly the same language experience a communication gap. The idioms and taken-for-granted knowledge of a person from New Jersey might not match those of someone from California – as someone from New Jersey discovers when he tries to order a hoagie at Tommy's Burgers in Los Angeles. Since English is an international language that is used by various cultures around the world, it has necessarily been stripped of its cultural underpinnings in England and the United States. It seems plausible to think that the blues might well be tied to a black culture whose linguistic nuances and idioms are not easily captured by the English spoken by most non-black Americans. Is there a gap of understanding that makes the blues inaccessible to musicians who are not black?

To answer this question we need to ask what is it that the lyrics of the blues express. How are these lyrics rooted in the unique experiences of those who 'get' the blues? Once again, Howlin' Wolf sheds some important light:

> A lot of people's wonderin', 'What is the blues?' I hear lots of people saying, 'The blues, the blues.' But I'm gonna tell you what the blues is: When you ain't got no money, you got the blues. When you ain't got no money to pay your house rent, you still got the blues. A lot of people's hollerin' about, 'I don't like no blues.' But when you ain't got no money and can't pay your house rent and can't buy you no food, you damn sure got the blues. That's where it's at, let me tell you. That's where it's at. If you ain't got no money, you got the blues, 'cause you're thinkin' evil. That's right. Any time you thinkin' evil, you thinkin' 'bout the blues.[8]

And at the second Ann Arbor Blues Festival, he said about the source for his blues:

> Some of you been mistreated and some of you have been drove from your door and some of you been treated like a dog. I know it, 'cause I been treated that way myself. Some of you, your folks is growing old. They didn't care about you. 'I have so much of worry. Sometime I could cry. But I'm going back to my mama's grave, fall on her tombstone and die.'[9]

Here he was talking about how his own mother turned him out at an early age and would not even acknowledge his existence later in life – all because he played the blues.

The experiences Howlin' Wolf is talking about are experiences human beings all have. We all feel mistreated at various times in our lives. Many of us have no money. Some of us lose our homes. A few of us are cursed by our mothers. We all hurt in various ways and understand what it is to hurt. The causes of our hurt may be different, but we all hurt in the same way. It is this common hurt that is the source of the blues. It is something we can all relate to and 'get' in both the experiential sense and the comprehension sense. If we go back to Howlin' Wolf's song 'I've Been Abused,' it is not hard to understand and identify with his complaints that 'he has caught it hard' and 'been abused' and 'been talked about.' All of us know what it is to 'feel so bad' and to have the hope 'this ain't gonna last' when we are hurt and sad. Of course, we do not feel the individual hurt and emotions Howlin' Wolf felt and sang about. But we feel the same type of hurt and emotion, so we can understand what Howlin' Wolf is singing about. Not all of us (in fact, very few of us) can put the hurt to music. The people who do this are the true blues musicians. But many of us, no matter our history or our racial group, can 'get' what the blues is about.[10]

NOTES

1 James Segrest and Mark Hoffman, *Moanin' at Midnight: The Life and Times of Howlin' Wolf* (New York: Pantheon Books, 2004), p. xvi.

2 Ibid., p. 300.

3 Interestingly, Miles Davis did not agree with Howlin' Wolf on this point. Miles Davis grew up in a well-to-do family (his father was a dentist). When he was at Julliard, pursuing classical music during the day and performing jazz and blues at night in New York City, one of his teachers connected playing the blues with being poor and picking cotton. In response, Miles Davis said he was not poor, never picked cotton, but played the blues.

4 See Alasdair MacIntyre, *After Virtue* (Notre Dame, IN: University of Notre Dame Press, 1984); Alasdair MacIntyre, *Whose Justice? Whose Rationality?* (Notre Dame, IN: University of Notre Dame Press, 1988); and Alasdair MacIntyre, *Three Rival Theories of Inquiry: Encyclopedia, Geneology, Tradition* (Notre Dame, IN: University of Notre Dame Press, 1990).

5 See Douglas Langston's discussion of these and related issues in his *Conscience and Other Virtues* (College Park, MD: Penn State Press, 2001), pp. 136–143, 179–184.

6 See, for example, Donald Davidson, 'On the very idea of a conceptual scheme,' *Proceedings and Addresses of the American Philosophical Association*, 47 (1973–1974), pp. 5–20.

7 Much of the following argument draws from chapter XIX of MacIntyre, *Whose Justice? Whose Rationality?* pp. 376–388.

8 Segrest and Hoffman, *Moanin' at Midnight*, pp. 235–236.

9 Ibid., pp. 275–276.

10 We wish to thank Constance Whitesell for critical editing help on this essay.

CHAPTER 16

DISTRIBUTIVE HISTORY

Did Whites Rip-Off the Blues?

Historical accounts often attempt to rectify past injustices, and this has especially been the case in recent decades. These injustices typically concern distributions of reputation rather than goods. Thus, E. P. Thompson's incomparable *The Making of the English Working Class* seeks to rescue 'the poor stockinger, the Luddite cropper, the "obsolete" hand-loom weaver, the "utopian" artisan [...] from the enormous condescension of history.'[1] Thompson does not glorify his subjects so much as rehabilitate them through sympathetic but careful analyses of their experience and behavior. Eugene Genovese did something similar in his classic *Roll, Jordan, Roll: The World the Slaves Made*.[2]

The white rip-off account of rock and roll offers up a cultural version of 'distributive history.' Its purveyors, as if in the name of justice, see another redistribution of reputation, this time from white artists to black artists. But, unlike Thompson and Genovese, they pay little attention to the very thing they want to redeem – black music. In their rush to condemn the white 'rip-off,' they take a lazy, stereotyped view of what they say was ripped off.

Blues – Philosophy for Everyone: Thinking Deep About Feeling Low, First Edition.
Edited by Jesse R. Steinberg and Abrol Fairweather.
© 2012 John Wiley & Sons, Inc. Published 2012 by John Wiley & Sons, Inc.

The result is an object lesson in the dangers of approaching culture with moral and political objectives, especially to the exclusion of aesthetic judgments. If the rip-off account attempts a justified form of reverse discrimination, it fails. An injustice is done, not only to those discredited but also to those *credited*. The supposedly positive stereotypes imposed on black artists and audiences look awfully like some long-discredited negative clichés. When encountered in the distributive history project, the 'positive' stereotypes turn out to be as unjust as the negative ones.

The Rip-Off Account

The rip-off account is a story – an appropriate word – about how white people stole, appropriated, or feebly imitated black music to create rock and roll. Until rock came along, we're told, white music was whitebread: repressed, stilted, and disconnected from reality, especially from the raw energy and sexuality that permeated black sensibilities.

Here are two samples of this view, the first from a recent American history textbook:

> Perhaps the most obvious symbol of the new youth was the emergence of rock and roll. Young adults added purchasing power to change musical taste in America by propelling 'rock 'n roll' to the top of the charts [...] A nineteen-year-old truck driver from Tupelo, Mississippi, [Elvis] Presley emerged in 1956 with his hit single, 'Heartbreak Hotel.' The young entertainer adapted the powerful rhythms and raw sexual energy of 'race music' to create his own unique style and sound.[3]

Black writers express fairly similar views. The respected *Billboard* music critic Nelson George wrote that

> Elvis' reverse integration [i.e., his 'immersion in black culture'] was so complete that on stage he adopted the symbolic fornication blacks had unashamedly brought to American entertainment. Elvis was sexy; not clean-cut, wholesome, white-bread Hollywood sexy but sexy in the aggressive earthly manner associated by white males with black males.[4]

George was hedging his bets: in the end he distanced himself from the stereotype, but he embraced it in the previous sentence.

Music historians generally avoid these inaccurate claims, which oversimplify black music and even take it for granted. But the flaws of the rip-off account go beyond inaccuracy. Its portrayal of black culture rests on unexamined assumptions that, in other contexts, are rightly considered racist.

Musical Traditions

Since black people were victims of discrimination, segregation, and worse, it is natural to suppose that black musical culture suffered complementary harms. For distributive historians, the rip-off account would therefore be a great moral convenience. But culture is no respecter of social boundaries, even rigid ones. The border between black and white music was always porous,[5] and it ran across a two-way street.

Even in Africa, black music was not purely African: the Wolof riffs that made their way into the blues had Arab origins.[6] In America, black blues and white music have intertwined since before the dawn of recording history. The banjo was originally a black instrument; the guitar, in America, a white one. Black gospel owed much to white religious music. Ragtime was developed by classically trained musicians, as were the so-called 'classic blues.' Whites went crazy for boogie-woogie at the end of the 1920s, but before that the music had been 'appropriated' by comparatively well-off black publishers whose sheet music, of course, used white notation. Among them was Clarence Williams, who back in 1923 issued a jazz tune with a boogie introduction called 'Tin Roof Blues.' The song was written by the New Orleans Rhythm Kings, an all-white group.

These interminglings should not be surprising: black blues musicians were people, not stereotypes. The jug bands of the 1920s showed a fondness for all kinds of white musical idioms. So did Blind Willie McTell, who covered such white tunes as 'Pal of Mine' and 'Wabash Cannonball.' Some of Washboard Sam's finest numbers, such as 'Good Old Cabbage Greens,' are as close to country as to blues. White music greatly extended the range of tempos and moods available to the blues performer – even if the record companies (and, later, white blues enthusiasts) preferred their 'race' artists to stick to a narrow conception of 'the blues.'[7]

Recorded Music: The Blues

No doubt the blues began as music created by blacks for blacks. But by 1920, when Mamie Smith offered up the first blues record, the genre was already something of a half-breed.[8] Her orchestra – a jazz ensemble, distant from blues roots – was probably the same one that backed the white (and sometimes blackface) singer Sophie Tucker.

These already 'sanitized' recordings help to explain the tact of blues historians, who introduce Papa Charlie Jackson as the first commercially successful 'race' artist to record outside the *orchestral* style of the 'classic' blues singers such as Bessie Smith.[9] You could also say that Papa Charlie Jackson was the first artist to record a blues not tailored to a night-club environment. He did that in 1924. In the same year – before Blind Lemon Jefferson, before Charley Patton, and twelve years before Robert Johnson – the white songster Uncle Dave Macon recorded 'Hill Billy Blues.' It was this song – a blues! – that brought the word 'hillbilly' into music. Jackson and Uncle Dave both accompanied themselves on the banjo. Years before the now-famous 'old masters' of the blues recorded, blues and country music were already interbreeding.

The commerce between black and white music never subsided. Nine years before Robert Johnson, Jimmie Rogers recorded several blues. A few white artists 'sounded black.' Many more developed their own very different versions of the music, for example the Jimmie Rogers tunes recorded nine years before Robert Johnson and decades before the rip-off account begins. Meanwhile the more urbanized black artists incorporated white idioms into their music. In one remarkable performance, 'Don't Say Goodbye,' Leroy Carr does about half the song as a perfectly nice but predictable blues and then – one almost imagines him saying, 'Oh, screw it' – finishes the track as what can only be described as a country song.

Rock and Race

The rock and roll era did not begin when this musical back-and-forth became a rip-off. Before there was theft, there was collaboration. Some of the very greatest R&B hits of the early 1950s – Little Willie Littlefield's 'Kansas City,' Big Mamma Thornton's 'Hound Dog,' Charles Brown's

'Hard Times,' The Robins' 'Riot in Cell Block 9' – were written by two whites, Jerry Lieber and Mike Stoller. A white man also wrote Nat King Cole's wonderful 'Route 66.' Johnny Otis, a white band leader who lived as if he was black, was central to the careers of several important R&B artists. Moreover, an astounding number of the greatest R&B hits came from white producers such as Sam Phillips and Ahmet Ertegun of Atlantic Records – this at a time when the studio owners didn't just sign papers and rake in cash, but might also help out with the writing chores, clap out a beat, or even join in on a chorus.

Much of the impression that black musicians 'founded' rock and roll is simply based on bad chronology. Such 'founders' as Chuck Berry, Little Richard, and Bo Diddley recorded their first rock-style numbers *after* Elvis' seminal 1954 Sun sessions. Besides, they were no more inclined to stick with stereotypically black tunes than were the earlier blues artists. Many of them loved country music.[10] Howlin' Wolf (Chester Burnett), taken to be the very epitome of an uncompromisingly black bluesman, was no exception:

> Chester first developed the howl that made him famous by listening to the first great country music star, Jimmie Rogers, the 'yodelling singer': 'I took that idea and adapted it to my own abilities,' Chester said. 'I couldn't do no yodelin' so I turned to howlin'. And it's done me just fine.'[11]

As for Chuck Berry, he said of himself around that time:

> Curiosity provoked me to lay a lot of our country stuff on our predominantly black audience and some of our black audience began whispering 'who is that black hillbilly at the Cosmo?' After they laughed at me a few times they began requesting the hillbilly stuff and enjoyed dancing to it.[12]

As for the great songwriter Otis Blackwell, he reported idolizing one of his 'early influences,' Tex Ritter.[13] Neither audiences nor writers nor performers were overly concerned about maintaining the racial purity of their culture.

The Music Business

But what of the music business itself? Weren't black musicians brutally exploited? They certainly were. But there was nothing particularly racial about this; it was mainly about making a quick buck. Among the worst exploiters of black artists was Don Robey, a black record company owner whose market was primarily black audiences.[14] Like his non-black (but sometimes Middle Eastern) counterparts, his relationships with his artists were complex: savior and exploiter all at once. The artists, understandably, were at least as hungry for cash. They broke contract by recording for different labels under false names and 'covered' others' material in the strict destructive sense of the word – to release someone else's song before the original had run its course in the market. One of the biggest black hits of 1953, the Orioles' 'Crying in the Chapel,' was covered by many white artists. However, it was itself a destructive cover version that stole sales from the original, a country number issued in the same year by Darrell Glen. Muddy Waters' 'Got My Mojo Working' (1957) exemplifies black-on-black musical exploitation: it blotted out the fine 1956 Anne Cole original. If these rip-offs were crimes, they were not white-on-black crimes. They were color-blind.

These practices invite caution about *cultural* exploitation – the accusation brought against white rock and roll. Even the boundaries between black and white musical cultures are not easy to define. Music is not classifiable by the skin color of its creators. Charlie Pride doesn't create black music, but Johnny Otis does. Audiences are what establish cultural origin. Black music is not the possession of some mythically homogeneous black community. It is the music of subcultures whose racial exclusivity dissipates almost as soon as they form.

This shows in the music itself. Though many songs clearly arise in and belong to a certain culture, their *ingredients*, as we've seen, frequently come from outside it. These ingredients don't dilute the song's claim to belong to its culture any more than their absence would make for a stronger claim. Music constructed entirely from elements present among the first generation of American slaves, even if contrived by a black person, might not be black music at all: it might be the fussy con-coction of someone who failed to connect to any living cultural stream. It might easily count as less 'black' than the 'impure' music of the great blues artists.

These complications can undermine accusations of cultural pillage. Would a white artist be 'stealing' a black song if it were suffused with elements taken from white culture? This would be like accusing you of theft if you were to 'appropriate' the boat I made partly from wood and fittings taken – without permission – from you. The difference is that, at the cultural level, it's not that both of us have done wrong: it's that neither of us have.

These nuances highlight the distinction between cultural theft and commercial exploitation. If you cover my record to 'steal' my sales, that's figurative theft but real wrongdoing. But the wrong, and the theft, are not in my performance but in the use of it. To accuse me of theft if I performed the song for myself, in my basement, would carry purism to fanatical extremes. This suggests that strict cultural pillage is almost impossible. What we may see as cultural theft resides, not in the imitation of others' work, but in the commercial exploitation of that imitation. The black–white cultural interchange that produced rock and roll involved lots of imitation. It also involved many commercial rip-offs. But it did not involve a white rip-off of black culture.

Sensibilities

Though the preceding arguments seem to undo the rip-off account, they only hint at the wrong done to *black* culture. White musicians are supposed to have 'appropriated' not just some licks and some tunes but a whole sensibility. Rock and roll supposedly delivered to white teenagers – in sanitized form – the alleged rawness, sexuality, and violence of black music.

These sensibilities are a key element in the rip-off account. No one could plausibly claim that rock and roll developed simply by copying blues progressions: this had been going on for decades before rock and roll. So the account must claim a rip-off of something more intangible: the sensibility of black music. Here is where the rip-off account moves from a specious attempt at rectifying injustice to a large injustice of its own. It rests on a portrayal of black musical sensibilities that is not only ludicrously distorted but shot through with prejudiced myth-making. This ironic case of unintended consequences exemplifies the dangers of even the best-intentioned distributive history.

To put it bluntly, the rip-off account feeds off racial stereotypes. Lots of black music has sexual content, of course. But it is ludicrously false to claim that white music was fundamentally different: the restraints of white popular music in the 1950s in no way reflected white musical traditions.[15] In the 1920s and 1930s, 'old timey' numbers such as 'Bang Away My Lulu' and 'My Sweet Farm Girl'[16] were as sexually explicit as any black blues. Closer to the dawn of rock and roll, Western swing bands produced quite a bit of what can only be called good-natured

MICHAEL NEUMANN

filth: Billy Hughes & His Pecos Pals, in 1946, recorded a number containing the line 'It's nice and nice [sic] and covered with cream / It's the best darn stuff you've ever seen' in their song 'Keep Your Hands Off It.' Bob Wills, the best-loved of all Western swing artists, contributed the 1937 'Oozlin' Daddy Blues,' with lines such as 'If she don't let my oozler be / They're gonna haveta lay a lily on me.' Just before the dawn of rock and roll, in 1953, Moon Mullican recorded a more sleekly sexual 'Rocket to the Moon.' But far more unjust than the stereotyping of white performers is the portrayal of black music itself.[17] The rip-off account, hell-bent on regarding black music as little more than a source of jungle sex and violence, ignores all its subtlety, variety, and charm.

The many dozens of sexually suggestive or explicit black blues say little about the genre, much of which is not at all sexual, macho, violent, or tough. Relations between the sexes in black music have all the emotional range you would expect of relations between males and females anywhere. Charlie Spand (in 'Good Gal,' 1929) doesn't have to 'get rollin' down the road,' doesn't have 'another mama over in Priceford,' and 'warn his woman she bettah change her ways or else.' He speaks with the very same direct, cruel honestly that you hear in any culture when love grows cold:

> You wonder why I treat you so,
> You should have sense enough to know,
> Good gal, good gal, I don't love you no more,
> Good gal, good gal, I don't love you no more.

His quiet, elegant, almost fragmentary piano somehow intensifies the chill of the lyrics. Josh White adds complex, delicate guitar fills, a thousand musical miles from the tough-guy licks that today form the public face of blues music. Nor do things have to get rough when the tables are turned. Robert Johnson's now-famous 'Love in Vain' is, like many blues, a stunningly beautiful tribute to lost love.

In thousands of blues numbers, the prevailing atmosphere is not raw defiance but – unsurprisingly – anxiety. Maceo Merriweather is terrified when he awakes to find his girlfriend standing over him with a .45; he pleads for his life. Jimmy Yancey's piano doesn't conjure up a violent or sex-charged world; he evokes an atmosphere of quiet contemplation. It is white music, not black, that has a whole category called 'murder ballads.' But blues is much more often concerned with 'romance without finance' than with lust. The idea that black blues was the musical equivalent of a porn emporium has no basis in fact.

The sex-and-violence stereotype fares no better when limited to Elvis sources. There is plenty of sex and violence in the R&B Elvis listened to. But none of the artists Elvis actually covered, nor any of the more famous of his black counterparts such as Big Joe Turner and Chuck Berry, ever surpassed the levels of sex and violence commonplace in white American popular music: that impression gains plausibility only if attention is confined to the Patti Pages and Pat Boones. Nor was it at all common for black performers to engage in suggestive stagecraft.

What's more, much of the raw/violent/sexual type of R&B was recorded by relatively unknown black artists *for white producers* such as Sam Phillips, whose primary interest was in the *white* market. (Pat Hare's 'I'm Gonna Murder My Baby' is an example.) Yet even Big Joe Turner, powerful voice and all, did quite a few polished, playful, and romantic numbers.[18] Someone can always insist that the less explicit, more restrained black performances were nevertheless smoldering with more-than-white sexual heat, but one should at least ask how much of that is in the eye of the beholder. One could just as well decide that it was whites, Elvis the Pelvis and his followers, who injected an almost breathless sexuality into black originals that were tame by comparison. Certainly no black record had anything like the orgasm noises of Mel Robbins' 1959 rockabilly number 'Save It.'

The Evolution of Taste

The rip-off account looks at black 'bluesmen' as sociological subjects, not as artists whose work is subject to aesthetic evaluation.[19] But, in fact, that account requires aesthetic judgments. Had the whites borrowed or stolen from black musicians yet created something far better than the originals, there would be no case for reputational redistribution: it would be like Shakespeare borrowing or stealing from his contemporary sources. So the rip-off account, as required, proclaims that the borrowings or thefts resulted in little or no improvement over the originals. The catch is that aesthetic judgments, once introduced, can be applied to black as well as to white music. When this is done, a whole different *historical* picture emerges. It is the aesthetics of black musical history – a story of

MICHAEL NEUMANN

the rise and decline of various forms of black music – that really highlights the injustices of the rip-off account.

Both in aesthetic terms and in the regard of black audiences, the music at the heart of the rip-off account was, by the mid-1950s, in decline. Blues did get tougher, but it also lost much of its – no need to apologize for the word – beauty. White audiences today may adulate such figures as Howlin' Wolf, John Lee Hooker, and Champion Jack Dupree. Pointing to Mississippi Fred McDowell and Lightin' Hopkins they may claim that, at least until very recently, blues was as vibrant as ever. But blues aficionados and black record-buyers alike tell a different story. Blues died, at least in part, because it lost its artistic and emotional range.

The musicians just mentioned are very good, honest performers. No blues historian, however, would ever put them on a level with the giants of earlier decades. In an odd way, it was the very brilliance of Robert Johnson that sowed the seeds of the decline. He became virtually the sole source of modern Chicago blues. Elmore James, a superb artist, all but built his entire career on a single Johnson lick. Muddy Waters all but defined the music by electrifying some small portion of Robert Johnson's guitar work. The whole rest of the blues – not only the blues of Texas, Atlanta, the Carolinas, and Mississippi itself, but also the piano blues that flourished in Northern cities such as Detroit and Chicago – became at best a sideshow and more often an obscurity. Virtually the whole range of black blues, though marginally available well into the 1950s, had a minimal public presence, even among blacks. People wanted to hear it Robert Johnson style, even if they'd never heard of the man.

More ominously, and increasingly, black audiences didn't want to hear it at all. By the time whites were covering 'tough' black material, they were also giving it new life. Black people, apparently unwilling to confirm expectations about their raw, sexual, violent nature, had to a great extent gone on to other things.

The abandonment of the blues loomed large in the career of Little Walter, perhaps the last of the blues' truly great exponents. By the start of the rock and roll era, his best work was almost behind him. St. Louis disk jockey Gabriel Hearns put it brutally when he described Little Walter's last days:

> The blues was sliding, [Little Walter] was seeing his career going to hell. Muddy Waters and John Lee Hooker had luck that Walter didn't have, they

were picked up by white promoters. I'll tell you something, if it weren't for white people there'd be no blues today. Black people are ashamed of the blues.[20]

Why so? Perhaps it was not that tastes had changed so much as that the music had stopped accommodating them. Blacks still wanted material that expressed, sometimes beautifully, a whole range of sensibilities. Blues no longer met that demand. When black audiences moved over to 'rhythm and blues,' they did not move toward that harsh, bluesy, but narrow segment of the genre that figures in standard histories of rock and roll. They moved toward music that provided more emotional and aesthetic range.

From just around the time of Robert Johnson's last recordings in 1938, new trends were taking over. Louis Jordan's work was quick, slick, witty, and almost joyfully lighthearted even when it tackled serious subjects. Its tasty professionalism commanded attention. So did the Ink Spots and other urbane blues combos. Black people loved them, just as they loved the jazzmen who collaborated not only with Jordan but also with Jimmie Rogers and Louis Armstrong. These artists offered a welcome change from the stark, dark, rough blues, which had begun to wear out its welcome.

This trend intensified as rock and roll emerged. Blacks paid scant attention to the music 'covered' by Elvis in his Sun sessions. Big Mama Thornton's white-authored 'Hound Dog' was her only entry in the R&B charts. Arthur Crudup, best known for the Elvis-covered 'That's All Right, Mama,' had just one week on the charts, in 1951, with an old-fashioned up-tempo number ten hit ('I'm Gonna Dig Myself a Hole'). Wynonie Harris' 'Good Rockin' Tonight' never made the charts at all;[21] neither did Junior Parker's 'Mystery Train.'[22] Black record-buyers preferred musicians who recaptured some of the range of sensibilities the blues had lost.

Among them were urbane and sophisticated pianists such as Cecil Gant, Willie Mabon, Camille Howard, and Amos Milburn. These artists did not fit the stereotype of the black bluesman any more than their audiences fitted the stereotype of the juke joint denizens. Charles Brown, for example, taught high school chemistry after finishing college. He scored a ninety-six on the Civil Service examination and worked at the arsenal in Pine Bluff, Arkansas, but found his supervision of white people made for an uncomfortable atmosphere. His break into the music business was propelled by a first-prize victory at the Lincoln Theatre on

Los Angeles' Central Avenue – LA's answer to the Apollo. After starting with an Earl Hines number, he blew his audience away with 'The Warsaw Concerto' and 'a little "Claire de Lune."'[23]

Then there was the sometimes naïve, unbluesy world of doo-wop. Doo-wop and its precursors drew on a variety of white music, including sacred songs and barbershop quartets. The new vocal groups 'stole' all sorts of white pop material – even Joyce Kilmer's 'Trees.' Doo-wop has been trivialized as the lovelorn music of cute but amateurish high-school kids. But the earlier groups were often composed of highly professional, thoroughly disciplined adults who not only held practices but imposed fines on those who missed them. The magnificent recordings of the Orioles, Dominoes, Flamingos, Five Keys, Five Royales, and other groups will not receive the broad recognition they deserve as long as white audiences care only for black popular music that fits the tough, sexual stereotype.

While white kids played hard-driving rockabilly and mined a blues tradition that no longer connected with black sensibilities, black kids went crazy for the sweet, gentle doo-wop sound. In the ghettos they formed hundreds of vocal groups whose songs had left the blues far, far behind. Doo-wop's success helps to explain the failure of black rock and roll artists to score big wins on the black musical scene. The leading blues-oriented black rockers of the fifties – Bo Diddley, Little Richard, and Chuck Berry – never did anywhere near as well with black record-buyers as Elvis. Far surpassing those three on the black charts were Ray Charles and Fats Domino, whose relaxed style fits awkwardly with the 'they stole black raw sexuality' doctrine. When the great harpist Sonny Boy Williamson (Rice Miller) at last attained some popular success, it was with those whitest of black music aficionados, the Yardbirds. The idea that he would have played with any popular black group recording at the same time is simply inconceivable.

Conclusion

In short, there was no rip-off. The context for it never existed. The racial barriers that poisoned America did not extend to its cultures. There was commercial exploitation of black musicians, but no cultural exploitation by white musicians. Musical traditions were too intertwined for that to be possible. Far more important, the assumptions behind the rip-off account – really a shameful collection of racial stereotypes – are false. Some black musicians were real or pretend tough guys singing of sex and violence, on occasion superbly. But the best black musicians were, unsurprisingly, sophisticated artists, out to produce beautiful music, and no more preoccupied with sex and violence than their white counterparts. Indeed the pervasive and intense sexuality of early rock and roll was something quite new. Rock and roll borrowed from contemporary black music in two ways: by tapping into a long-established common heritage and by infusing some few black songs with a peculiarly frantic sexuality not found in the originals. That sensibility was not some copy of the raw sexuality of black music. It couldn't be, because 'black' music – understood as what black people actually listened to – didn't *have* that character.

The rip-off account is an object lesson in the dangers of approaching culture with moral and political objectives, especially to the exclusion of aesthetic judgments. Because cultural divides are not as rigid as racial or class divides, rewriting cultural history to champion the oppressed is an unpromising venture, prone to generating counterproductive stereotypes. The picture of white musicians ripping off black musicians required the construction of cardboard blacks and whites whose portrayals draw on the most tired and vulgar of racial prejudices. Perhaps those who do not seek to right social injustices through cultural analysis need not fear making such mistakes.

NOTES

1   E. P. Thompson, *The Making of the English Working Class* (Harmondsworth, UK: Penguin Books, 1968), p. 12.
2   Eugene Genovese, *Roll, Jordan, Roll: The World the Slaves Made* (New York: Vintage, 1974).
3   Steven M. Gillon and Cathy D. Matson, *The American Experiment: A History of the United States*, vol. 2 (New York: Wadsworth, 2002), p. 1106.
4   Nelson Geroge, *The Death of Rhythm and Blues* (New York: Dutton, 1988), 62f. Nelson George also won the approval of Kevin Chappell in 'How blacks invented rock and roll: R&B stars created foundations of multibillion-dollar music industry', *Ebony* (January 1997, http://findarticles.com/p/articles/mi_m1077/is_n3_v52/ai_18980636). The article places greater emphasis on the 'rip-off' aspects of the process.
5   One historian, pointing to a large repertory of shared material, says: 'Why this shared repertoire should have existed is clear enough. [...] it is not in the

nature of such songs and tunes to be segregatable, and, firm and ubiquitous though racial divisions may have been, they could not prevent – and probably few would have wished to prevent – the use of by blacks or white, or by whites of black material' (Tony Russell, *Blacks, Whites and Blues* (London: November Books, 1970), p. 30).

6 See Robert Palmer, *Deep Blues: A Musical and Cultural History of the Mississippi Delta* (Harmondsworth, UK: Penguin Books, 1982), p. 26.

7 Often non-blues numbers such as Leroy Carr's 'Carried Water for the Elephant' are found only in the artist's earlier or unissued tracks. However, Paul Oliver is agnostic about the role of record companies in emphasizing the blues genre, at least in the early years of recorded black music. Instead he emphasizes the vast range of material, mostly forgotten, that *was* recorded. See Paul Oliver, *Songsters & Saints: Vocal Traditions on Race Records* (Cambridge, UK: Cambridge University Press, 1984).

8 As for blues, so for country music. The very first song on the Grand Old Opry in 1926 was 'Pan American Blues,' performed by the black harmonica player DeFord Bailey.

9 See, for example, Michael Agresti, 'William Henry "Papa Charlie" Jackson,' *Tell it Like it Is – An intermittent publication of the Wisconsin Blues Society* 1:2 (1990), p. 2 (http://www.paramountshome.org/index.php?option=com_con tent&view=article&id=82:william-henry-qpapa-charlieq-jack-son&catid=45:new-york-recording-laboratoriesartist&Itemid=54).

10 So says Little Richard's guitarist Bill House in Charles White, *The Life and Times of Little Richard: The Quasar of Rock.* (New York: Harmony Books, 1984), p. 37.

11 James Segrest and Mark Hoffman, *Moanin' at Midnight: The Life and Times of Howlin' Wolf* (New York: Da Capo Press, 2005), p. 20.

12 Chuck Berry, *Chuck Berry: The Autobiography* (New York: Harmony Books, 1987), p. 89.

13 Brandon Harris and Ralph Newman, 'The Otis Blackwell interview,' *Time Barrier Express Magazine* (July 1979, http://www.kyleesplin.com/jllsb/jllsb-dir/pages/68apage.htm).

14 Little Richard said of Don Robey: 'I was telling people how rude he was, how nasty he was, how he didn't pay me, and that he was a crook and was just using all these people – using them up' (White, *The Life and Times of Little Richard*, p. 37). Little Richard contrasts this behavior with the conduct of white promoter Alan Freed, described in the most glowing terms (Ibid., p. 84).

15 Even English and Scottish songwriting were full of sexual innuendo, and more. Robert Burns collected and imitated some of it in James Barke and Sydney Goodsir Smith (Eds.), *The Merry Muses of Caledonia: A Collection of Bawdy Folksongs, Ancient and Modern* (New York: Grammercy Publishing Company, 1959).

16 For example: 'I trim her hedges / I clean out her back yard / She loves her daddy / Because I'm long and hard.'

17 Western Swing, popular but regional and lower-class, offers up much more sexual material than other white popular music. The numerically greater incidence of black sexual recordings in the 1930s and 1940s was probably the product of racial prejudice, not greater sexual interest. Mainstream white audiences and musicians were the targets of censorship. Blacks, considered animalistic, were not. As black music became more mainstream, in the late 1950s, its explicitly sexual content diminished sharply.

18 On 'You Know I Love You,' the B side of 'Shake, Rattle and Roll' (1954), Big Joe falls across his bed and cries himself to sleep.

19 The refusal to evaluate black blues artists aesthetically is probably some expression of North American guilt. European reviewers have no such qualms: witness, for example, the reception of some performances by J. B. Hutto and Little Walter on their European tour. See Tony Glover, Scott Dirks, and Ward Gaines, *Blues with a Feeling: The Little Walter Story* (New York and London: Routledge, 2002), 260f.

20 Glover, Dirks, and Gaines, *Blues with a Feeling: The Little Walter Story*, p. 266.

21 See John Witburn, *Top Rhythm & Blues Records, 1949–1971* (Menomonee Falls, WI: Record Research, 1973).

22 'Mystery Train' was co-authored by the white producer Sam Phillips, and apparently 'stole' its first lines from the Carter Family's 'Worried Man Blues.'

23 Chip Deffaa, *Blue Rhythms: Six Lives in Rhythm and Blues* (Urbana, IL: Da Capo Press, 2000), 106f.

MICHAEL NEUMANN

CHAPTER 17

WHOSE BLUES?

Class, Race, and Gender in American Vernacular Music

> *when you hear me singing my blue lone some song,*
> *These hard times can last us so very long.*
> (Nehemiah Curtis 'Skip' James, 1931)

Questioning Ourselves

The Socratic imperative, 'know thyself,' is the philosophical burden of every free mind. Yet it is a burden we more easily bear together, reflecting on our common humanity, than each alone, pondering existence in solitary curiosity. In fact, were there no other people, there would not be much in the way of a self for you to know, would there? We learn to sing through the voices of others as we learn to see through their eyes, and we tell their histories in order to find ourselves. We can be misled. Sometimes we lose our way. This means that our personal freedom and self-direction depend in no small measure on correctly understanding the origins of our collective plights and predicaments. In what follows I argue that the historical

Blues – Philosophy for Everyone: Thinking Deep About Feeling Low, First Edition.
Edited by Jesse R. Steinberg and Abrol Fairweather.
© 2012 John Wiley & Sons, Inc. Published 2012 by John Wiley & Sons, Inc.

reception of blues music in America reveals a deeply troubling failure to understand ourselves, our culture, and our contemporary social aspirations. If I'm right, it is no marginal failure: uncorrected, we cloud the business of our individual self-knowledge and inhibit the progress of our mutual flourishing.

My argument is that the story of American blues is beset by bad habits of thinking about differences between people – habits that stem from a mistaken confidence in the notion that a people's music will tell the tale of their shared identity. Not only does this confidence ignore stubbornly important facts about the makers of blues music; not only does it leave us ill-equipped to make much sense of ourselves as consumers of blues music; but it also conspires to perpetuate exactly the sort of material and emotional oppression from which blues songs have always sought deliverance.

A Twice-Told Tale

People invented the blues by making music; people invented blues history by making up people. Both music and musicians are, in this sense, cultural artifacts; products of collective imagination and shared belief. People make up people, as Canadian philosopher Ian Hacking says,[1] by devising schemes for sorting individuals into groups. Such schemes work by exploiting the constant interplay between our talk and behavior – between conventional labels and actual lives. Hacking's idea is that the labels we use to group ourselves collectively inform the ways we think about ourselves individually. Our labels, in other words, tell us what *kinds* of people we are and, in turn, how people *like us* are supposed to act. If you happen to regard someone as a generous sort of person, for instance, you can expect her to exhibit a particular kind of behavior: precisely the kind you'd *not* expect from a miserly person. According to Hacking, this process of making up people is, moreover, interactive: we adjust our actions to fit the labels we inherit, while at the same time we configure our labels to match the ways we actually live.[2]

Because these schemes for grouping ourselves into kinds of people are both dynamic and interactive, so too are the stories we tell about our past. They are rather like home movies, these stories: portraits of our social worlds in motion. In looking to blues music historically, then – as having shaped the contexts in which we understand ourselves today – it

RON BOMBARDI

seems we inevitably make up people; and, from the kinds of people we make, we inherit the kinds of people we can become. My argument says that there are two stories of American vernacular music, and that different kinds of people inhabit each of them. Blues history in particular is, I think, a twice-told tale: a pair of incompatible narratives that nevertheless fuel the social dynamics of our own time.

The two tellings I have in mind are more than variant perspectives on the same events. Neither translates well into the other. One story tells the invention of blues music as central to the creation of black racial identity in the Americas from the colonial period into the twenty-first century. We might call this the *orthodox* tale because it is widespread, familiar, and figures prominently in contemporary political discourse. On the orthodox telling, blues musical forms were born in bondage, liberated by emancipation, matured in segregation, appropriated by rock, and inherited by the likes of rhythm and blues, soul music, hip-hop, and rap.[3] Within this narrative, we find innumerable episodes of denial and recompense, of struggle and survival, the sum total of which expresses the emergence of black American culture from servitude into the era of civil rights. But this story is incomplete. It is incomplete because between the worlds of black and white Americans there has always been multi-cultural interchange and cross-talk. And once we begin to examine the interchange, and listen closely to the cross-talk, a second story emerges. If it is not outright heretical, it is at least *unorthodox*, or, as we more often say nowadays, *alternative*.

Although marginalized from the start by the promoters of minstrel shows and later by the producers of segregated record catalogs, this alternative tale whispers a fierce complaint from what blues historian Christopher Waterman calls the 'excluded middle of the American racial imagination.'[4] Blues music developed in the late nineteenth and early twentieth centuries, by Waterman's lights, in a cosmopolitan atmosphere of ready hybridization across musical genres. Yet this middle ground between black and white, urban and rural, folk and popular music is nowadays all but excluded from historical accounts.[5] If so, we might well ask what music and musicians occupied this hybrid territory.

Consider the career of the Mississippi Sheiks, perhaps the most commercially successful of the many versatile black string bands playing throughout the southeast during the heyday of 'race records.' By 1930, for example, their repertoire included such pieces as 'Sitting on Top of the World' and 'Yodeling, Fiddling Blues' – the former became a gift to bluegrass, and the latter a fashionable tribute to hillbilly star Jimmie

Rogers.[6] Principal family members Lonnie, Bo, and Sam Chatmon, along with their colleague Walter Vinson and other local musicians from the Bolton-Edwards area, west of Jackson, Mississippi, played lucrative engagements, mainly for white audiences, and also recorded in various combinations as the Mississippi Mud Steppers, the Mississippi Blacksnakes, The Jackson Blue Boys, and the Down South Boys.[7] In the composition both of their ensemble and their songs, the Sheiks exemplify a striking alternative to the orthodox telling of blues history – precisely the sort of alternative that falls between white and black racial identity profiles, as much today as in their own time. I think that is because the Sheiks composed themselves and their music from the individual genius of their members, whose tastes ranged far and wide across the American musical landscape. Their work illustrates the often paradoxical character not just of blues but of nearly all American vernacular music between the great wars. At once folk and commercial, sacred and profane, gendered male and female, spoken freely and enslaved, enriching and forfeited, the music we call blues fused divisions among *kinds* of people. But not just any kinds.

Let's call the kinds that matter 'social kinds.' They matter because, while inseparable from resistance to the indignities and ravages of slavery, early blues and spirituals alike were also marked by a persistent disregard for the reigning categories of color, class, gender, and religion into which both black and white Americans sorted themselves once European colonialism gave way to the rise of democratic institutions in the New World. Despite their divergence, what these particular categories have in common, even today, is that they play a pivotal role in making up what constitutes dominant and submissive people, with each polarized category serving to legitimate unequal distributions of power – especially power over the material and emotional conditions of individual well-being.

Insofar as blues songs began in protest, however, their inspiration was nevertheless conspicuously personal; and this feature in turn supports a general claim: the original creative drive in blues innovation and development was toward overcoming *individual* differences in power based on *collective* differences in social kinds – differences in class and status, race and ethnicity, gender and domestic cohesion, as well as religious and spiritual practice. That is to say, when blues forms first emerged from plantation field hollers and prison work songs, their purport was intensely personal, and their performances were more matters of self-creation than expressions of social discontent. This alternative telling of blues history

RON BOMBARDI

says that the overriding oppression against which blues songs gave and continue to give voice is the oppression of having to conform to the expectations of other people – expectations generated by attributing *accidental* differences in personal freedom to *essential* differences in social kinds.

What Makes Us Different?

Suppose we ask, then, what, after all, does make us different? The question may seem simple enough, but we cannot hope to answer it, even provisionally, unless we first divine its target. Are we asking, in other words, what makes each person different from every other person? Or are we asking what makes one kind of person different from another kind? These are very old questions. Together, they worried the ancient Greek philosophers mightily,[8] and, because the efforts of those early thinkers shaped the problems that have occupied Western philosophy ever since, our intellectual horizons nowadays still reflect ideas and accounts that first saw the light of day in ancient Athens, over two thousand years before the birth of the blues.

One of these ancient ideas is that everything in nature comes sorted into kinds.[9] What troubled the early philosophers, however, weren't so much questions about *what* kinds of things there are in the world, but questions about *how* kinds are to be distinguished from one another. These were among the questions that famously divided the philosophies of Plato and Aristotle, and it is my contention that the legacy of that division still troubles us today when we ask after the origins of *our* social kinds.

Now, the central point of dispute between Aristotle and Plato in this regard was over how best to understand differences between individuals. To Plato's mind, individual differences simply reflect differences in kind. On this understanding, moreover, both natural and social kinds actually *generate* the very traits and behaviors that make individuals of the same kind, well, the *same*. We can recognize a robust survival of this reasoning in much of our contemporary thinking about the relation between biological species and their genomes. Accordingly, if we apply Plato's view to the blues, we are bound to come up with something close to what I've been calling the orthodox account of blues history. That is to say, from Plato's perspective we should expect blues musical forms to have been the artistic product of a distinct *kind* of people. In accordance with Aristotle, however, I argue that Plato's view is at best inadequate and at worst seriously flawed.

The cardinal tenet of Aristotle's objection to Plato is this: only individuals exist. General terms – the nouns we use to label kinds, forms, types, and so on – do not name things, he thought, but instead refer to attributes of things and relations between them. Kinds, we might say, are things *in name only*.[10] Now, if we think through blues history as Aristotle might have done, we should not regard the people who made blues music as mere tokens of a general type at all, but as unique and autonomous individuals. In turn, we should see the creative efforts of each individual artist as accumulating *into* blues forms rather than having been generated *by* those forms.

Similar reasoning applies, surely, to our understanding of genomes and biological species. Where followers of Plato tend to see genes forming individuals, the Aristotelian sees only individuals copying various traits from their ancestors and passing them along to their descendants. The analogy in play here – between biological and cultural evolution – further illustrates how blues forms came to settle into relatively stable patterns (such as the familiar use of twelve-bar rhythms, and melodies turning on minor thirds and sevenths) without having recourse to any Platonic ancestors to serve as their models. Instead of copying models, blues musicians simply copied each other; but never entirely, never without the perpetual spin of individual variation. Working from Aristotle's rather than Plato's understanding of human differences, we can additionally make better sense, I think, of the widespread practice among both traditional and commercial blues singers of claiming compositional credit for songs all of whose elements were unoriginal.[11] These credits were claimed, and are surely deserved, not for having invented the elements of this or that blues form but for having recombined those elements into novel expressions, often of great power and beauty.

At this point, I claim two things. The first is that the tension between Aristotle's and Plato's deeply opposed views about difference accounts perfectly for the parallel tension between what I have rendered as two incompatible histories of the blues, each occupied by different kinds of people. The second says that blues were never, and are not now, the artistic product of any particular *kind* of people at all. These assertions may at first appear contrary to one another; the remainder of my argument will aim to show that they are not, and also why that matters to the kinds of people we can hope to make of ourselves.

RON BOMBARDI

Whose Blues?

Earlier I said that the primordial drive in making up blues was toward overcoming individual differences in power based on collective differences in social kinds. I want next to address the implications of this claim once we train it on overlapping kinds – specifically, kinds involving our ideas about color, class, gender, geography, age, and religion. My thesis is that blues history, however it is told, must be a history of people with conflicted identities.

The elements of inevitable conflict can be traced, I think, to the very first blues forms to emerge from the traditional call-and-response patterns West African slaves adapted to preserve their endangered religious sensibilities in colonial America. This means that the early blues singers were often in the covert business of transforming sacred song into secular rituals – rituals whose primary social function was, wittingly or unwittingly, to engender social cohesion. But at the same time, because blues performance was from the start local, intimate, and intensely personal, blues forms came to represent a triumph of the individual voice over collective song. This striking tension is quite evident, for example, in L'il Son Jackson's analysis of his own conversion from bluesman to preacher:

> You see, it's two different things – the blues and church songs is two different things. If a man feel hurt within side and he sing a church song, then he's asking God for help. It's a horse of a different color, but I think if a man sing the blues, it's more or less out of himself [...] He's not askin' no one for help.[12]

This uneasy conflict between fostering social cohesion and expressing personal complaint might have spawned little more than a few short-lived idiomatic contributions to Southern vernacular culture, were it not for the hugely unequal distributions of political, social, and economic power that marked Reconstruction and its aftermath throughout the Americas in the twentieth century. Folklorist Alan Lomax, citing an unnamed singer, reports an especially informative commentary:

> The blues is just *revenge*. Like you'll be mad at the boss and you can't say anything. You out behind the wagon and you pretend that a mule stepped on your foot and you say, 'Get offa my foot, god-dam sonafabitch!' You won't be talkin' to the mule, you'll be referrin' to the white boss [...] That's the way with the blues: you sing those things in a song when you can't speak out.[13]

There is thus in blues music a veritable template for generating conflicted identities. On the one hand, traditional blues singers learned to pose their unique experiences and went against the grain of the group. But, on the other hand, the many variations from which these same singers incessantly fashioned their songs came to represent the common experience of various powerless people, never able to address the powerful directly, in plain speech, and with a clear understanding of each other's worlds in mind.

As a consequence of this dual artistic trajectory, it becomes virtually impossible for us to interpret with any confidence whose blues is actually being sung in any given performance, or even performance style. We might ask, for instance: Whose blues was sung by the urban divas that rose from poverty in the 1920s crooning torch songs for desolate, rural black women, thanks to the financial interests of white male record producers? A generation later, whose blues exactly was Big Bill Broonzy singing when performing his seething indictment of racist ideology, 'Black, Brown and White Blues,' dressed in sharecropper's overalls, before polite, well-heeled, middle-class Europeans with a taste for exotic imports? I argue that such questions do not have definitive answers because the likes of Mamie Smith and Big Bill sang from unstable centers of artistic vision. That is one reason. There is another and perhaps deeper reason, having less to do with the invention of blues forms as with their reception; that is, with the telling of blues history. It concerns the elevation of some blues over others on grounds of greater authenticity.

The very idea that some songs embody more authentic experiences than others, and can therefore be trusted to speak for entire communities of otherwise voiceless people, is probably nowhere better enshrined than in the commonplace, nearly universal, maxim, 'to play the blues, you have to pay the dues.' Despite its allure, however, I think this is a pernicious maxim. It is effectively counterproductive because the notion of appealing to authenticity as the preeminent measure of artistic worth in the blues serves inevitably to perpetuate the very same unequal distributions of power against which blues songs have, in one way or another, always complained. In order to see how this happens, we have only to tell blues history entirely by Plato's lights, and to invent the kinds of people that inhabit what I've called the orthodox tale – people whose individual traits and behaviors are seen to typify, and consequently to stand for, the collective experiences of their class, their race, their gender. But, if authenticity demands the paying of dues, and if the dues amount to suffering in submission to the domination of those having the upper

RON BOMBARDI

hand, we make a living museum of disempowered voices. Worse still, if we determine to define the divas or the bluesmen or their descendants solely as illustrative instances of their kin and kind, we inevitably narrow the margins of our own understanding to the reigning stereotypes of their day. That is, we deny to them a part of our common humanity: the right to difference – to variety, plurality, and multiplicity; the right to invent ourselves freely; and unlike stereotypes, the right to engage in open conversation with anyone we may happen to meet.

Our Blues

Because the blues emerged in history as both secular ritual and personal testament, and because both forms of expression matured in social settings fraught with uneven distributions of power across lines of class, race, gender, geography, culture, and religion, all at once, it seems blues history, no matter how we tell it, must leave us perplexed about what makes blues, blues. However well we may cobble together enough similarities between blues recordings to satisfy even Plato's ghost with genuine original blues forms, we shall in the end find only a ghostly handful of Aristotle's individuals, still chanting in the modern sound-scape, each unhappy in a different way, in a different voice. That the blues resists definition, then, does not represent a failure of our ingenuity; it follows because, given the multiplicity of social conditions in which both traditional and contemporary blues were and are composed, the blues simply has no essence.

Even if there is no one satisfactory definition of blues music on offer today, perhaps our descendants may craft one. I think that is unlikely. The blues frustrates our many efforts to define it, I think, not because it is elusive but because it is pervasive. From their inception, blues forms grafted hybrids from several musical strains at once. We know, for example, that more than a few contemporary hillbilly standards derived, like 'Old Joe Clark' and 'Cripple Creek,' from mixing the remembered rhythms of African ritual dance with the parlor melodies of Scots-Irish immigrant culture on strange and various readymade instruments in remote locations.[14] That is why the blues and the blues singer alike lack convincing paradigms: because both trade massively in borrowed ideas and techniques. The elements of the blues have been taken apart, reshuffled, and rebuilt so often, in fact, that their only internal drive would appear to be downright *evolutionary*. Where nature seems to reshuffle good ideas in the form of genes, cultures likewise seem to copy and adapt good musical ideas, one from another. And, because musical ideas seem best to us when they vividly portray the most intimate scenery of our inner lives, music is probably the most direct form of human communication we ever share with one another. This is precisely the analysis St. Louis bluesman Henry Townsend offered to Paul Oliver when he observed that

> there's somethings that have happened to me that I wouldn't dare tell – but I would sing about them. Because people in general they takes the song as an explanation for themselves – they believe this song is expressing their feelings instead of the one that singin' it.[15]

If this analysis indeed fits blues history as I've sketched it twice over, then it seems to me that there is only one proper answer to the question of whose voices sing the blues. And that is: ours.

Unfinished Business

My conclusion is two-fold. Both parts concern the stories our descendants may have to tell about us. First, because the blues was born in paradox, and nurtured on ironies from which it has not yet been weaned, the idea of blues music as an art form thoroughly unified by the common experiences and mutual sensibilities of its practitioners has a strong hold on contemporary thought and imagination. But this idea is mistaken, as I've argued, because it derives from bad habits of thinking about human differences – habits that reduce individuals to instances of their type, their social kind. In the long run, this sort of thinking must inevitably frustrate our every aspiration to reinvent ourselves on principles of genuinely equal opportunity for all quarters of our society. That is because so long as we remain unable to address one another uniquely, as free and autonomous persons, our differences will continue to cluster around expressions of power, both material and symbolic, to advance the interests of our *own* kind.

Second, while the rights and privileges to reproduce historic blues compositions remain, as they are today, scattered among the beneficiaries of past distorted power relations, there is unfinished business in the telling of blues history. That is to say, we are not done with asking *whose* are the blues. Furthermore, if we are ever to know ourselves as well as the Socratic imperative with which I began demands, I believe we shall be asking this question for a long time to come.

NOTES

1 Hacking adopts this strategy in numerous studies of social classification schemes. He introduced the central idea in a 1986 article, 'Making up people.' In T. C. Heller, Morton Sosna, and David E. Wellbery (Eds.), *Reconstructing Individualism: Autonomy, Individuality and the Self in Western Thought* (Stanford, CA: Stanford University Press, 1986), pp. 222–236.

2 This is what Hacking calls the 'looping effect of human kinds.' The notion is developed at length in *Rewriting the Soul: Multiple Personality and the Sciences of Memory* (Princeton, NJ: Princeton University Press, 1995).

3 Variations on this theme can be found in any number of blues histories. Among the more influential are Leroy Jones [Amiri Baraka], *Blues People* (New York: Morrow, 1963); Robert Palmer, *Deep Blues* (New York: Viking, 1981); Peter Guralnick, *The Listener's Guide to The Blues* (New York: Facts on File, 1982); Albert Murray, *The Omni-Americans: Black Experience and American Culture* (New York: Vintage, 1983); Julio Finn, *The Bluesman: The Musical Heritage of Black Men and Women in the Americas* (London: Quartet, 1986); and Jon Michael Spencer, *Blues and Evil* (Knoxville, TN: University of Tennessee Press, 1993).

4 Christopher A. Waterman, 'Race music: Bo Chatmon, "Corrine Corrina," and the excluded middle.' In Ronald Radano and Philip V. Bohlman (Eds.), *Music and the Racial Imagination* (Chicago, IL: University of Chicago Press, 2000), pp. 167–205.

5 Ibid., p. 177.

6 See Francis Davis, *The History of the Blues: The Roots, the Music, the People, from Charley Patton to Robert Cray* (New York: Hyperion, 1995), p. 88.

7 See Andrew Leach, 'Sam Chatmon.' In Edward Komara (Ed.), *Encyclopedia of the Blues* (New York: Routledge, 2006), pp. 697–698.

8 Often referred to as 'the problem of the one and the many,' this was one of the central concerns of the earliest Greek philosophers, whose interests in natural phenomena settled on understanding the general relation between singular and plural forms of nouns. That is why they did not consider 'one' to name a number at all – we need not count things unless we have two or more on hand.

9 The first Greek word for a kind of thing was probably *genos*, derived from the Indo-European stem *gen-* or *gene-*, meaning 'to bear' or 'to give birth.' From the Latin form, *gens* (the clan), comes a sizable host of modern English terms,

not the least interesting of which are gender, progeny, gene, gentry, ingenuity, engineer, benign, and pregnancy. See John Ciardi, *A Browser's Dictionary* (New York: Harper and Row, 1980), p. 148.

10 For this reason the Aristotelian view has since been called 'nominalism.' The designation first surfaced in debates the early mediaeval philosophers had over the import of what they called 'universal' terms. They considered expressions such as 'beauty is in the eye of the beholder' and 'honesty is the best policy,' worrying about whether words such as 'beauty' and 'honesty' name real things, concepts, or just collections of things.

11 See Samuel Charters, *The Country Blues* (New York: DaCapo, 1975) and David Evans, *Big Road Blues, Tradition and Creativity in the Folk Blues* (New York: DaCapo, 1982).

12 Paul Oliver, *Conversation with the Blues* (New York: Horizon Press, 1965), pp. 164–165.

13 Alan Lomax, *The Rainbow Sign: A Southern Documentary* (New York: Duell, Sloane, and Pearce, 1959), pp. 7–8.

14 See Elijah Wald, *Escaping the Delta: Robert Johnson and the Invention of the Blues* (New York: Amistad, 2004), p. 57.

15 Oliver, *Conversation with the Blues*, p. 165.

PHILOSOPHICAL BLUES SONGS

The songs below were identified by the authors as those that inspired their written contributions to this volume. We thus offer our readers the following informal list, identifying the artist, title, and album. Enjoy!

Blind Blake. 'He's in the Jailhouse Now,' *Blind Blake Vol. 2*.
Barbeque Bob. 'Goin' Up the Country,' *Chocolate to the Bone*.
Big Bill Broonzy. 'Black, Brown, and White Blues,' *Trouble in Mind*.
Big Bill Broonzy. 'Terrible Operation Blues,' *Do That Guitar Rag*.
John Lee Hooker. 'No Substitute,' *The Healer*.
Son House. 'Death Letter,' *The Original Delta Blues*.
Son House. 'John the Revelator,' *The Original Delta Blues*.
Son House. 'Preachin' the Blues,' *The Original Delta Blues*.
Mississippi John Hurt. 'Spike Driver Blues,' *Essential Recordings*.
Skip James. 'Hard Time Killing Floor Blues,' *Hard Time Killing Floor Blues*.
Blind Lemon Jefferson. 'Rising High Water Blues,' *Sings the Blues*.
Robert Johnson. 'Cross Road Blues,' *King of the Delta Blues*.
Robert Johnson. 'Smokestack Lightnin',' *Moanin in the Moonlight*.
Robert Johnson. 'Sweet Home Chicago,' *Single*.
B. B. King. 'How Blue Can You Get?' *Live At the Regal*.
B. B. King. 'Lucille,' *Lucille*.

Blues – Philosophy for Everyone: Thinking Deep About Feeling Low, First Edition.
Edited by Jesse R. Steinberg and Abrol Fairweather.
© 2012 John Wiley & Sons, Inc. Published 2012 by John Wiley & Sons, Inc.

Leadbelly. 'Leaving Blues,' Leadbelly's *Last Session*.
Blind Willie McTell. 'Ticket Agent Blues,' *Last Sessions*.
Jelly Roll Morton. 'Original Jelly Roll Blues,' *The Piano Rolls*.
Charlie Patton. 'High Water Everywhere Pt. 1,' *Hang It on the Wall*.
Charley Patton. 'Mississippi Bo Weavil Blues,' *Founder of the Delta Blues*.
Blind Joe Reynolds. 'Outside Woman Blues,' *Roots of Rock*
Mississippi Sheiks. 'Sitting on Top of the World,' *Stop and Listen*.
Mississippi Sheiks. 'Yodeling, Fiddling Blues,' *Mississippi Sheiks: Complete Recorded Works*.
Mamie Smith. 'Crazy Blues,' *The Best of Mamie Smith*.
Frank Stokes. 'Downtown Blues,' *The Best Of Frank Stokes*.
Muddy Waters. 'You Can't Lose What You Aint Never Had,' *The Anthology*.
Howlin' Wolf. 'How Many More Years,' *Howlin' Wolf Album*.
Howlin' Wolf. 'I've Been Abused,' *The Anthology*.

NOTES ON CONTRIBUTORS

ROBERT ABRAMOVITZ, MD, is distinguished lecturer and co-director of the National Center for Social Work Trauma Education and Workforce Development at Hunter College School of Social Work. He was trained in adult and child psychiatry at Yale University and the Yale Child Study Center, where he was an associate professor of pediatrics and psychiatry. Dr. Abramovitz is a child trauma specialist focusing on the impact of adversity, violence, poverty, and racism on individuals, communities, and organizations, and has a strong interest in individual and community resilience. He has authored numerous book chapters and journal articles, and co-written and produced ten child development films/videos, including 'The Discovery Year,' a television special about the first year of life hosted by Christopher Reeve. He has also been a consultant for children's television programs and for the Academy-award-winning animators Faith and John Hubley. He received the Sarah Haley Memorial Award for Clinical Excellence from the International Society for Traumatic Stress Studies. Avid listening and regularly seeking out blues clubs have honed his long-time affection for every blues style.

RON BOMBARDI has been teaching logic and philosophy at Middle Tennessee State University since 1984. He is now professor and chair of the Department of Philosophy. As a child born in New York City at

Blues – Philosophy for Everyone: Thinking Deep About Feeling Low, First Edition.
Edited by Jesse R. Steinberg and Abrol Fairweather.
© 2012 John Wiley & Sons, Inc. Published 2012 by John Wiley & Sons, Inc.

the height of the Cold War on the very day Woody Guthrie turned forty years old, Bombardi found more friends on subways than in classrooms, more music worth feeling on street corners than on the airwaves. To this day he has a hard time telling lecterns from music stands. Nobody knows why he took to ragtime like a famished fruit fly to a Georgia peach – another of Guthrie's gifts, perhaps. Hypnotized for a time by the exquisite discipline of Celtic dance, Bombardi found a fiddle and found fiddling irresistible. But it was the ghost of Big Bill Broonzy that finally woke him from his dogmatic slumbers and that taught him to think in shades of blue and play to the musical phrase, not the metronome. Nowadays Bombardi regularly teaches courses in the philosophy of music. He wonders why the entire Western tradition all but completely ignores the philosophy of musical performance, preferring instead to worry exclusively over questions of interpretation, reception, or creation. He thinks it may have something to do with matters of race, class, and gender. He thinks these are very old matters; older even than the blues.

KIMBERLY R. CONNOR's identification with the blues grows daily along with her hipster teenage son, who appears to have also made a deal with the devil at the crossroads but not to have been rewarded with any gift other than the ability to drive her crazy. Luckily several decades of studying, researching, and teaching the improvisatory genius of African-American artists have helped her to keep on keeping on: to keep telling the stories, to keep playing the songs, to keep listening in prayer. Currently she worries the line at the University of San Francisco, where she is an associate professor in the College of Business and Professional Studies. She also edits a book series for Oxford University Press and is associate editor of the *Journal of the American Academy of Religion*. But when she really wants to get her mojo on you can find her putting on a pirate swagger to lead field trips at 826 Valenica, a non-profit organization dedicated to supporting school-age students in learning writing skills and helping teachers to get students excited about the literary arts.

DAVID C. DRAKE is a lifelong lover of blues and jazz music who has studied philosophy at National Chengchi University in Taipei, Taiwan as well as the University of Utah. He currently resides in Seattle.

BRIAN DOMINO first met the blues in the form of British invasion rock and roll at the same time that he began reading philosophy. The two never sat comfortably next to each other in his mind. While he went on to pursue the love of wisdom formally by earning PhD in philosophy at the Pennsylvania State University, he remains haunted by Robert Johnson's warning, 'Well, it's hard to tell, it's hard to tell / When all your love's in vain.' He is currently an associate professor at Miami University.

ABROL FAIRWEATHER teaches philosophy in the Bay Area (University of San Francisco, San Francisco State, Las Positas College) and has published in the area of virtue epistemology. In addition to his interest in various intellectual excellences, he has published on more-popular topics including Facebook and philosophy, and *Dexter* and philosophy. A number of years ago, Willow told him to 'check out Mississippi John Hurt' and that was it; it was all over – he done sold his soul to the blues.

BEN FLANAGAN is a working rock musician with a degree in philosophy. He currently lives in San Francisco. When he is not saturated in existential crisis and pondering his wildly non-lucrative passions, he is rooting for his Duke Blue Devil basketball team and touring with his band The Trophy Fire, who will be putting out their third release in the fall of 2011.

OWEN FLANAGAN is James B. Duke Professor of Philosophy at Duke University. The musical talents of his son, Ben Flanagan, are all from his mother's side.

WADE FOX has worked as a writer and an editor at Ten Speed Press, Lonely Planet Publications, and the Whole Earth Review. Heartbroken and lonely, he is currently paying his dues as a professor of English at Community College of Denver.

RICHARD GREENE is a professor of philosophy at Weber State University. He received his PhD from the University of California, Santa Barbara. He has published papers in epistemology and metaphysics, and has edited a number of books on philosophy and pop culture. His woman left him, his dog died, he's poor, and his guitar aint got but two strings.

BRUCE IGLAUER is the founder and president of Chicago's forty-year-old Alligator Records. He has personally produced or co-produced over 125 blues albums. He has been inducted in the Blues Hall of Fame, has won two Keeping the Blues Alive awards, is a co-founder of *Living Blues Magazine*, and chairs the Blues Community Foundation. For more information on Alligator Records visit www.alligator.com.

PHILIP JENKINS is an assistant professor of philosophy at Marywood University in Scranton, Pennsylvania. His current areas of research are philosophy of art (especially music and expression) and philosophy of mind (especially questions surrounding the social nature of the self and emotions). Jenkins has had a lifelong interest in psychology and the arts, particularly painting, photography, dance, and theater, as well as rock, alternative, classical, and avant-garde music. He is also a drummer and has been a member of many rock bands over the years, including the space rock combo Surface of Eceon, with whom he recorded two full-length records and several compilations in the early 2000s.

DOUGLAS LANGSTON teaches at New College of Florida, where he is a professor of philosophy and religion. He specializes in medieval philosophy and philosophy of religion. He has listened to the blues for years, but, without any musical talent, he's had to limit himself to supporting those who can play the blues and learning as much as he can about the genre.

NATHANIEL LANGSTON is a student at Warren Wilson College. He has been playing the blues since he was sixteen. Originally self-taught, he has been able to work with a number of fine musicians over the years. Nat has performed in Sarasota, Florida as well as Asheville, North Carolina.

JOSEPH J. LYNCH learned to play guitar and helped to set up equipment for a local blues-rock band in high school in the Washington, DC area. Occasionally the band would let Joe onto the stage to play harmonica on their blues numbers, for example 'Baby Please Don't Go.' Prior to this, most of his musical performances were confined to singing bass in the choir at the Baptist church. While he loved to play guitar and listen to rock and blues music, he went to a small Baptist college to study for the ministry. It was here he learned that the music he loved was the devil's music, and, soon enough, he was invited to leave. After a period of time hitch-hiking, playing music, and working odd jobs, he decided to give college a second try and discovered philosophy. His passion for philosophy grew as large as his passion for rock and blues, so before long he received his PhD in philosophy and became a professor at California Polytechnic State University in San Luis Obispo.

ROOPEN MAJITHIA completed his schooling in India and his higher education in the United States and Canada. He holds a PhD in philosophy from the University of Guelph and is currently head of philosophy at Mount Allison University in Canada, where he teaches widely in the history of western philosophy and Indian philosophy as well as in ethics. He has written and published on Plato, Aristotle, and Shankara.

MICHAEL NEUMANN writes on moral and political philosophy; he teaches at Trent University. His work on popular music has made its mark. For example, a leading rock critic has remarked: 'Who is this asshole Neumann and how can I kill him before Christmas?'

ROBERT S. PYNOOS, MD, MPH, is Professor in Residence at the Department of Psychiatry and Biobehavioral Sciences, David Geffen School of Medicine at the University of California, Los Angeles (UCLA). He is co-director of the UCLA-Duke University National Center for Child Traumatic Stress, which coordinates a nationwide network of academic, hospital, and community service sites in order to improve the standard of care for traumatized children and their families. He is an internationally recognized expert on the developmental consequences of child, adolescent, and young adulthood trauma. Throughout his career, he has had a special interest in the impact of traumatic experiences on the lives of artists and cultures, and the process by which these are creatively transformed in literature, painting, and music. He is grateful for the partnership with two blues aficionados that permitted this exploration of the profound impact of interpersonal and societal violence in the evolving creative force of the great blues musicians.

JOEL RUDINOW teaches philosophy and pop culture at Santa Rosa Junior College in northern California and moonlights as a musician in San Francisco Bay Area roots music bands (achieving fifteen minutes of fame as the piano player in Elvin Bishop's touring band at the end of the twentieth century). His most recent book, *Soul Music: Tracking the Spiritual Roots of Pop from Plato to Motown*, a philosophical meditation on the essence of soul in music, was published in 2010 by the University of Michigan Press. Happily married, with two grandchildren, and approaching retirement in California's beautiful wine country, he realizes he's way too blessed, privileged, and comfortable to have the blues.

ALAN M. STEINBERG holds a PhD in philosophy from Cornell University. He is currently associate director of the UCLA-Duke University National Center for Child Traumatic Stress in the Department of Psychiatry and

Biobehavioral Sciences at the University of California, Los Angeles. He is a recognized authority in the areas of child traumatic stress and the design and analysis of a broad spectrum of biological, psychological, and social research across this field. Over the years, he has published more than 100 theoretical and empirical articles in highly prestigious psychiatric journals and books. In addition, he has made contributions to the medical ethics literature on issues related to competency to consent to medical treatment and biomedical research, and mandated reporting of child abuse. Dr. Steinberg has worked around the world to assist in the development and implementation of post-war and post-disaster mental health recovery programs. He endeavors to play lead and rhythm blues guitar, albeit with varying degrees of proficiency and success – but always with a deep love and appreciation for the history and meaning of the blues.

JESSE R. STEINBERG is currently an assistant professor of philosophy and the director of the Environmental Studies Program at the University of Pittsburgh at Bradford. He has published articles on a range of topics including philosophy of mind, metaphysics, and moral philosophy. Jesse has played guitar in various blues bands over the years, has attended numerous blues festivals, and is an all-around blues fanatic.

BENJAMIN A. STOLOROW has been active as a pianist and teacher in the San Francisco Bay Area for over ten years. After studying both classical and jazz music at University of California, Berkeley; the Manhattan School of Music; and with numerous private teachers, Ben has become one of the most sought-after jazz pianists in the Bay Area. He has always been attracted to highly emotionally charged music, and the blues has become an integral aspect of his music making. The power of musical expression to transform emotions that cannot be expressed verbally into sounds that can be felt continues to draw him to the piano. In whatever music he plays he tries to understand the emotional meaning behind it. The influence of the blues and other deeply expressive musical genres can be heard on Ben's first trio album, 'I'll Be Over Here,' which features seven original compositions and a fresh arrangement of the jazz standard 'Stella by Starlight.' In addition to performing in the Bay Area, he has also performed extensively in Japan and other parts of Asia.

ROBERT D. STOLOROW is a psychoanalytic and philosophical author who holds doctorates in both clinical psychology and philosophy. Having loved the blues since he was a boy, he has become even more drawn to it since his theoretical interest became focused on emotional trauma (eventuating in his book, *Trauma and Human Existence*) and, especially, since the music of his son, Ben, became more bluesy. Robert practices psychoanalysis in Santa Monica, California, where he also teaches philosophy and psychoanalysis to clinicians and trainees.

KEN UENO's life was saved by Jimi Hendrix when he was convalescing from an injury that redirected his life from West Point and a career in politics toward a life in music and academia. Since the time he was inspired by Hendrix to pick up electric guitar, Ken has become a Rome and Berlin Prize-winning avant-garde composer, picking up a PhD from Harvard along the way. He is currently an assistant professor at the University of California, Berkeley.

MEGHAN WINSBY received her master's in philosophy from Dalhousie University. Bitten by the East Coast blues bug, she has been lending her vocals to jams from Halifax, Nova Scotia to Tucson, Arizona ever since. Her current gig as doctoral student in the Department of Philosophy at the University of Western Ontario has her researching autonomy, responsibility, and the nature of conscience. Though, after midnight, she may be found at any of a number of local jam sessions.